CROSS-EXAMINATION ON TRIAL

Advocacy and Vulnerability in Criminal Trials

Jonathan Doak, John Jackson, Debbie Cooper, Candida Saunders and David Wright

BRISTOL UNIVERSITY PRESS

First published in Great Britain in 2026 by

Bristol University Press
University of Bristol
1-9 Old Park Hill
Bristol
BS2 8BB
UK
t: +44 (0)117 374 6645
e: bup-info@bristol.ac.uk

Details of international sales and distribution partners are available at bristoluniversitypress.co.uk

DOI: 10.51952/9781529227253

British Library Cataloguing in Publication Data
A catalogue record for this book is available from the British Library

ISBN 978-1-5292-2722-2 hardcover
ISBN 978-1-5292-2724-6 ePub
ISBN 978-1-5292-2725-3 ePdf

Cover design: Liam Roberts Design
Front cover image: Priscilla Coleman
Bristol University Press uses environmentally responsible print partners.
Printed and bound in Great Britain by CPI Group (UK) Ltd, Croydon, CR0 4YY

FSC
www.fsc.org
MIX
Paper | Supporting responsible forestry
FSC® C013604

Bristol University Press' authorised representative in the European Union is:
Easy Access System Europe, Mustamäe tee 50, 10621 Tallinn, Estonia,
Email: gpsr.requests@easproject.com

Contents

List of Figures and Tables

Figures

Tables

Acknowledgements

This book would not have been possible had it not been for the generous funding provided by the Nuffield Foundation. We would like to thank Ash Patel, Christopher Milton (formerly of the Nuffield Foundation), and Ellen Wright for their guidance, support, and advice throughout the project. We would extend our thanks to Bristol University Press for agreeing to publish this book, which is based on our research, and particularly to our Commissioning Editor, Grace Carroll, for her patience and flexibility throughout the process.

We are also grateful for the support we received from our respective universities at all stages of this project, from the initial phases of the grant application in early 2019 through to the completion of this manuscript in December 2024. At the University of Nottingham, we would like to thank Hilary Sanders for her support with the grant application, and the late Agnes Flues and Kobie Neita in the School of Law for their assistance with project management and finances. Special thanks go to Laura Wills, who, as a research assistant for the first 15 months of the project, showed remarkable fortitude in observing trials across England and Wales during the COVID-19 pandemic. At Nottingham Trent University, we would like to thank Beatriz Gómez Fariñas, Selbi Durdiyeva, Xingxing Wei, Nisan Alici, and Xiaocong Liu for their research assistance at various stages, as well as Kerri Gilbert for her administrative support.

We express our sincere gratitude to all members of our advisory group, who played a key role throughout the project by advising the research team on various issues, including access to data in different jurisdictions, providing feedback on the research questionnaires, and introducing us to key stakeholders. Many also contributed to colloquia and associated events organised during the research period. The members were: Professor Penny Cooper, Barrister-at-Law and former Chair of The Advocate's Gateway; Tim Jebb, Solicitor and Barrister-at-Law at the Northern Ireland Bar; Professor Shane Kilcommins, Provost and Deputy President of the University of Limerick and expert in Irish criminal law and procedure; Dr Alison May, Lecturer in English Language at the University of Leeds and expert in corpus linguistic analysis; Dr Sarah Poppleton, HMCTS, Head of Crime

Insight and Research; Her Honour Judge Catarina Sjölin Knight (Lincoln Crown Court); and Louise Taylor, Lecturer in Law at the Open University and expert in Scots criminal law and victims' rights. We also thank former members of the group, Rozanna Franklin, formerly of HMCTS, and the late Professor Pete Duff, an expert in Scots criminal law and procedure at the University of Aberdeen, who provided much advice and support at the outset of the project.

Thanks are due to the Senior Presiding Judge for England and Wales, the Lord Justice Clerk in Scotland, the Lady Chief Justice of Northern Ireland, and the Legal Research and Library Services Committee of the Irish Courts Service for giving their approval in principle for the research. Conducting research during the COVID-19 pandemic was challenging, and we are extremely grateful to the judges and court staff across the jurisdictions who facilitated our trial observations and provided transcripts despite the restrictions.

The success of the project depended on the goodwill and cooperation of those with direct court experience. We thank all the judicial, advocate, and intermediary interviewees who generously gave their time for often lengthy interviews. In order to preserve their anonymity, we have used the female pronoun when referring to judicial and intermediary interviewees and the male pronoun when referring to advocate interviewees. We also thank the resident judges in the court centres in England and Wales, Aliza Catlin (formerly of the Judicial Office England and Wales), Tom Sadler (formerly of the Scottish Judicial Office), Kim Elliott (Head of Reform, Lady Chief Justice's Office in Northern Ireland), and Laura Butler (Head of Legal Research and Library Services in the Irish Courts Service), for arranging interviews with judges. We are grateful to the Ministry of Justice, the Intermediary Cooperative, and Janet Smith for helping arrange interviews with intermediaries in England and Wales, and to various sets of chambers and the Criminal Bar Association of Northern Ireland for their assistance in arranging interviews with advocates. Special thanks go to Dr Miriam Delahunt, Barrister-at-Law, for introducing us to barristers and judges during our visit to the Criminal Courts of Justice in Dublin in October 2022.

We also thank the School of Law at the University of Limerick for co-hosting and funding the project's international conference on *Adversarialism, Participation, and Voice in the Criminal Process*, held in Limerick on 22–23 June 2023. Dr Alan Cusack, Associate Professor of Law, went to considerable lengths to ensure its success. We are also extremely appreciative of those who attended the launch of the research report at the Nuffield Foundation in London on 1 February 2024, with particular thanks to our keynote speakers, including HHJ Sarah Whitehouse KC (Senior Circuit Judge at the Old Bailey, who chaired the event), Professor Penny Cooper (Co-founder and former Chair of The Advocates' Gateway), HHJ Patricia Smyth

(Recorder of Belfast), Mary Prior KC (formerly Vice Chair and now Chair of the Criminal Bar Association), and Geraldine Hanna (Northern Ireland Victims' Commissioner).

In addition to the above, many other friends and colleagues provided helpful insights at various stages of the project. Special thanks to members of the Northern Ireland judiciary, Lord Beckett, Dr Liz Curran, Dr Alan Cusack, Dr Miriam Delahunt, HHJ Greg Dickinson, Dr Samantha Fairclough, Dr Emily Henderson, Professor Tyrone Kirchengast, Professor Yvonne McDermott Rees, Dr David Plater, Rob Street, Dr John Taggart, Dr Matt Thomason, and Connor Doak Sr (for proof-reading). Needless to say, the authors assume responsibility for any errors contained in the book.

Preface

The research underpinning this book took place during a period of uncertainty and flux, and as such our experiences have been both challenging and enlightening. Cross-examination, once considered a cornerstone of the adversarial model of justice, is now under scrutiny for two main reasons: its inherent capacity to effectively test evidence and whether its benefits outweigh the distress and trauma it can cause vulnerable witnesses. Despite numerous legal and policy initiatives over the past 30 years to address these concerns, the fundamental nature of cross-examination has remained largely unchanged.

However, the last two decades have seen the gradual erosion of the conventional 'advocacy' model and the emergence of a new 'best evidence' model, focusing on producing the best evidence rather than simply winning cases. Notable innovations during this period have entailed the roll-out of intermediaries, the introduction of pre-trial 'ground rules hearings' (GRHs), the expansion of pre-recorded cross-examination, and the development of specialised training for advocates and judges. Despite these changes, there is a lack of recent research on their practical impact. It remains unclear how well judges manage cross-examinations, enforce GRH decisions, and the extent to which traditional adversarial questioning techniques are still prevalent.

This project sought to ascertain the extent to which recent efforts to change the nature of cross-examination of vulnerable witnesses are being reflected in practice within criminal courts. The overarching goal was to map the precise nature and extent of these new approaches, identify specific issues and problems, and develop evidence-based solutions to enhance the capacity of vulnerable people to participate in trials.

To achieve this, we adopted a mixed methodology, including an international review of the law, policy, and practice of cross-examination across common law jurisdictions, and focused observations at eight courts across the UK and Ireland – five in England and Wales, and one each in Scotland, Northern Ireland, and Ireland. This involved observing entire trials with vulnerable witnesses, interviewing judges, advocates, and intermediaries, and conducting corpus linguistic analysis of transcripts containing cross-examinations of vulnerable witnesses.

The research was conducted during a time when all studied jurisdictions were adapting their processes to deal with the COVID-19 emergency. This sudden shift to new ways of working significantly impacted our plans and caused some delays but did not prevent us from obtaining a substantial body of data. Initially, the pandemic halted jury trials altogether, leading to an increased use of remote evidence to clear the backlog of cases. Many special measures for questioning vulnerable witnesses involve remote evidence, such as live link or video evidence. COVID-19 allowed all manner of witnesses, including defendants, to testify outside the courtroom, enabling trials to continue.

This book is a collaborative effort by multiple authors, analysing their findings across different work packages in the study. We frequently use the first person in our narrative when discussing our interview and observational data. Although we strive for epistemological objectivity in reporting our findings, these research methods are inherently susceptible to observer, confirmation, and interpretive biases (Podsakoff et al, 2012). By using the first person, we acknowledge that different interviewers or observers might have perceived the data differently. Readers may notice variations in writing styles, tones, and 'voices' across each chapter. We hope that these stylistic differences do not detract from the overarching arguments of the book; they reflect the diverse backgrounds and perspectives of the authors, which we believe enhance the depth and richness of the research. The final synthesis of our findings and conclusions is very much the product of a fully collective endeavour.

Throughout the book, we critically reflect on how recent innovations such as special measures, GRHs, and associated case law have affected a cultural shift among legal practitioners aimed at achieving best evidence and minimising secondary victimisation for vulnerable witnesses. We also highlight ongoing challenges related to inconsistent practices, challenges posed by new technologies, resource constraints, and issues of equality for vulnerable defendants, who are treated differently from non-defendant witnesses. In conclusion, although a unified 'best evidence' model has not yet fully materialised, there is a strong commitment among legal professionals to enhance the experience for vulnerable witnesses and improve the evidential quality of their testimony. Going forward, the aim is to ensure that the evidence provided by these witnesses is received by the judicial process in an optimal, high-quality, and fair manner, without compromising the fair trial rights of the accused. We hope that our book offers valuable insights for academics, legal practitioners, and policy makers interested in reforming cross-examination practices to create a fairer and more just system for all.

Jonathan Doak, Nottingham Trent University
John Jackson, University of Nottingham
Debbie Cooper, University of Nottingham
Candida Saunders, University of Nottingham
David Wright, Nottingham Trent University

1

Mapping the Changing Face of Cross-Examination

Cross-examination – the questioning of a witness by an opposing party during a trial – has long been considered an 'iconic' feature of adversarial criminal proceedings used to test oral evidence (Roberts, 2022: 311). It has also been regarded as often crucial in determining the outcome of a contested trial because it is the point at which there is a 'direct confrontation of one point of view by the other' and the 'conflict becomes explicit' (Stone, 1984: 296). However, many now question the view that it is 'the greatest legal engine ever invented for the discovery of the truth' (Wigmore, 1940: §1367; see Roberts, 2019). Over the course of the past 30 years, research studies have consistently reported that many witnesses find the process distressing. Such distress is particularly acute among the most vulnerable witnesses: children, complainants in sexual offence cases, and witnesses with learning disabilities (Doak, 2008; Kirchengast, 2016).

Many previous studies on the cross-examination of vulnerable witnesses have tended to focus on questions of witness satisfaction (Hamlyn et al, 2004; Burton et al, 2006; Wood et al, 2015). Such studies provide important insights but they do not give an indication as to how language is used as a tool of advocacy. Additionally, sociolinguistic studies have amassed a body of evidence on the types of questions which can prove problematic for witnesses, and the impact of responses on the trial fact-finder (Brennan and Brennan, 1988, Davies and Seymour, 1998; Kebbell and Johnson, 2000; Hanna et al, 2012; Zajac et al, 2018). Useful practical suggestions have also been made as to how their experiences might be improved (for example, Plotnikoff and Woolfson, 2009, 2019; Jacobson and Cooper, 2020), and a more muscular role for the judiciary or professional regulators has also been suggested (Hunter et al, 2018).

Increasingly, governments around the world have introduced a range of special or alternative measures as a tool to achieve 'best evidence' and to ease the burden of giving evidence (Hayes and Bunting, 2013). Some of the most prominent examples include the use of screens, the removal of wigs/gowns, live video link, pre-recorded evidence, supporters who accompany vulnerable witnesses while testifying, and intermediaries or communication experts who facilitate communication with a witness or a defendant. Although these reforms have helped alleviate some of the stress and anxiety associated with giving evidence (Burton et al, 2006; Plotnikoff and Woolfson, 2009, 2019), they have not altered the fundamental nature of cross-examination or its underpinning epistemic assumptions. However, in the course of the past decade, there has been a growing acknowledgement that there is a need for more fundamental change to the nature of cross-examination itself. Spearheaded originally by the senior judiciary in England and Wales (but increasingly with the support of senior judges in other jurisdictions), a new paradigm is emerging which shifts cross-examination away from party control towards a 'best evidence' model. Whereas cross-examination has traditionally been used by advocates as a means of winning cases, it is now restricted, particularly when it comes to vulnerable witnesses, to producing the 'best evidence' for the court (Henderson, 2015b). In what has been described as a new 'revolution' in practice (Lord Judge, 2013), advocates are now being required to adapt their forensic techniques to suit the needs of the witness.

Some of the most notable innovations in recent years have been the rise of intermediaries[1] and the introduction of pre-trial hearings, known as 'ground rules hearings' (GRHs), which are used to set the rules of trial advocacy and aim to improve the language advocates use to cross-examine the most vulnerable witnesses. The roll-out of pre-recorded cross-examination is now becoming a prominent feature of trials involving vulnerable witnesses in both England and Scotland (where it is referred to as 'evidence on commission'). There has also been a promulgation of training initiatives and guidelines to inform advocates of best practice in questioning vulnerable witnesses and 'toolkits' have been devised setting out guidance for judges and advocates on the questioning of vulnerable witnesses (Cooper, 2018).

Although many of these changes were considered to be anathema to traditional cross-examination, Henderson (2015a, 2015b, 2016) detected a shift in professional attitudes towards cross-examination from her interviews in 2013 with judges, advocates, and intermediaries in England and Wales soon after the changes there began to take effect. However, ten years on there is a dearth of research exploring the extent to which changes in

---

[1] Other jurisdictions use alternative terms including 'children's champion' (New South Wales), 'communicator' (Western Australia), 'communication partner' (South Australia), 'communication assistant' (New Zealand), 'youth interrogator' (Israel).

practice in England and Wales have influenced cross-examination on the ground. Many earlier studies are now outdated given the breadth and depth of the changes that have occurred in intervening years (Doak et al, 2021). In particular, it remains unclear the extent to which judges are managing cross-examination in trials or whether directions made at GRHs concerning the manner and content of questioning are subsequently being enforced at trial. Above all, it is uncertain whether the traditional 'tools of the trade' are still being used by advocates in cross-examining vulnerable people. The same is generally true of other jurisdictions which have followed in the path of the changes introduced in England and Wales. As changes are introduced, a robust evidence base is needed to evaluate how reforms are being received on the ground, whether they truly enable vulnerable witnesses to give best evidence, and what further improvements might be made.

Mapping cross-examination

Beginning in April 2020, our project 'Mapping the Changing Face of Cross-Examination' set out to ascertain the extent to which recent changes to cross-examination are reflected in criminal practice. The overarching aim of the research was to map the precise nature and extent to which new approaches towards cross-examination are producing change on the ground and to identify specific issues and problems and develop evidence-based solutions that enhance the capacity of vulnerable people to participate in the trial.

Funded by the Nuffield Foundation, the three-year project was underpinned by a mixed methodology to provide a rounded picture of cross-examination in practice across a number of jurisdictions and allow the impact of changing approaches to cross-examination to be measured in a variety of ways. The project began with an international review of the law, policy, and practice across common law jurisdictions (Doak et al, 2021). It was felt important to locate the research in the context of international best practice, given that many of the changes have been predicated on the concept of best evidence. Field research was conducted over a 27-month period at eight research sites in the UK and Ireland – five in England and Wales and one each in Scotland, Northern Ireland, and Ireland. These jurisdictions were chosen because they share a strong adversarial tradition but have each been making changes to accommodate the cross-examination of vulnerable witnesses in recent years. At the same time, they differ in size and in the ways that they are implementing change. While there is considerable legal and procedural overlap between these jurisdictions due to their shared history, each jurisdiction is also unique with differing procedural rules, special measures, and approaches to judicial case management. It was considered that a cross-jurisdictional approach could serve as a useful comparison regarding the attitudes of professionals involved, how changes have been implemented in practice and how best practice is being developed. The research centred on courts where the most serious (often sexual) offences are contested because this is where concerns about the impact of cross-examination on vulnerable witnesses have been concentrated and where many of the changes to practice have been targeted.

A detailed treatment of our methodology can be found in our final research report to the Nuffield Foundation (see Jackson et al, 2024, Part 2). Essentially, the empirical limb of the project comprised three main qualitative strands. The first strand entailed trial observation, which helped the researchers to understand the evidential case as a whole and to observe defence and prosecution advocates' approach to cross-examination for both vulnerable and non-vulnerable witnesses, as well as judicial interventions and jurors' (apparent) reactions to the various parties and evidence. Altogether 40 trials were observed, yielding more than 2,500 pages of detailed contemporaneous notes of proceedings. A sizeable proportion (62.5 per cent) of the trials involved rape and serious sexual offences (n = 25). We observed 194 witnesses giving testimonial evidence, including adult and child, vulnerable and non-vulnerable, lay, professional, and expert witnesses, called by both the prosecution (n = 150) and the defence (n = 44). Of the defence witnesses observed, 34 were defendants. Approximately one third of all prosecution witnesses (n = 50) were considered vulnerable, along with three vulnerable defendants.

Secondly, the research team conducted 60 semi-structured interviews across six court centres with 21 judges, 24 advocates, and 15 intermediaries, who had a wide range of experience working with vulnerable witnesses in trial settings. Participants were asked whether, in their experience, there has been a change of approach to the cross-examination of vulnerable witnesses and whether this has led to an improvement in the practice of cross-examining such witnesses. The interviews generated over 72 hours of recorded data.[2]

Thirdly, corpus linguistic analysis was applied to 56 cross-examinations involving 34 vulnerable witnesses and 22 'non-vulnerable' witnesses from 23 observed trials, comprising complainants (n = 29), defendants (n = 18), prosecution witnesses (n = 8), and defence witnesses (n = 1). Corpus linguistic techniques combine quantitative identification of the frequency of particular linguistic phenomena such as words, phrases, or grammatical structures with a qualitative examination of how language is being used in context. Although the technique has been used previously in courtroom discourse, this is the first time it has been applied to contemporary cross-examinations of vulnerable witnesses in an interdisciplinary triangulated research context.

[2] To ensure the anonymity of research participants, all interview excerpts are presented using a coded format. These codes are designed to convey minimal identifying information while maintaining confidentiality. Each code consists of three components: the participant's jurisdiction and region (first two digits), their professional group (third digit), and a unique numerical identifier (fourth digit).

To complete the triangulation, we adopted a 'grounded theory' methodology in our data analysis (see Charmaz, 2006) to identify key themes from the different sets of observational, interview, and linguistic data such as: the support available to vulnerable witnesses, including special measures; the use of GRHs to manage cross-examination; the role of intermediaries; the impact of pre-recorded cross-examination; and the various adaptations being made to the structure, tone, and content of questions put to witnesses. These themes provided the framework for the structure of the book, which is set out later in this chapter.

The fieldwork for the research was conducted during the COVID-19 pandemic. This had a significant impact on our proposed methodology and caused some delay. However, the research team was still able to obtain a significant amount of data. Moreover, the data provided unforeseen but important new insights into how the jurisdictions studied adapted their processes in order to deal with the emergency. The pandemic had the initial effect of stopping jury trials altogether and then led to an increase in the use of remote evidence to help clear the backlog of cases. Many of the special measures that are used to question vulnerable witnesses involve the use of remote evidence, whether this takes the form of live link or video evidence. The effect of COVID-19 was to permit all manner of witnesses, including defendants, to testify outside the courtroom to enable trials to continue (Hoyano, 2021; Jackson, 2023).[3]

This raises the question of whether, during our fieldwork, a fundamental shift in the nature of cross-examination occurred, only to revert to the status quo ante once the pandemic subsided. Over the two-year period, we observed both vulnerable and non-vulnerable witnesses being questioned inside and outside the courtroom (using remote technologies). This allowed us to compare how cross-examination was conducted in both settings. However, the increase in the use of digital technologies has continued in the post-pandemic world, with legislation now empowering courts in England and Wales to 'require and permit' any person to take part in criminal proceedings including summary and Crown Court trials by live link.[4] In England and Wales there is a significant backlog of cases which was evident even before the pandemic,[5] remote evidence has continued to be relied upon more than before the pandemic and this now seems to be a feature of the 'new normal' that has changed the nature of criminal hearings for the foreseeable future.

---

[3] See for England and Wales Coronavirus Act 2020, s 53; sch 23.

[4] Police, Crime, Sentencing and Courts Act 2022, s 200; sch 20.

[5] Godfrey et al (2022).

Terminology

So far we have used the terms 'vulnerable' and 'non-vulnerable' witnesses without explaining their meaning. Vulnerability is both a contested concept and an imprecise measure; individuals who experience or witness crime will inevitably respond differently (Green, 2007; Shapland and Hall, 2007; Cooper, 2018). It has also been argued that vulnerability is not a condition inherent only to – or found within – certain groups or individuals but is a condition to which we are all subject and is shaped by structures and institutions in society (Fineman, 2008, 2013; Dehaghani, 2019). While recognising that some witnesses will be more 'vulnerable' than others irrespective of whether or how the law pigeonholes them, in the absence of consensus on what constitutes a 'vulnerable' witness, we found it convenient to operationalise 'vulnerable' to reflect the criteria for eligibility for special measures set out in the legislation governing special measures in the various jurisdictions studied.

As mentioned earlier, 'special measures' is the term that has been given to procedural adjustments that are made to enable witnesses to give their 'best evidence'. In England and Wales and Northern Ireland witnesses eligible for special measures are classified as 'vulnerable' if they satisfy the criteria relating to 'age and capacity' and are classified as 'intimidated' if they satisfy criteria relating to 'fear or distress about testifying', whereas in Scotland all witnesses who are eligible for special measures are classified simply as 'vulnerable'.[6] In our research, for the purposes of simplicity, we have opted to follow the Scottish approach, thus using the term 'vulnerable' to encapsulate all eligible witnesses. Over the years, all jurisdictions have expanded the criteria of eligibility for special measures to reflect evolving societal attitudes towards vulnerability and there is now a presumption that particular kinds of witness, such as children and sexual offences complainants, are entitled to certain measures.[7] It has been estimated that around 54 per cent of witnesses in English Crown Court trials meet the criteria for special measures (Burton et al, 2006). We were confident that using these criteria as the basis for our definition of vulnerability would enable us to identify sufficient numbers of vulnerable witnesses in the trials we observed, and indeed this proved to be the case (total n = 53).

Although much of the focus in the literature has been on the experiences of vulnerable witnesses who give evidence as victims or as witnesses for

6 See Youth Justice and Criminal Evidence Act 1999, ss 16–17; Criminal Evidence (NI) Order 1999 arts 4–5; Criminal Procedure (Scotland) Act 1995, s 271(1).

7 See eg in Scotland Victims and Witnesses (Scotland) Act 2014 and in Ireland the Criminal Law (Sexual Offences) Act 2017 and the Criminal Justice (Victims of Crime) Act 2017. For a detailed analysis of these measures see Keane and Davidson (2018: 38–42); Cusack (2020); Doak et al (2021).

the prosecution, our research includes vulnerable defendants who give evidence. Evidence suggests that considerable numbers of defendants suffer from mental illness, a learning disability, cognitive impairment, or communication difficulties (for example, Jacobson and Talbot, 2009; Hoyano and Rafferty, 2017; Fairclough, 2018a). The Equality and Human Rights Commission (2020) underscores how these conditions can impact defendants during trials, manifesting as memory loss, short attention spans, anxiety, and difficulty understanding legal processes. Vulnerable defendants were originally excluded from the special measure regimes across the four jurisdictions (see Fairclough, 2018a for England and Wales). The English legislation was later amended to permit defendants to avail themselves of certain special measures, although only under stricter eligibility criteria than other vulnerable witnesses: in the case of child defendants, only where they have a compromised ability to participate effectively as a witness due to their level of intellectual ability or social functioning; and in the case of adults, only where they suffer from mental disorder or otherwise have a 'significant impairment of intelligence and social function' and 'are *unable* to participate effectively as a witness'.[8]

The asymmetry in the eligibility criteria for vulnerable defendants and other vulnerable witnesses gives the impression that 'defendants whatever their age are somehow less deserving of assistance to give their best evidence than are other witnesses with the same communication difficulties' (Hoyano, 2010: 366). By contrast, in Scotland accused children and adults are now afforded the same access to special measures (with the exception of screens) as other vulnerable witnesses.[9] In Ireland there is no explicit legislation that enables defendants to avail themselves of special measures. The differentiation in the treatment of vulnerable witnesses and vulnerable defendants emerged as a persistent theme throughout our research, as outlined in the course of this book (see further Cooper et al, 2024; Jackson et al, 2024; and also Dehaghani et al, 2023). For the purpose of our research, we chose to classify defendants as 'vulnerable' witnesses when they gave evidence in circumstances where they appeared to meet the eligibility criteria for special measures of other vulnerable witnesses.

Structure

Following this introduction, Chapter 2 examines the theory and function of cross-examination within the adversarial trial structure. In many respects it is the pinnacle of the criminal process, through which the defence can

8 See Youth Justice and Criminal Evidence Act 1999, s 33A(4)(5) inserted by Police and Justice Act 2006, s 47.

9 See Vulnerable Witnesses (Scotland) Act 2004, s 271F.

'put the case' to prosecution witnesses, and is an essential component of the accused's right to a fair trial (Hostettler, 2006). The chapter critiques the normative justifications underpinning the practice and considers how it has impacted vulnerable witnesses. It also outlines the current legal and policy context and discusses current juridical trends which indicate a shift away from combative advocacy towards a grander quest to ensure effective participation and enable best evidence.

Chapters 3–6 are ordered according to the relevant stage in the criminal process and seek to integrate the key insights from the study's three separate but complementary strands of qualitative investigation: trial observations, corpus linguistic analysis, and semi-structured interviews exploring the experience and attitudes of criminal justice professionals. Chapter 3 focuses on the pre-trial stage, analysing the roll-out of pre-recorded cross-examination and GRHs. Our focus then shifts to the trial itself. In Chapter 4 we critically assess the role of the intermediary, while Chapter 5 provides an account of our observations in Crown Courts (or their equivalents in other jurisdictions). The use of language in cross-examination is the focus of Chapter 6, whereby corpus linguistic analysis (adopting both quantitative and qualitative methods) was adopted to analyse trial transcripts with a view to identifying any emergent and recurring patterns across different trials while also focusing on particularly significant exchanges between advocates and witnesses.

Drawing on the findings discussed in the previous chapters, Chapter 7 reflects on the impact of legal professional culture upon the conduct of cross-examination. For many decades, advocacy training positioned prosecution and defence counsel as gladiatorial combatants, with training manuals alluding to 'butchering', 'breaking', and 'destroying' opposing witnesses (Ellison, 2001: 104). Focusing on the changing attitudes of judges and advocates, this chapter considers the extent to which changes to law and practice have impacted upon such a characterisation of trial advocacy. The chapter explores the challenges professionals have encountered in the pursuit of best evidence and evaluates the extent to which these efforts have positively impacted the ability of vulnerable witnesses to provide it.

In conclusion, Chapter 8 synthesises our key findings. While the changes discussed throughout this book have likely improved both the quality of evidence and the experience of witnesses, it is too early to claim that a 'best evidence' model of cross-examination has become the norm; a coherent and consistent set of practices is still on the horizon. The chapter also explores the implications of new trends, including international best practices, new directions in human rights law, and emerging discourses around therapeutic jurisprudence, international convergence, and managerialism. These influences challenge normative assumptions about the adversarial model of proof and encourage experimentation with innovative approaches across traditional procedural boundaries.

2

Reform in Context

This chapter provides a contextual overview of how cross-examination evolved from being a widely accepted core tenet of the adversarial model of proof to being widely viewed as one of the most problematic aspects of the criminal trial. It begins with a brief overview of the core principles underpinning it, before exploring its pretext and traditional justifications. The chapter then considers how, from the latter years of the twentieth century up to the present day, the apologia for cross-examination have been cast into doubt. Concerns were reflected not only in legal literature but also in mounting evidence from criminologists, linguists, and psychologists, highlighting the acute difficulties vulnerable witnesses encounter when testifying. This emerging body of research percolated various international fora, ploughing new directions in human rights law, casting fresh light on the concept of fairness of criminal proceedings, and propelling new notions of best practice such as 'effective participation' and 'best evidence'.

The chapter then explores the policy response across all four jurisdictions in our study, which entailed a discernible shift towards a witness-centric approach, heralding the introduction of new measures to protect witnesses and enable best evidence. This, in turn, brought about a juridical turn, whereby the appellate courts in England and Wales (and to a lesser extent in Scotland) adopted a markedly more muscular approach in seeking to regulate the perceived excesses of cross-examination. The chapter concludes by noting the influence of an international shift towards a modern concept of a fair trial, which favours optimising reliable evidence and seeks to ensure fair participation for all witnesses.

Principles and parameters

One of the most salient features of the adversarial system is the concept of freedom of proof, which grants parties extensive rights to present their cases and arguments as they choose, within the bounds of the rules of evidence. This freedom has fundamentally shaped the evolution of cross-examination, allowing parties to question all witnesses on any relevant issue or matters concerning a witness's credibility (*Hobbs v Tinling* [1929] 2 KB 1). By the end of the nineteenth century, courts recognised cross-examination as a fundamental right of defence counsel, and lawyers commonly understood it as having superseded the oath as the primary method for uncovering the truth by exposing unreliable witnesses (Langbein, 2003).

The rule in *Browne v Dunn* ((1894) 6 R 67), which mandates that advocates must 'put the case' (that is, challenge a witness with an alternative version of events), remains a landmark case across much of the common law world. Any sworn witness is expected to undergo cross-examination as a matter of course. If no cross-examination is conducted, evidence-in-chief is still admissible but may be deemed to carry less weight (*R v Doolin* [1882] 1 Jebb CC 123). If such testimony is significant to the case's outcome, the verdict may be overturned on appeal (*R v Lawless* (1993) 98 Cr App R 342). Failing to conduct an effective cross-examination may be seen as accepting the witness's version of events (*R v Wood Green Court, ex p Taylor* [1995] Crim LR 879; *R v Farooqi* [2013] EWCA Crim 1649).

As the fervent nature of cross-examination became deeply rooted in trial advocacy in the nineteenth century, it became apparent that this new-found zeal in criminal courtrooms needed to be tempered by responsibility (Cairns, 1998: 165). To this end, new evidential rules and concepts began to emerge which also imposed explicit new duties on both judges and counsel. As such, it is widely recognised that this freedom of proof is not unfettered and is subject to a number of controls. First of all, there is a nuanced difference in a criminal trial between the role of prosecution and defence counsel:

> If the advocate is appearing for the Crown ... he cross-examines in order to get as near to the truth as he can and not to secure a verdict. [But] if he is defending in a criminal case ... he is under no duty to continue with questions which might establish facts unfavourable to his client and favourable to his opponent. (Du Cann, 1993: 112; see also *R v Puddick* (1865) 4 F&F 497)

This is not to say that prosecutors are necessarily 'softer' in cross-examining witnesses; they remain bound by a duty to put the case and the high standard of proof obliges them to eviscerate any reasonable doubt that might remain in the minds of the jury.

Secondly, the scope of cross-examination may be curtailed under the inherent powers of the court at common law to control its own procedure. Judges have discretion in determining if a witness should be compelled to answer a question put to them in accordance with the principles laid down in *Hobbs v Tinling*. Judges also have a duty to curtail unnecessarily protracted cross-examination (*R v Kalia* (1974) 60 Cr App R 200; *Mechanical and*

General Inventions Ltd and Lehwess v Austin and Austin Motor Co Ltd [1935] AC 346, 360). Counsel must not engage in 'aggressive, repetitive or oppressive questioning'; the purpose 'is not to discomfort, harass or abuse a witness for the sake of it' (*Le Brocq v Liverpool Crown Court* [2019] 4 WLR 108 EWCA Crim 1398 [at 62]).[1]

Thirdly, the contemporary Bar Code of Conduct (Bar Standards Board, 2024) sets out rules which reflect these common law restrictions. Under Rule C7, advocates have four primary obligations:

1) you must not make statements or ask questions merely to insult, humiliate or annoy a witness or any other person;
2) you must not make a serious allegation against a witness whom you have had an opportunity to cross-examine unless you have given that witness a chance to answer the allegation in cross-examination;
3) you must not make a serious allegation against any person, or suggest that a person is guilty of a crime with which your client is charged unless:
   a. you have reasonable grounds for the allegation; and
   b. the allegation is relevant to your client's case or the credibility of a witness; and
   c. where the allegation relates to a third party, you avoid naming them in open court unless this is reasonably necessary.
4) you must not put forward to the court a personal opinion of the facts or the law unless you are invited or required to do so by the court or by law.

These constraints on cross-examination have been tempered, however, by the fact that adversarial trials have traditionally prioritised judicial passivity and judges have remained wary of intervention; case law also suggests that 'interventions should be as infrequent as possible' lest it give witnesses 'time to think out the answer to awkward questions' (per Denning LJ, in *Jones v National Coal Board* [1957] 2 QB 55 at 65). In *R v Sharp* ([1993] 3 All ER 225), frequent interruption by the judge resulted in a conviction being quashed by the Court of Appeal, with a warning issued on the dangers of 'seeming to enter the arena … in the sense that he may appear partial to one side or the other' (at 235). This apparent reluctance to intervene has been evidenced through many empirical studies (Davies and Seymour, 1998; O'Kelly et al, 2003; Smith and Skinner, 2012; Zajac et al, 2012).

There is an inherent source of tension between the need for judicial intervention to ensure that controls on cross-examination are adhered to, and the duty in *Browne v Dunn* for the advocate to 'put the case' and

[1] See also *R v Milton Brown* [1998] 2 Crim App R 364, 371.

challenge witnesses who provide testimony which potentially undermines it. In his handbook, Colman (1970) illustrates how some degree of latitude is necessary to ensure that counsel are able to protect their clients' interests first and foremost. Direct questions such as 'are you sure?' are unlikely to be successful. Hence the constant refrain, 'if your lordship will bear with me'. The cross-examiner may find it best to begin by asking questions about the witness himself, or about some matter which is 'no more than marginally relevant to the inquiry [in order to get] the measure of his witness' (156–7). It may be his duty to inquire 'into details which are of no great importance in themselves' in order to bring out conflicts between his opponent's witnesses and to try to break down a well-rehearsed, shrewd or dishonest witness' (158). While judges are notionally duty-bound to intervene where necessary to enforce the rules of conduct, they are inherently prone to give counsel a wide degree of latitude lest they are perceived to enter the arena (Jackson and Doran, 1995; Auld Review, 2002: 527).

Critiquing cross-examination

While cross-examination is widely accepted as a fundamental cornerstone of the adversarial system, this in itself does not provide a rationale for its place in trial. However, the practice has been both staunchly defended by its proponents and heavily scrutinised by its critics.

Cross-examination has been largely justified on two broad grounds: its potential to uncover truth and its corollary to the principle of natural justice. The process was famously lauded by Wigmore (1940: §1367) in the following terms:

> Cross-examination is beyond doubt the greatest legal machine ever invented for the discovery of the truth. However difficult it may be for the layman, the scientist or the foreign jurist to appreciate its wonderful power, there has probably never been a moment's doubt upon this point in the mind of a lawyer of experience.

Wigmore's statement has been widely endorsed in judicial dicta. According to Viscount Sankey LC, in *Mechanical and General Inventions*, '[c]ross-examination is a powerful and valuable weapon for the purpose of testing the veracity of a witness and the accuracy and completeness of its story' (359). According to Colman (1970: 4), there is only one aim of cross-examination: 'to assist in the administration of justice by revealing the truth to the court'. However, establishing the facts is not necessarily a straightforward task since 'there is frequently the danger that the testimony offered may be untruthful. And, even more often, it can be misleading because it is mistaken or presented in an incomplete or inaccurate form' (Colman, 1970: 1).

Colman elaborates, noting that:

> There are witnesses who testify, with the appearance of candour, to what they know to be false; there are witnesses who, because they are biased, or for other reasons, have deceived themselves into believing that what they say is true; there are witnesses who are honest, but mistaken; there are witnesses whose evidence in chief, although it is true and accurate, tends to mislead because material facts are omitted ... there are witnesses whose evidence ought to be received with caution because of their temperaments, their habits, their history, or their interests. (Colman, 1970: 4–5)

The idea that cross-examination can shed new light on assertions made by witnesses is shared by psychologists. Saks and Spellman (2016: 113–35) note that cross-examination helps the trier of fact assess witnesses' truthfulness, accuracy, confidence, and judgement. In this sense, it complements other means of evaluating testimony, such as the weight attached to the oath, witness demeanour, and character evidence.

Beyond these epistemological arguments, cross-examination is widely considered a corollary of the common law principle of natural justice, which holds that parties should have the opportunity to call their own witnesses and cross-examine opposing witnesses (see *Al-Rawi v The Security Service* [2011] UKSC 34 [14] per Lord Dyson). It is often conflated with the right to confrontation enshrined in the Sixth Amendment to the US Constitution. However, these rights can be distinguished: confrontation implies more than the defendant's right to examine opposing witnesses. As stated in the Sixth Amendment, it extends to 'be confronted with the witnesses against him', which has been interpreted as a right to physically confront one's accusers. The scope of the Sixth Amendment is broad, encompassing several aspects: testimony should be given under oath, subjected to cross-examination, and presented in the presence of both the accused and the trier of fact (see further Friedman, 1998).

As well as being an aid to truth-finding, cross-examination can claim then to represent an important process value in adversarial procedure enabling the defendant to participate fully in the presentation of evidence to the fact-finder linked to his right to autonomy and dignity (Dennis, 2010: 266). Like the right to confrontation, however, this must be weighed against the affront to dignity that can be caused to victims and witnesses when they are subjected to cross-examination by defendants. Dennis has argued that the defendant's claim to be treated with dignity does not apply uniquely to defendants. Such a claim can also be made by other participants, namely witnesses and victims (see further Wemmers, 2012; Giannini, 2016). It is true that defendants, unlike other participants, are distinctively in the position of potentially losing their liberty if the verdict goes against them. But this goes more to the epistemic need, linked to the presumption of innocence, that witnesses against them are properly tested before their testimony is relied upon. As the Canadian Supreme Court stated in *Osolin v R* ((1993) 86 CCC (3d) 481, at 516–17):

> [cross-examination] is the ultimate means of demonstrating truth and of testing veracity. Cross-examination must be permitted so that an accused can make full answer and defence. The opportunity to cross-examine witnesses is fundamental to providing a fair trial to an accused. This is an old and well-established principle that is closely linked to the presumption of innocence.

Notably, however, the Canadian Criminal Code does not give an unfettered right to defendants to personally cross-examine witnesses against them, and indeed it is commonly considered that a skilled advocate is much better able to fulfil this role.[2]

Although international human rights instruments do not explicitly reference 'cross-examination', they do state that the defendant has a right to examine witnesses against them,[3] which effectively means a right to cross-examination. However, it is important to underline that the European Court of Human Rights (ECtHR) has never interpreted this right to entail the kind of adversarial, party-driven cross-examination seen in common law courts (Jackson, 2005). In developing this right, the court has had to navigate fundamental differences between common law adversarial approaches and civil law inquisitorial systems, placing increasing emphasis on the specificities of national models (De Wilde, 2013). While most civil law jurisdictions require some form of oral evidence, they lack a conceptual equivalent of cross-examination. Instead, the general principle of 'contradiction' ensures that all parties have the right to present their case and challenge the opposing side's case. Traditionally, this is achieved through submissions to the court, which may include suggested lines of questioning. A number of systems, such as France, Germany, Spain, Portugal, and Italy, now allow parties to directly question witnesses at the discretion of the court (Colson and Field, 2011; Bachmaier, 2019). These changes have introduced an element of 'collective performance in search of an objective truth' (Grande, 2019: 79) but have not fundamentally altered the inquisitorial nature of these systems (Grande, 2019).

Despite being regarded as a useful truth-finding tool by many during the previous century, Langbein (2003: 270) notes that legal historians

[2] Criminal Code (Canada), s 463.2.

[3] See eg Art 14(3)(e) ICCPR; Art 6(3)(d) ECHR; Art 8(2)(f) IACHR.

increasingly came to view cross-examination as a 'blunt instrument' rather than a precise or rigorous method for uncovering the truth. Similarly, Jerome Frank (1949: 85), the American realist who coined the phrase 'fact-skepticism', famously likened the adversarial trial method to 'throwing pepper in the eyes of a surgeon when he is performing an operation'. Cross-examination has been a significant focus of this scepticism, with a growing body of experimental psychological research questioning its effectiveness as a fact-finding tool. This critique is not limited to vulnerable witnesses, with studies having shown that it is often less complete and less accurate than direct examination (Greer, 1971; Loftus, 1975). Concerns generally include the reliability of eyewitness memory (Valentine and Maras, 2011), suggestibility (Loftus, 1975; Wheatcroft and Ellison, 2012), memory and recall, acquiescence (Valentine and Maras, 2011), and the use of complex legal language (Kebbell and Johnson, 2000; Kebbell et al, 2010; Jack and Zajac, 2014; Jacobson et al, 2015) which may undermine the quality of evidence of all witnesses.

Such factors are also likely to act as stressors; while the literature focuses on the strains and anxieties experienced by vulnerable witnesses, cross-examination can be stressful for all types of witnesses regardless of their background or experience. Few are likely to relish the prospect of cross-examination, and even those who regularly experience it, such as police officers and experts, may also experience a sense of trepidation (Brodsky et al, 2017; Brian and Cruickshank, 2019). Nevertheless, heightened vulnerability is likely to exacerbate the impact of underlying distress. Evidence indicates that heightened fear or stress can impair a witness's ability to provide complete and coherent answers (Goodman et al, 1992; Rush et al, 2012; Zajac et al, 2012). Ellison and Munro (2017) note that trauma victims often have fragmented memories, lacking specific details and a linear narrative. The study found that fragmented or incomplete responses may be misinterpreted as dishonesty. Additionally, nervousness, hesitancy, and other physical reactions during questioning might be perceived by the trier of fact as signs of lying, when they are often just stress responses to testifying (see also Segovia et al, 2017).

Questioning techniques for child witnesses have been found particularly wanting, with the use of complex language, age-inappropriate jargon (Brennan and Brennan, 1988; Davies and Noon, 1991; Hayes and Bunting, 2013), and the exploitation of children's increased exposure to suggestibility (Flin, 1990; Davies et al, 1997; Zajac et al, 2012). Plotnikoff and Woolfson (2004) reported that over half of child witnesses found some questions confusing, and the same researchers subsequently reported that many children described defence counsel as 'aggressive' and did not understand all questions. A follow-up study in 2019 indicated some improvements in practice, though disparities in advocacy quality remained. In Australia, meanwhile, research suggests that questioning formats have changed little since the 1950s (Zajac et al, 2018).

Witnesses with learning disabilities face similar challenges. These disabilities range from mild to severe, with those having profound and multiple learning disabilities (PMLD) often not deemed competent to testify (Doak and Doak, 2017). For those who do testify, there are significant concerns around their reduced ability to recall events (Gudjonsson and Henry, 2003; Agnew and Powell, 2004), limited vocabulary, and difficulty understanding courtroom language (Ericson and Pearlman, 2001; White et al, 2015). Like children, such witnesses are often more suggestible, especially when responding to leading questions (Bowles and Sharman, 2014). Some may also be inclined to acquiesce to authority figures to avoid stress (Drake, 2010; Gooding and O'Mahony, 2016). Studies show that cross-examiners often fail to adjust their questioning style due to a lack of knowledge or skills (Kebbell et al, 2004; Henderson, 2015a). Judges also rarely intervene to clarify questions for these witnesses (O'Kelly et al, 2003; Zajac et al, 2012). A systemic review by Morrison et al (2019) highlighted ongoing communication challenges, including suggestibility, negative feedback, and difficulties with court language.

The adversarial nature of trials necessitates that witnesses are closely controlled by counsel, with their testimony managed to align with the case theory. Danet and Bogoch (1980) conducted an empirical study of six US criminal trials, measuring the degree of combativeness in attorney questioning. They categorised questions as either 'coercive' or 'non-coercive' based on the extent of control exerted over the witness, finding that 87 per cent of cross-examination questions were coercive. In the English context, Hamlyn et al (2004) reported that less than half (46 per cent) of prosecution witnesses felt they could give their evidence 'completely accurately'. The remaining 54 per cent felt interrupted, cut off, or unable to fully explain or provide all facts, indicating that cross-examination can obscure or filter out relevant evidence. In a simulated study, Wheatcroft and Ellison (2012) found that mock witnesses who received prior guidance on cross-examination and advocacy techniques provided more accurate evidence and made fewer factual errors than those without such familiarisation. This contrasts with the 'achieving best evidence' (ABE) approach for police interviews (Ministry of Justice and National Police Chiefs' Council, 2022), which emphasises breaks, open-ended questions, and free narrative. In a similar vein, Fielding (2013) criticises the controlled question-and-answer approach of cross-examination, advocating for courts to be more open to receiving evidence in narrative form, similar to the ways in which people naturally recount events in everyday interactions. Despite Wigmore (and many others besides) asserting the potential for cross-examination to uncover truth, Roberts (2022: 315) contends that it is now widely regarded as an 'obstacle to effective forensic fact-finding rather than its guarantee'.

Towards the end of the twentieth century, the potential for secondary victimisation through cross-examination became increasingly apparent. Beyond concerns about cross-examination undermining the truth-finding function of trials, the wellbeing of witnesses became an increasingly important issue. Witnesses often feel like outsiders in a professionalised process, experiencing stress and anxiety, which can be exacerbated by insensitive treatment, sometimes likened to bullying or harassment (Ellison, 2001; Sanders and Jones, 2007; Doak, 2008). Rock (1993: 50) highlighted how witnesses were often coerced into breaking language taboos, with courts hearing details of violent and profane speech from private and public settings. For many judges and legal professionals, distress was seen as a natural aspect of criminal trials (Fielding, 2006, 2013).

As the visibility of victims and witnesses grew, a moral question emerged about exposing vulnerable people to the traumatic effects of cross-examination. Many witnesses, especially in cases of personal offences, faced 'victim-blaming' tactics by the defence to cast them in a negative light (McBarnet, 1983; Brereton, 1997). The plight of complainants in rape and serious sexual offence (RASSO) cases became a focal point in academic debates. Research shows that cross-examination in these cases can be particularly invasive and traumatic, leading to long-term emotional and psychological harm (Chambers and Millar, 1986; Adler, 1987; Lees, 1996; Victim Support, 1996). Rape trials often focus on consent rather than the occurrence of intercourse, leading to credibility battles between the complainant and the accused (Ellison, 2001; Doak, 2008; Smith, 2018). Defence tactics frequently aim to discredit the complainant by portraying them as morally questionable (Grohovsky, 2000; Temkin, 2000). High attrition rates in these cases are partly due to complainants' reluctance to testify, fearing the distress of cross-examination (Smith, 2018; Molina and Poppleton, 2020; Iliadis et al, 2021a). The vulnerability of complainants remains a significant concern, with evidence that intrusive cross-examination tactics persist despite changes in social attitudes and stricter rules on the admissibility of sexual history evidence (McGlynn, 2017; Smith, 2018; Booth et al, 2019).

The legal and policy response

International norms and benchmarks

In addition to academic interest, media coverage of high-profile cases involving vulnerable witnesses has pushed the issue onto the policy agenda in various jurisdictions (Doak, 2008). But it is also worth underlining the growing influence of international trends and developments which have also acted as important drivers for reform towards more effective forms of witness participation and their subsequent impact on fair trial rights. Criminal justice policies are no longer restricted to the boundaries of individual nation states (Misileglas et al, 2015; Colson and Field, 2016), and this had the effect of breaking down the adversarial/inquisitorial dichotomies that have long characterised national criminal procedures and encouraged greater experimentation with mixed models (Jackson, 2021). The International Criminal Court (ICC), established in 2002, exemplifies this trend. The ICC's rules of evidence and procedure were designed to minimise the trauma of giving evidence in cases of genocide, crimes against humanity, or war crimes (Lara, 2011). From the outset, these were created to conform with emergent best practice, drawing from international human rights standards to protect the physical and psychological integrity of witnesses (Beriqi, 2017).[4] Although such standards tend to steer away from prescribing how exactly testimony should be given, there has been a clear overall trend towards a victim/witness-centric and more inclusive approach, which aims to minimise trauma while maximising the quality of evidence (Doak, 2008).

The European Union Victims' Directive 2012/29/EU is another significant milestone. Article 10 grants all victims the right to be heard and provide evidence, and where the victim is a child, due account must be taken of the child's age and maturity. Member states must protect victims and their families from secondary and repeat victimisation and ensure their dignity during questioning and testimony (Article 18). Additional protections are outlined in Articles 21 (privacy), 22 (individual assessment of protection needs), 23 (protection for victims with specific needs), and 24 (protection of child victims). This Directive has been a catalyst for reform across various jurisdictions, leading to legislative changes in Scotland and Ireland and being extensively cited by the Gillen Review (2019) in Northern Ireland.

Various instruments have been developed to enhance standards for vulnerable witnesses, including children and victims of sexual violence. Child witnesses are protected by the well-established 'best interests' principle, with numerous hard and soft law standards mandating significant adaptations to conventional trial processes to enable their effective participation. Similar standards have emerged for witnesses in RASSO cases. The Istanbul Convention on Preventing and Combating Violence Against Women and Domestic Violence (2011) requires measures to protect the privacy of complainants. Signatory states must enact legislative changes to ensure

[4] There are, however, significant concerns surrounding how effectively these measures operate in practice (see eg McGonigle Leyh, 2011; Beriqi, 2017; Hirst and Sahyouni, 2020; Doak et al, 2021).

victims can be heard, provide evidence, and have their views, needs, and concerns considered, either directly or through an intermediary. In *VK v Bulgaria* (C/49/D/20/2008), the United Nations Committee on the Elimination of Discrimination Against Women (CEDAW) held that states must protect women in criminal proceedings from gender stereotypes and misconceptions about rape and sexuality. Similarly, in *Y v Slovenia* (App No 41107/10, 28 May 2015), the ECtHR ruled that cross-examination by the accused in person could breach the complainant's Article 8 rights, stating that cross-examination should not be used to intimidate or humiliate witnesses. Witnesses with disabilities are protected under Article 13 of the UN Convention on the Rights of Persons with Disabilities, which calls on states to facilitate their effective participation as witnesses and ensure appropriate training for all involved in the administration of justice.

Effective participation as an emerging international human rights norm

The ECtHR has recognised that effective participation is essential for the accused's fair trial rights under Article 6 (*Colozza v Italy* (1985) 7 EHRR 516; *Stanford v UK* (1994) App No 16757/90). The English model has previously been found to be in breach of the Article 6 rights for juvenile defendants for failing to adapt its procedures to enable effective participation (see *T and V v United Kingdom* (1999) 30 EHRR 121; *SC v United Kingdom* (2005) 40 EHRR 10). Beyond the generic observations made by the Court in these cases, there is little certainty about the types of measures that might enable all defendants to participate more effectively, irrespective of whether they are considered 'vulnerable'. Yet there is growing evidence of an emergent right to 'effective participation' for all witnesses, both defendants and non-defendants, regardless of individual vulnerabilities (European Commission, 2013). Although the precise meaning of such a right remains imprecise and contested (Owusu-Bempah, 2018), Sixsmith (2024: 56) argues that the test for effective participation requires defendants to understand the case against them, follow the course of proceedings, instruct their legal representatives, and give evidence in their defence.

'Balancing' of rights

The ECtHR has ruled that Article 6(3)(d), which guarantees a criminal defendant the 'right to examine or have examined witnesses against him', enshrines the principle that all evidence against him must normally be produced in his presence at a public hearing with a view to adversarial argument (*Al-Khawaja and Tahery v UK* (2012) 54 EHRR 23, [118]). But in common with other Convention rights, it has adopted a proportionality approach towards limitations on this principle and, crucially, has recognised that, 'in appropriate cases, principles of fair trial require that the interests of the defence are balanced against those of witnesses or victims called upon to testify, in particular where life, liberty or security of person are at stake, or interests coming generally within the ambit of Article 8 of the Convention' (*Doorson v The Netherlands* (1996) 22 EHRR 330, [70]).[5]

Unlike the US, where the Sixth Amendment's 'confrontation clause' has been interpreted to grant the accused the right to a face-to-face encounter with opposing witnesses (*Dowdell v United States*, 221 US 325, 330 (1911)), the ECtHR has long recognised that deviations from traditional oral testimony (including pre-trial hearings) do not violate fair trial rights under Article 6 of the Convention, provided there are effective counterbalancing measures in place to challenge the evidence (*Kostovski v Netherlands* (1989) 12 EHRR 434, [41]; *Baegen v Netherlands*, App No 16696/90, 27 October 1995). In *Mraović v Croatia* (App No 30373/13, 14 May 2020), the Court held that excluding the public from a rape trial did not infringe the applicant's Article 6 right to a public hearing; the state had an obligation to protect the complainant from embarrassment and stigmatisation, which could lead to secondary victimisation. Given that the cross-examination involved highly sensitive matters related to her private life, it was reasonable to restrict the applicant's Article 6 rights to protect the complainant's Article 8 rights. The Court dismissed the applicant's argument that only the relevant part of the proceedings should have been closed, noting that sensitive information could have been mentioned at any point during the trial.

However, the rights of the accused should not be diminished lightly, as the accused stands to lose significantly more than the victim if the trial process is flawed. In rare instances where such a balancing act is necessary, the rights of the defence 'must be curtailed as little as possible' and cannot be simply 'balanced away' (Campbell et al, 2019: 48). In *Van Mechelen v Netherlands* ((1998) 25 EHRR 657), it was held that any measures restricting the rights of the defence should be strictly necessary, and if a less restrictive measure can suffice, then it is that measure which should be applied (at [59]). Breaches of the right to a fair trial are unlikely to be found on the basis of evidential or procedural rules per se, with the Court looking instead at the trial process as a whole in order to ascertain whether the fundamental requirements of fairness have been observed (*Barbera, Messegue and Jabardo v Spain* (1988) 11 EHRR 360).

Crucially, the defence must be afforded an opportunity to challenge the complainant's evidence, albeit not necessarily through direct questioning. In *SN v Sweden* (App No 34209/96, 2 July 2002), the Court held that, while

[5] See also *Finkensieper v Netherlands* (App No 19525/92, 17 May 1995); Art 8 imposed a positive obligation which did not interfere with the fair trial rights of the accused.

the pre-recorded testimony of the child was virtually the sole evidence on which the defendant had been convicted, the fact that the defence had been allowed to test the evidence by putting questions indirectly to the victim through a police officer acting as a conduit meant that the applicant had not been denied a fair trial.[6] However, such cases highlight that the outcome of the balancing exercise is not always predictable. Burton (2023: 23–4) raises the general question of how far a defendant's right to question opposing witnesses should be balanced against a vulnerable witness's right to restrictions on how that cross-examination should occur. While the case law outlines measures that have been deemed not to interfere with fair trial rights, new and innovative methods of receiving evidence may not always be considered compliant.

This evolving normative stance has been described as a model of 'participatory proof', which encourages member states to develop less adversarial practices to enable all witnesses to provide their best evidence (Jackson and Summers, 2012). Three well-established common law principles have often been cited as barriers to reform: the principle of open justice, the right to confrontation, and the principle of orality, which dictates that live testimony should be given under oath in open court in the presence of the accused and the trier of fact (see Doak et al, 2021). However, international fora consider that proportionate departures from these principles can be justified without prejudicing the accused's right to a fair trial (Jackson, 2023). Such departures have been upheld by appellate courts in many common law jurisdictions, including Canada, New Zealand, and South Africa. As noted by the Gillen Review (2019: 155–65) and observed in our own research (see Chapters 3 and 7), many objections to procedural innovations, such as pre-recorded cross-examination, have not been based on matters of principle but rather on the practical difficulties of implementing new innovations.

Law and policy in the surveyed jurisdictions

Developments at the national level have mirrored the international trend towards a more inclusive and witness- and victim-centric approach. There has been a clear shift from the conventional 'advocacy' model of cross-examination to a 'best evidence' model, which focuses solely on testing the veracity of witnesses' evidence. While the scale and pace of reform have varied across jurisdictions, initial limited exceptions to normal trial procedures – such as the use of screens or the removal of wigs and gowns – have evolved into more significant departures. These include the use of video

[6] Cf *Bocos-Cuesta v The Netherlands* (App No 54789/00, 10 November 2005); *Kovač v Croatia* (App No 503/05, 12 July 2007).

platforms that allow witnesses to give live or recorded evidence outside the courtroom, often with the assistance of an intermediary.

As noted earlier, the traditional 'umpireal' role of the adversarial trial judge often conflicts with the duty to intervene and prevent overzealous, irrelevant, or protracted cross-examination. Historically, appellate courts have avoided providing specific guidance on how and when judges should control advocates' questioning styles or lines of inquiry. However, the following discussion reveals a marked change in direction. Judicial assertiveness, led by the Court of Appeal in England, has significantly influenced a broader cultural shift within the legal profession (see further Chapter 7).

England and Wales

Special measures for child witnesses were first introduced in the 1980s. The Court of Appeal indicated that courts had a common law discretion to order the use of screens (*R v X, Y and Z* (1989) 91 Cr App R 36), while the Criminal Justice Act 1988 introduced live links, followed by the introduction of pre-recorded evidence-in-chief under the Criminal Justice Act 1991. The Pigot Committee (Home Office, 1989) made a far-reaching recommendation that the entirety of children's evidence in serious cases should be pre-recorded in advance of the trial, although the proposal was met with stiff opposition (see further Spencer and Flin, 1993: 415). The idea resurfaced a decade later as part of a series of recommendations from a government interdepartmental review on the treatment of vulnerable or intimidated witnesses in the criminal justice system, *Speaking Up for Justice* (Home Office, 1998). This led to an enhanced range of special measures being introduced under the Youth Justice and Criminal Evidence Act 1999 for broader categories of vulnerable and intimidated witnesses, excluding defendants.[7] As noted in the previous chapter, the introduction of pre-recorded cross-examination has replaced live cross-examination at trial for certain witnesses, and the powers of intermediaries to rephrase questions mark a significant departure from the adversarial principle of party control;[8] these reforms are considered in some depth in the next two chapters.

---

7 Eight special measures are contained within Part 2 of the Act: screens; live links; giving evidence in private; removal of wigs and gowns; pre-recorded evidence-in-chief; pre-recorded cross-examination or re-examination; examination through an intermediary; aids to communication. For early evaluations see Hamlyn et al (2004); Burton et al (2006). The legislation was accompanied by Home Office guidance (see currently Ministry of Justice and National Police Chiefs' Council, 2022).

8 See generally Damaška (1973), distinguishing the adversarial model whereby parties generally control the evidence from the inquisitorial model wherein it is controlled by state officials.

In the years that followed the introduction of special measures, it became apparent to many intermediaries that their recommendations were not being consistently applied at trial. As such, they began to meet with the Crown Prosecution Service (CPS) and advocates pre-trial to discuss and agree their recommendations on how witnesses should be questioned (Cooper et al, 2015; Henderson et al, 2019). These 'bottom-up' pre-trial meetings evolved into what are now known as ground rules hearings (GRHs), wherein the trial judges, in consultation with counsel and the intermediary, predetermine the nature and extent of proposed questioning as well as any adaptations to trial procedure that may enable vulnerable witnesses to give best evidence (see further Chapter 3).

While England and Wales has been an international trail-blazer in many respects, the appellate courts have considered several cases where it was argued that accommodations made for vulnerable witnesses at trial interfered with the fair trial rights of the accused. In a leading 2008 decision, the House of Lords reaffirmed the common law principle that a defendant in a criminal trial should be confronted by their accusers to cross-examine and challenge their evidence (*R v Davis* [2008] UKHL 36). However, English courts have long accepted that the right to cross-examination does not necessarily entail physical confrontation (*R v Smellie* (1919) 14 Cr App R 128),[9] preferring the proportionality approach adopted by the ECtHR. To date, there has been no indication that any aspects of the special measures regime would be potentially incompatible with fair trial rights. As Lady Hale observed in *R v Camberwell Green Youth Court ex p D (a minor)* ([2005] 1 WLR 393, [49]):

> The evidence is produced in the presence of the accused, some of it pre-recorded and some of it by contemporaneous television transmission. The accused can see and hear it all and has every opportunity to challenge and question the witnesses against him at the trial itself. The only thing missing is face-to-face confrontation, but the appellant accepted that the Convention does not guarantee a right to face-to-face confrontation.

Here the court considered a challenge to child witnesses being examined-in-chief by pre-recorded video and cross-examined by live link, but had the witness's cross-examination been pre-recorded this procedure would not be any less compliant with Article 6 (see *R v PMH* [2018] EWCA Crim 2452). Nor is there any reason to believe that when an intermediary who has been appointed to facilitate the communication of a vulnerable witness interjects

[9] See also Wigmore (1940: §1397); Home Office (1989: §230).

during cross-examination that this would not be considered compatible with the Convention.

In *R v Jonas* ([2015] EWCA Crim 562), the Court of Appeal considered whether the defendant's fair trial rights were unduly infringed when the trial judge intervened to restrict the cross-examination of a complainant in a case involving trafficking and sex offences with multiple defendants. The complainant had been cross-examined for two weeks, mostly in relation to the veracity of her life 'backstory' in Hungary. The judge subsequently prevented counsel for the co-accused from pursuing a similar line of questioning, stating that it would be repetitious and unfair to the complainant. Dismissing the appeal, Hallett LJ stated that 'in our view her timely and sensible interventions ensured that the whole process was fair to everyone. She protected the witness from unnecessary and oppressive questioning, but not at the expense of a fair trial for the defendants' (at [37]).[10]

Scotland

Paralleling calls for reform in England and Wales, the Scottish Law Commission (1990) advocated for a series of reforms regarding the evidence of vulnerable witnesses. Their report led to the Criminal Procedure (Scotland) Act 1995, which introduced screens and live televised links for child witnesses under 16 giving evidence-in-chief and under cross-examination. Subsequent reforms to the 1995 legislation followed. The Vulnerable Witnesses (Scotland) Act 2004 extended the categories of vulnerability to include complainants in RASSO cases and adults whose live testimony in court might be diminished by mental disorder, fear, or distress. The range of alternative measures was broadened to include the taking of evidence by a commissioner (a pre-trial hearing comprising both examination-in-chief and cross-examination overseen by a judge), the use of a supporter, and giving evidence-in-chief in the form of a prior statement.

Further amendments to the 1995 Act were introduced by the Victims and Witnesses (Scotland) Act 2014, which extended the categories of vulnerability, and by the Vulnerable Witnesses (Criminal Evidence) (Scotland) Act 2019, which enabled courts to take children's evidence in full in advance of the trial in 'solemn' cases via a commissioner. Witnesses who fall under other vulnerable categories may also apply to the court to give evidence in this way, and it has become the norm for complainers in RASSO cases to give evidence in this manner. While many of these alternative measures bear some similarity with those which have been introduced in England and Wales, one difference lies in the fact that there is no conceptual equivalent of an intermediary. The role of a 'supporter' is markedly different from that of an intermediary; supporters may not

[10] See also *R v Pipe* ([2014] EWCA Crim 270).

intervene or rephrase questions or answers; their sole purpose is to provide moral support by being present alongside the witness while s/he is giving evidence.

The Dorrian Review (2021) on the management of sexual offence cases recommended, inter alia, the creation of a specialist non-jury court for sexual offences, where trauma-informed practices would be embedded and a presumption of early pre-recorded cross-examination would apply in all cases. Many of these recommendations which require legislation have been introduced in the recent Victims, Witnesses and Justice Reform (Scotland) Bill 2023, although the proposals for juryless trials have since been dropped.

Northern Ireland

Northern Ireland mirrored England and Wales in implementing special measures for vulnerable witnesses. During the 1990s, live link and pre-recorded evidence became available to child witnesses. The Criminal Evidence (Northern Ireland) Order 1999 then provided the same range of special measures as the Youth Justice and Criminal Evidence Act 1999. Initially, defendants were excluded from these measures, but subsequent amendments allowed certain vulnerable defendants (children under 18 and those with disabilities) access to live link and intermediaries. The roll-out of intermediaries and pre-recorded cross-examination faced significant delays; after initial pilots based on the English approach, intermediaries were introduced across Northern Ireland in 2016, and pre-recorded cross-examination was partially introduced in 2017 for piloting.

Reform efforts gained momentum following the publication of the Gillen Review (2019), which examined the law and procedures in serious sexual offences in Northern Ireland after a high-profile trial where two professional rugby players were acquitted of rape. The Review proposed transformative changes, advocating for 'a new culture of cross-examination, which departs from the conventional adversarial approach' (at 149). The Review highlighted the need to redefine conventional rules for cross-examining children and vulnerable people in criminal trials and directed advocates to change their current practices (at 480). It recommended piloting GRHs in all cases involving pre-recorded cross-examination, with the aim of eventually extending them to hearings involving child complainants and vulnerable adult witnesses (including the accused). Training was identified as a key priority.

The first major changes were outlined in a Practice Note (Lord Chief Justice's Office, 2019), emphasising that the principle of best evidence applies to all witnesses, including the accused. It stated that 'this may mean departing radically from traditional questioning techniques in the cross-examination of a vulnerable witness. The form and extent of the cross-examination of a vulnerable witness will vary from case to case' (at [25]). Two separate protocols are appended to the Practice Direction. The

Protocol for Vulnerable Witnesses (Annex A) outlines the additional steps and provisions necessary to encourage, facilitate, and support the attendance and participation of vulnerable witnesses to give their best evidence in all trials. It details the purpose and nature of GRHs, as well as the roles of Registered Intermediaries (RIs) and the Witness Service/Young Witness Service in preparing for and during their evidence in court. Annex B contains a similar protocol specifically outlining support and special measures for both adult and juvenile vulnerable defendants.

Ireland

The first significant statutory protections for vulnerable witnesses were introduced in the Criminal Evidence Act 1992, which aimed to make it easier for children and persons with 'mental handicap' to give evidence in cases of physical or sexual abuse. This legislation remained largely unchanged for a quarter of a century. As in many other jurisdictions, heightened awareness of the issues facing vulnerable witnesses and the advent of the European Union Victims' Directive (Directive 2012/29/EU) acted as catalysts for a major overhaul of the law. The 1992 Act was significantly revised by two new pieces of legislation: the Criminal Law (Sexual Offences) Act 2017 and the Criminal Justice (Victims of Crime) Act 2017. These Acts extended the range of measures available and broadened eligibility requirements to cover a wider pool of witnesses, including complainants in sexual assault cases. Irish law now recognises a full range of special measures, including: live link; pre-recorded evidence-in-chief; the removal of wigs/gowns; and the use of screens. Despite calls by Rape Crisis Ireland (2018) and the Oireachtas Joint Committee on Justice (2021) to introduce a pilot of pre-recorded cross-examination, no such statutory provision exists. The proposal was rejected by the O'Malley Review (2020) due to concerns about sufficient disclosure to the defence, though it was noted that this merited future consideration.

Ireland was one of the first jurisdictions to make statutory provision for the use of intermediaries under the 1992 legislation. However, despite its place on the statute books, the procedure was rarely utilised until recently due to vague wording in the original legislation and the lack of subsequent guidance in Irish courts (Rape Crisis Network Ireland, 2018: 10–11). The measure is available to all witnesses under the age of 18, as well as to adults with a 'mental disorder', who are delivering, or about to deliver, testimony through a live television link in respect of a sexual or violent offence (that is, a 'relevant offence').[11] The relevant offence gateway does not apply where the witness, in respect of whom the special measures application is

[11] Criminal Evidence Act 1992, s 14(1A).

being made, is the victim of the alleged offence and is a child or an adult with a 'mental disorder'. In each case, the court has jurisdiction to grant an application for an intermediary if it is satisfied that such an accommodation is in the 'interests of justice'.[12] Additionally, pursuant to section 19(2)(c) of the Criminal Justice (Victims of Crime) Act 2017, the intermediary facility is open, at the discretion of the court, to all victims who are adjudged to have a 'specific protection need', regardless of the nature of the offence allegedly committed against them. There are indications that intermediaries are active in a growing, though still small, number of cases following their successful roll-out across England and Northern Ireland (Delahunt, 2024). Following the recommendation of the O'Malley Review on the need for a cohort of appropriately qualified intermediaries, a Professional Diploma in Intermediary Studies was launched at the University of Limerick in September 2022, and the Department of Justice is currently in the process of creating a national panel. The O'Malley Review also served as the impetus for a new legislative framework for pre-trial hearings. Under the Criminal Procedure Act 2021, courts have the discretion to hold one or more preliminary hearings in all cases involving indictable offences, provided the court is satisfied that such a hearing 'would be conducive to the expeditious and efficient conduct of the proceedings' and 'is not contrary to the interests of justice' (section 6(1)). Notably, section 6(2) mandates this approach for certain particularly serious offences (see further Cusack, 2022).

As in other jurisdictions, recent decisions of the Irish Court of Appeal have endorsed the constitutionality of certain special measures following concerns that they could interfere with the constitutional right to a fair trial. In *DPP v VE* ([2021] IECA 122), Ms Justice Ní Raifeartaigh noted that the fairness of the trial might require some accommodations for vulnerable complainants and in *DPP v O'Driscoll* ([2022] IECA 4), the Court upheld a ruling allowing the principal prosecution witness to give evidence by video link and be supported by an intermediary. However, a more recent decision concluded that:

> If matters have reached a point where a child witness no longer remembers the events which gave rise to the prosecution by reason of the delay between the video-recording and the trial, matters may have reached a point where cross-examination would be in effect meaningless, and the accused person may be said to have been deprived of his right to cross-examine. (*DPP v MT* [2023] IECA 65 [86])[13]

[12] Ibid, s 30(c)(ii).

[13] Cf the English Court of Appeal decision in *R v DL* ([2019] EWCA Crim 1249).

Juridical flux

As previously noted, the traditional umpireal role of the adversarial trial judge often conflicts with the duty to intervene and prevent overzealous, irrelevant, or protracted cross-examination. Historically, appellate courts have avoided providing specific guidance on how and when judges should control advocates' questioning styles or lines of inquiry. This remains true in Northern Ireland and Ireland. However, the situation in England and Wales, and to a lesser extent in Scotland, is now quite different. Here, courts have increasingly exercised judicial authority to ensure the best evidence is obtained, which has significantly influenced a broader cultural shift within the legal profession (see further Chapter 7).

This juridical turn was spearheaded by the Court of Appeal in England in four decisions between 2010 and 2012, all involving sexual offences on young children, and marked the beginning of an era of fundamental change for the cross-examination of vulnerable witnesses: *R v Barker* ([2010] EWCA Crim 4); *R v E* ([2011] EWCA Crim 3028); *R v W and M* ([2010] EWCA Crim 1926); and *R v Wills* ([2012] 1 Cr App R 2). This line of case law elicits three key rules that cross-examiners ought to bear in mind. First, age-appropriate language must always be used. As the court remarked in *Barker*, 'the task of the advocate is to formulate short, simple questions which put the essential elements of the defendant's case to the witness' (at [42]). Secondly, cross-examiners must restrict the use of suggestion and use 'short and untagged questions' (at [30]), and there is a corresponding duty on the judge to ensure that any limitations are complied with' (*Wills*, at [36]). Thirdly, cross-examiners should adopt a cautious approach when challenging or seeking to undermine the testimony of a vulnerable witness. In *E*, the Court noted that 'direct challenges', such as accusations of lying, are unhelpful and risk confusion (at [28]). As the court explained in *Wills*, such necessary limitations to protect witnesses impact upon the traditional approach to cross-examination insofar as comment should not be made on any inconsistencies (at [39]). Instead, the evidence could be challenged after the witness had finished providing testimony.[14]

In the years that followed, best practice guidelines were issued urging judges and magistrates to control the questioning of vulnerable witnesses. In some cases, this meant breaking from the rule in *Browne v Dunn*, which held that a failure to cross-examine should be taken as tacit acceptance of the witness's evidence. As the Court of Appeal stated in *R v Lubemba; R v JP* [2015] 1WLR 1579, these developments represent a radical departure from the traditional style of advocacy. To ensure justice for both the vulnerable

[14] See also *R v E* ([2011] EWCA Crim 3028).

witness and the accused, '[a]dvocates must adapt to the witness, not the other way round' ([45]).

Significant steps have also been taken to train advocates in questioning vulnerable witnesses. The Inns of Court College of Advocacy, in conjunction with the Bar, has developed a national programme of Advocacy and the Vulnerable Training. This programme, based on '20 Principles for Questioning' vulnerable people and children, is designed to become mandatory for any advocate wishing to undertake publicly funded work in serious sexual offences cases involving vulnerable witnesses (see further Cooper et al, 2018).

An independent body known as The Advocate's Gateway has also published 20 toolkits to assist judges, lawyers, and other criminal justice professionals in dealing with vulnerable court users.[15] These toolkits provide advice and illustrative examples of optimal approaches on various issues such as questioning witnesses with a range of disabilities, young children, and ensuring the effective participation of young defendants. In addition to being referenced by the Inns of Court College of Advocacy, the toolkits have been endorsed by the Crown Prosecution Service (2021) and the Judicial College (2024), and have been cited as a source of best practice by the Court of Appeal (see *R* v *Grant-Murray and Others* [2017] EWCA Crim 1228; *R* v *RK* [2018] EWCA Crim 603) and advocacy manuals (Cowe and Cavender, 2020: 114). They were also frequently mentioned by many of the practitioners we interviewed in the course of the research.

The Scottish courts have also become increasingly vocal concerning the role of the court in intervening to prevent inappropriate cross-examination. In *Begg (Duncan William) v HM Advocate* ([2015] HCJAC 69), a rape complainant had been subject to a lengthy cross-examination, which opened with the question: 'you are a wicked, deceitful, malicious, vindictive liar?' The advocate continued with comments such as 'because you've been trying to get [the appellant] into trouble for the last twenty years? … and this is your last hurrah?'

Lord Carloway issued a stern rebuke to this line of questioning:

> Due regard must be had to the right or privilege under domestic law to test a witness's evidence by properly directed and focused cross-examination. That right, however, does not extend to insulting or intimidating a witness … It also requires to be balanced against the right of a witness to be afforded some respect for her dignity and privacy … The court must be prepared, where appropriate, to interfere when cross-examination strays beyond proper bounds, both in terms

[15] www.theadvocatesgateway.org/toolkits-1-1-1.

> of the nature of the questioning and the length of time for which a complainer can be expected to withstand sustained attack. In this case, it is doubtful whether the ubiquitous informed bystander would have regarded the conduct of this trial as affording due respect for this complainer's rights.

Citing *Inch v Inch* (1856) 18 D 997, referring to the power of the judge to stop questioning that was 'protracted, vexatious and unfeeling', as well as the English cases of *Lubemba* and *Jonas*, he concluded that where a proper balance cannot be achieved by the representatives of the Crown and defence, the court had a duty to intervene (at [40]).

The rapid roll-out of GRHs, extension of the use of evidence on commission and significant appellate rulings[16] have introduced a 'sea change' in the court's readiness to control cross-examination in sexual offences cases (Lord Beckett, 2023), notwithstanding some disquiet around the apparent erosion of the 'unfettered right to ask any question of any witness' (Scottish Courts and Tribunals Service, 2016). Particularly since the COVID-19 pandemic, the High Court has also been making use of its existing powers to take the evidence of many vulnerable witnesses, including complainers in sex offence cases, on commission as early as possible (Lord Beckett, 2023). Practice Notes issued by the High Court of Justiciary (2017, 2019) provide for a Scottish equivalent of the GRH, requiring all parties to consider which measures should be put in place and which rules should govern the questioning. Several indicative good practices are set out for taking evidence on commission, including endorsement of the English Court of Appeal's decision in *Lubemba*, the toolkits issued by The Advocate's Gateway, and the power to order the pre-submission of written questions.[17] As in England and Wales, professional bodies and regulators have taken separate steps to introduce training in respect of the new measures introduced under the 2019 Act to help practitioners understand its provisions, apply them in practice, and access necessary support and resources (Scottish Government, 2023).

Conclusions

Cross-examination plays a crucial role in truth-finding, ensuring that the defence can challenge prosecution evidence. However, research over the past few decades has highlighted that this procedure can also be detrimental

16 See eg *Begg*; and *Donegan v HM Advocate* [2019] JC 81.

17 The 2019 Practice Note creates a presumption that written questions will be prepared for all children under 12.

to truth-finding and to the rights and interests of victims and witnesses. Recently, there has been a clear shift from its traditional adversarial roots – where the goal was to advance a case and undermine an opponent – towards using it as a purely forensic tool for testing a witness's evidence to achieve the 'best evidence'. This new paradigm is evolving against the backdrop of an increasing emphasis on international human rights norms that recognise the rights and interests of victims and witnesses alongside those of defendants.

At the national level, special or alternative measures and procedures are entrenched in legislation across all four jurisdictions. Over time, both the range of measures and the categories of witnesses eligible to apply for them have increased considerably. In addition to children, complainants in sexual offence cases are now presumed or deemed eligible, as are witnesses with developmental disorders and those in fear or distress (Doak et al, 2021). More recently, legislation has expanded to cover witnesses in trafficking, modern slavery, and domestic abuse cases (Doak et al, 2021). These measures have become more innovative, significantly impacting the 'art of the advocate' (Du Cann, 1993) and challenging some of the epistemological assumptions around the function of the adversarial trial and the principle of orality.

The overall direction is clear: there is a strong consensus that the traditional 'gladiatorial' approach to cross-examining vulnerable witnesses is now essentially redundant. In this respect, at least on paper, England and Wales appears to be a trail-blazer, having the most extensive range of measures in place, with the pace and success of their roll-out attributable in significant measure to a series of assertive decisions by the Court of Appeal. Scotland has followed suit to a large degree, with evidence on commission being pre-recorded, although there is no provision for intermediaries. Similarly, Northern Ireland has the same mechanisms in place as England and Wales, although pre-recorded cross-examination is still not operational. Ireland appears to lag behind in some respects, with no provision currently for pre-recorded cross-examination or GRHs, although efforts towards further reform have gathered momentum over the past decade.

In broad terms, the reforms outlined have not only made legislative inroads into the orality principle but, with the active participation of the judiciary, have also begun to change the fundamental nature of cross-examination itself. The introduction of GRHs, pre-recorded cross-examination, and the increasing use of intermediaries to mediate how questions are put represent significant changes to the traditional 'advocacy' model of cross-examination. These developments are explored further in the following chapters.

3

Pre-recorded Cross-Examination and Ground Rules Hearings

Introduction

The previous chapter highlighted the justifications and critiques of cross-examination, emphasising the importance of new mechanisms to facilitate the effective participation of witnesses and defendants. International developments, such as the EU Victims' Directive,[1] case law from the European Court of Human Rights, and other international instruments, have acted as catalysts for change in domestic systems. For many years special measures have been in place to ease the ordeal that witnesses face when giving testimony in court. In contrast to what might be loosely termed 'first-generation measures', such as the use of screens, live link, and pre-recorded evidence, which have been subject to considerable analysis and critique for some three decades now, considerably less is known about the operation in practice of 'second-generation' measures which impact directly on cross-examination, particularly pre-recorded cross-examination and the use of intermediaries. Both mechanisms have proven notably more contentious than the first, and their roll-out was a significant factor in the evolution of ground rules hearings (GRHs).[2] As we shall see, these measures are not yet in place across all the jurisdictions and may operate in different ways, but they are having a profound impact on the way cross-examination is conducted. This chapter explores pre-recorded cross-examination, the operation of GRHs, and our fieldwork findings, which provide valuable insights on their operation in practice. While the role of intermediaries is

[1] Directive 2012/29/EU (the Victims' Rights Directive).

[2] Note that GRHs are not special measures per se. As discussed later, they emerged as a bottom-up initiative by intermediaries and the Crown Prosecution Service (CPS).

also integral to these processes, their role at the trial is discussed separately in the next chapter.

Pre-recorded cross-examination

Pre-recorded cross-examination was generally received positively by most practitioners, albeit judges and intermediaries were more supportive than counsel (one judge even described herself as a 'massive fan' (AAJ3)). Many highlighted benefits such as reducing trial delays and capturing fresher, more reliable evidence by mitigating the risk of memory fading over time. In Scotland, there was considerable support among judges and advocates for taking the evidence of vulnerable witnesses on commission in advance of trial, with the reduction in stress commonly cited as a key benefit (English judges were less certain on this point). In the longer term, there was support for capturing all evidence given by children early, similar to the *Barnahus* (Children's House) system used in Nordic countries (see further Chapter 8). Counsel, particularly in England and Wales, had more mixed views. Some expressed reservations about its use with adult witnesses, concerned that it might isolate evidence from the trial's holistic context. Intermediaries found pre-recorded cross-examination effective for young and elderly witnesses, but some noted concerns around the risk of cracked trials.

The dynamics of pre-recorded cross-examination

In theory, there should be no material difference between pre-recorded and live cross-examination of a witness at trial. Most counsel agreed, noting that 'everything should be dealt with in the same way' (AAJ1) and it was 'no different' (ABC2). Interviewees in both jurisdictions said that cross-examination took exactly the same form as if it were given before a jury in the actual trial and, in England and Wales in particular, there was unlikely to be any significant change in the anxiety or stress felt by witnesses. However, there was a general consensus in both jurisdictions that without a jury questioning was shorter, more focused, and less theatrical (see further Chapter 8).

Pre-recorded cross-examination is conducted differently in England and Wales and in Scotland. In England and Wales, pre-recorded cross-examination is received through a 'section 28 hearing' which is notionally part of trial itself.[3] However, it cannot stand alone as a special measure. A special measures direction (SMD) for video-recorded cross-examination may only be granted if there already exists an SMD for video-recorded

[3] Youth Justice and Criminal Evidence Act 1999, s 28.

evidence-in-chief under section 27 of the Act. Accordingly, pre-recorded cross-examination as a special measure is conditioned upon a police 'Achieving Best Evidence' (ABE) interview having already been recorded and admitted as the witness's evidence-in-chief. Thus, the use of section 28 pre-recorded cross-examination depends on police recognition of a particular witness's vulnerability. A failure by the police to recognise that vulnerability or to video-record an ABE interview has the additional consequence that section 28 pre-recorded cross-examination becomes unavailable to that witness.

Section 28 hearings proved to be contentious and were the last of the special measures under the 1999 Act to be implemented (Cooper, 2005). They were subsequently omitted from the first phase of implementation in July 2002 and original plans to pilot them in 2003 were repeatedly delayed, meaning that the measure was not piloted until 2013 and was only made available for certain categories of witnesses in all Crown Court centres in November 2020 (see Doak et al, 2021; Fairclough, 2023). Section 28 was rolled out nationally for vulnerable witnesses in late 2020.[4]

Some concerns were logistical in nature, relating to issues such as the expedited case preparation timeframe and the availability or functionality of technology (Munro et al, 2024; see later discussion), while others were directed at the potential negative ramifications on the fair trial rights of the defence, including how to deal with late disclosure (Cooper et al, 2018; Kyneswood, 2022). Other objections centred on the apparent erosion of the principle of orality, whereby the accepted norm is for live testimony to be given under oath in open court, subjected to cross-examination, in the presence of the accused and in the presence of the trier of fact. In short, the adversarial model's primary mechanism for testing evidence appeared to be threatened (Lazer, 2021). The objections to pre-recorded cross-examination from the legal profession, however, have not tended to be based on the principle of orality per se but rather on the practical difficulties of accommodating pre-recorded cross-examination within a trial system dedicated to orality (see, for example, Gillen Review, 2019: 155–65).

During such a hearing, the witness sits in a room adjoining the courtroom and gives evidence via video link. The hearing is recorded and played at trial in place of live cross-examination. Few interviewees suggested that this was any less trying than giving evidence in open court. While one judge

[4] Data on the use of s 28 shows that in the period June 2016–June 2023, section 28 was used in 4,392 cases, though its use increased substantially from 2021 following the implementation of s 28 for child and other vulnerable witnesses in all courts and the piloting, roll-out and implementation of s 28 for adult witnesses when it was used in 3,610 cases (Thomas, 2024).

acknowledged that stress might be exacerbated 'when there's a jury and there's a judge and the whole thing is underway' (ACJ3), another stated that it was 'just as traumatic for them whether there's a jury there or not' (ABJ2). An intermediary noted that requiring hearings to be conducted in the court building was an example of how technology drives procedures to the detriment of obtaining the witnesses' best evidence (AXR1). In her view, many witnesses would prefer to give evidence from a location remote from the court building, but existing technology could not facilitate this.

In Scotland, pre-recorded cross-examination is taken on commission by a High Court judge and, unlike in England and Wales, is regarded as a separate pre-trial hearing.[5] Practice Notes issued by the High Court of Justiciary (2017, 2019) require all parties to consider which measures should be put in place, and which rules should govern the questioning. A number of indicative good practices are set out for taking evidence on commission, including endorsement of the English Court of Appeal's decision in *R v Lubemba; R v JP* [2015] 1 WLR 1579, the toolkits issued by The Advocate's Gateway (2015a, 2015b, 2019, 2024), and the power to order the pre-submission of written questions as part of GRHs (see later in the chapter).

Usually, the witness's evidence-in-chief will have been recorded in a joint investigative interview, now the norm for child witnesses, meaning that both evidence-in-chief and cross-examination will be pre-recorded. The environment is quite different from the live link room used in English proceedings. In Glasgow, evidence is taken at a bespoke commission suite away from the main court building, described by one judge as 'an average-sized living room with a desk' (BAC2) or, in other parts of Scotland, in the well of a small courtroom (BAC2, BAC3). The informal environment was seen by many as an important factor in enabling best evidence:

> There's a specially designed commission room used in Glasgow for a great many commissioners, and it's a circular room. Everyone gets a seat at a desk. The judge, the commissioner, wears a lounge suit. We're all in lounge suits, no gowns and wigs and the like, so it's much less formal, much less intimidating than a courtroom. (BAC5)

The intimacy of the setting was also seen as instrumental in tempering the questioning style, acting as a constraint on the 'theatrical gene within advocates' which would ordinarily be 'inflamed' by the presence of a jury. There is 'absolutely no grandstanding because the absence of the jury stops any grandstanding' (BAJ4). It also prevented counsel from being 'aggressive or intimidating or nasty in any sense to a witness who you're directly facing,

[5] Criminal Procedure (Scotland) Act 1995, s 271.

particularly someone who has any sort of vulnerability' (BAJ3; see further Chapter 8).

According to one advocate, the witness usually sits alongside five other persons: the judge, the judge's clerk, two advocates, and the witness's supporter, with the proceedings beamed to the accused and his solicitor in another building (BAC2). This advocate acknowledged that some witnesses might prefer to give evidence in this manner, but underlined that it was quite different from the way the joint investigative interview would have been conducted, and it could be quite intimidating, for example, for a teenage girl to sit in a room with five men who are strangers and have to recount intimate details to them.

Added value

The most commonly cited advantage of pre-recorded cross-examination and evidence on commission is the avoidance of delay, with some judges expressing relief that the witness's evidence is already secured:

> I'm about to do [a section 28 hearing] with about nine victims, and they're all going to be pre-recorded Section 28 cross-examinations. I think they can work very well indeed and spare these little boys, who have been raped multiple times by a local man. He's basically groomed them, and there are multiple victims from very dysfunctional families, limited IQ, just very vulnerable, on the street really, these boys. All of them are being cross-examined ahead of the trial, which is next year. Because there's a real danger that you will lose them, that they will just disappear, and that's why it's important to get their evidence recorded as soon as you can. (ABJ1)

> There are delays in bringing cases, not necessarily anyone's fault. It's just the volume of cases and other pressures they bring to bear, but the real advantage here is the evidence is captured. You've got it. So that if the case does proceed to trial 18 months later, you've still got the evidence. (BAC1)

Many also identified that the evidential quality of the witnesses' evidence was considerably enhanced as it was recorded in a much more proximate timeframe to the incident in question, when memories are likely to be fresher and more accurate, and reduces problems caused by memory lapse:

> It is sooner so yes memories have not faded. That much is a great advantage to the witness. (ACJ1)

> It gets the evidence recorded early … That means that it's recorded when it's fresher in the witness's memory. It also means that the evidence is secure if the witness then decides to be unsupportive. (ABJ3)

> There are massive advantages to [section 28]. It's the fact that the witness is able to give their version of events closer to the incidents themselves. At the moment I'm listing cases 18 months to 2 years down the line. It's just not fair. And everybody forgets that with time, memory fades. And you're going to be a much better witness nearer the time. (ABJ2)

However, this advantage rests on the assumption that the hearing actually takes place close to the incident; some Scottish advocates pointed out that even though evidence is taken on commission pre-trial, some form of delay is still inevitable: 'all we're really doing is perhaps allowing a complainer to give their evidence two years after the event rather than two and a half or three years' (BAC5).

As the backlog of trials has continued to increase in the years since the pandemic, the importance of organising pre-recorded cross-examination at an early stage is particularly apposite. However, there was a view that section 28 hearings decreased the priority for a timely trial date:

> And my only concern about it from a practical point of view is whether, as it were, with the cross-examination and the examination-in-chief of the complainant in the can, that the court thinks that they can just boot it back a bit further [in the court schedule] and deal with some other stuff. (AAC2)

> I think section 28 is being seen as a panacea to the court backlog because it's like, oh, well, we'll get the witnesses heard earlier, and it doesn't matter when the trial goes on. (ABC1)

Another compelling advantage alluded to previously concerned the brevity and highly focused nature of the questioning. In contrast to live cross-examination, pre-recorded questioning is 'much shorter, more focused, and less confrontational' (ABJ4). A similar opinion was expressed by another judge: '[W]hat I'm really an ardent fan of is the style of cross-examination that this has introduced. Short, focused, pre-prepared, and I don't think the forensic process is damaged to any extent by that; in fact, it's enhanced' (AAJ3). One interviewee (AAJ2) cited a recent six-year-old who had been asked only four questions in cross-examination, which was 'over in less than 10 minutes', while another recalled a young child being asked just five questions (AAC3).

But while the brevity of cross-examination may be less stressful for the witness, and more efficient from the perspective of the professionals involved, it does raise the issue of whether this new approach may be less robust in terms of testing the evidence. This was alluded to by interviewees in both jurisdictions:

> It's almost like sometimes the advocate feels as though they're going through the motions. Now, you know, whether they are or not is ultimately irrelevant because what they're doing is they're abiding by the new rules that we have … And with a non-vulnerable witness, there may be lots of scope to ask questions in reaction to an answer. Well, that doesn't really happen with vulnerable witnesses because the answer tends to be what you could foresee it to be and the advocate's less entitled to go off piste anyway. (ABJ4)

> My experience is an unhappy one in taking evidence on commission … thus far the ones I've dealt with, the witnesses have been put so much at their ease that they have been able to give … and often their evidence can be given simply by use of their prior statement to the police … that will be read at the trial. And the prosecutor might have a few questions for them and then I have to try and suggest to them in this cosy wee room where we're all informal that perhaps she's not being entirely truthful and there's not a great deal of places you can go in that environment. (BAC5)

However, two Scottish advocates made the point that the aim is not to remove the ability to test evidence, simply to create the conditions in which evidence can more reliably be tested.

> It's making it quite difficult for [witnesses] to be challenged in the way that [advocates] used to challenge it. And maybe that's a good thing because sometimes the way in which evidence was challenged previously had an artificiality about it. (BAC2)

> Turning to the question of how effective one can be cross-examining at the commission in a very unnatural setting for the court practitioner. That's the whole point of them. They're not meant to be as intimidating as a court. (BAC5)

One English advocate suggested a more radical reframing of how defence testing of a vulnerable witness's evidence could be carried out.

> I wonder whether section 28 is anything more than the appearance of cross-examination rather than anything of real value … If there

> are points the defence want to raise like, 'We want to ask about what happens at a particular time or a particular place. You say this happened at the backseat of the car, in fact it was just a two-seater car with only a seat in the front, is that right?' Then that that could be done by an intermediary as a sort of follow-up ABE rather than cross-examination in a courtroom. (ACC3; see also discussion in Chapter 8)

Another advantage of pre-recorded cross-examination is that it can be edited for trial. As one judge noted, this means she would not need to decide whether to discharge a jury if a witness disclosed inadmissible evidence, such as, 'He did it to my sister and he served two years' (ABJ1). A Scottish advocate added that the ability to edit recordings allows objections regarding the relevance or admissibility of questions to be raised with the judge after the witness has given evidence, preventing the witness from having to 'hang around' while the point is argued (BAC3).

Obviously, there are also significant benefits for witnesses. Many judges emphasised the relief for vulnerable witnesses in giving their evidence in advance of the trial without a jury, thus sparing them the trauma of testifying at trial (ABJ2, BAC3, AAC3). Advocates and intermediaries recognised the significant benefits for young children and elderly complainants, whose evidence needs to be recorded early. However, they noted that the advantages for adults might be more nuanced, as many continue to feel anxious until the trial's conclusion (ABC1). Some witnesses preferred to give their evidence quickly and move on, while others feared the 'double trauma' of a section 28 hearing followed by the trial, during which they might not testify but would still anxiously await the verdict (AAR3). This intermediary also highlighted that section 28 hearings require witnesses to undergo early cross-examination, which would prove unnecessary if the defendant entered a guilty plea prior to trial, sparing the witness cross-examination altogether.

Despite these benefits to the witness, many counsel were uncomfortable with pre-recorded cross-examination as it isolated the main witness from the rest of the trial. One counsel explained: 'You are isolating a part of the evidence. Whereas when you're doing a trial, it has to be looked at holistically. And you still have to know how to weave the threads together, and I don't think you can do that when you cross-examine one witness' (ABC1). Rather than fast-tracking cross-examination, many believed a better solution to the problems of delay would be to fast-track vulnerable witness trials altogether:

> Section 28s are only necessary because the whole system is so badly funded that we can't get a trial with a vulnerable witness on quickly enough. If the system worked properly, we wouldn't be saying to that

person, 'We're going to separate your evidence off from the trial'. We'd be saying to that person, 'Well, because you're vulnerable, we can hold the trial in four months' time, that's not too long to wait'. So we'll have the trial and it's all sorted, the whole thing is dealt with. But because we can't do that, we've come up with this halfway house which is just turning the whole thing into a sort of adjunct to the trial. (AAC1)

Logistical issues

A general concern among judges and counsel in England and Wales was that section 28 hearings were being rolled out excessively without sufficient consideration of the significant logistical problems that could lead to adverse consequences. One judge, a supporter of section 28 hearings when they work well, noted the impact of a lack of resources on the smooth operation of section 28 hearings and opined that there had been insufficient investment in the quality of recordings, computer equipment, staff training, and funding for advocates to be paid for time spent drafting questions in advance (ABJ1).

The use of an outsourced service provider in England and Wales further complicated matters due to restrictions on playback. One judge (ACJ2) cited a case where the cross-examination could not be played as scheduled on the first day of the trial. The requirement to give 24 hours' notice to the service provider for a new slot meant that the playback was delayed until the third day, which was inefficient in terms of valuable court time. Another judge (ABJ4) noted that the inability to pause the playback was also an impediment to efficiency. Unlike in England and Wales, in Scotland it was unnecessary to pre-book time slots in courtrooms, which prevented disruption to other court business.

While some practitioners had few concerns about the technical standard of pre-recorded cross-examination, others were less impressed:

> I find that just staggering, that we have equipment that's so out of date … We should have state-of-the-art equipment, we should. And then if [we] had the Wi-Fi, broadband, and all of that stuff working, it would be brilliant. But we don't. (ABJ1)

> The technology at the moment is still in its infancy. Often the videos that are recorded are of poor quality, they are sometimes of poor visual quality, sometimes of poor audio quality. (ABC3)

There were fewer concerns expressed in Scotland, where the view seemed to be that this was now a legacy issue: 'The only problem is does the technology work? That's the only drawback it seems to me. It's not so bad now' (BAJ2).

A further difficulty commonly mentioned was the original requirement for the same judges and counsel to appear in GRHs, section 28 hearings and trials. Steps have been taken to obviate this difficulty by not requiring the same judge to appear in both section 28 hearings and trials. We were told that most court centres now have designated section 28 judges and the case then gets released to another judge for trial (ABC1). In March 2022 the Criminal Practice Directions were amended so that it is no longer mandatory for the same judge to conduct the GRHs and the section 28 hearing or for the same advocate to appear at the GRH, the section 28 hearing, and the trial.[6] But interviewees said this was far from ideal: '[t]he ground rules hearing had been done by a different judge a couple of weeks earlier who'd made rulings, some of which had been recorded, some of which hadn't. Some other judge again is going to deal with a trial … that's not the way to do it' (ACC1). From counsel's point of view, it was also ethically problematic, because 'I would never be allowed to step into a trial where a witness has already been cross-examined, it would have to be a re-trial, so I don't see why you should be doing that as an advocate for a section 28' (ABC1).

In Scotland, practitioners seemed less concerned about the same personnel not being used for GRHs, evidence on commission, and the trial. One judge said that the lack of continuity of judges was not a problem so long as there is the clarity about what the decisions reached are at each stage (BAJ1). An advocate referred to the problem that he may not be able to cross-examine a witness on commission if he were involved in another trial, which meant that the cross-examination would be done by someone without a full grasp of the case (BAC5). But he accepted that there was a 'huge advantage' for witnesses in getting their evidence heard early and there seemed to be more acceptance on the part of advocates that evidence on commission was the best way forward for vulnerable witnesses.

Many practitioners believe that the strict timetables for section 28 hearings are often unsuitable for complex cases involving older witnesses, where extensive third-party material disclosure (such as social services and medical records) is necessary. A judge noted that this can lead to the police delaying charges until they complete their disclosure, thus simply moving the delay before the child can give evidence to a different part of the criminal justice process (AAJ1). Additionally, if full disclosure is not made in time for the section 28 hearing, there is a reluctance to schedule a second pre-recorded cross-examination. As a result, any later disclosure may be admitted as an agreed fact, preventing the prosecution addressing the new information. Judges and advocates in Scotland also identified issues with late disclosure by the Crown Office after evidence had been given on commission. As in

[6] Criminal Practice Directions 2023, [6.3.50]–[6.3.53].

England and Wales, there was a reluctance to organise a second pre-recorded cross-examination, which can be unfair to complainants as the defence can use the new material to their advantage (BAJ1).

Both counsel and judges expressed concerns about the additional workload involved in appearing in GRHs and section 28 hearings alongside other ongoing trials. Preparing for section 28 hearings requires the entire case to be prepared twice – once for the hearing and again for the trial – effectively doubling the workload (AAC1). This also means preparing for two cases simultaneously. As one judge explained, '[i]f you're part-heard in a guns case, but you've got a section 28 hearing and need to cross-examine a vulnerable nine-year-old, you have to spend the evening before reminding yourself of the questions, the tone, and the approach, while also preparing the cross-examination of the principal witness in the guns case' (ABJ1). One counsel mentioned that he, along with other senior members of the Bar, had stopped doing section 28 hearings due to the workload involved. He warned that the system would grind to a halt if section 28 were extended to all vulnerable witnesses, including every complainant in sexual offences cases, because 'people like me will say, I can't do those cases because I have such a heavy workload, I can't work in those time frames' (ACC4). One Scottish judge noted that although the process is resource-intensive, requiring defence lawyers, prosecutors, and judges to invest almost double the time compared with having a witness testify during the trial (BAJ1), this process made the trial itself more efficient, as time was saved through the relative brevity of evidence on commission.

In general, Scottish practitioners tended to raise fewer logistical problems regarding evidence on commission than their English counterparts did in relation to section 28. This may be explained by the fact that the procedure has been much more embedded in Scotland, with the government having invested significantly in bespoke commission facilities, sidestepping some of the issues reported in England and Wales regarding the need to pre-book slots, which can subsequently disrupt other court business. Additionally, the recording and editing of evidence on commission is handled by an in-house team rather than an external service provider, resulting in greater efficiency and fewer technical problems and postponements.

Extending the reach of pre-recorded cross-examination

There has been a recent push to extend the remit of section 28 to include adult sexual offence complainants as well as children. In England and Wales, it was noted that the push for section 28 hearings has come from senior judges and is becoming ingrained in the practices of the Crown Prosecution Service (CPS) and police (ABJ1). This judge was concerned that the practice was becoming an automatic choice rather than one based on the individual needs of the witness. Before expanding the reach of the scheme, she felt that issues such as technological failures, inadequate staff training, and insufficient remuneration for advocates need to be addressed. General unease and a sense of unreadiness were common themes alluded to by both judges and counsel, with defence counsel in particular being sceptical about the politically motivated nature of the roll-out to improve conviction statistics or to 'speed up the process' (ACC4), even in cases where complainants were not classified as vulnerable or where a less drastic measure would be more appropriate (ABC2). As discussed in Chapter 7, such concerns may stem more from fears about the impact on counsel workloads and scheduling than from doubts about the deservedness of complainants.

In Scotland, the exacerbation of trial delays by the pandemic seems to have been a driving factor in the uptake of evidence on commission to mitigate the harm of long waits for complainers (BAJ1). The drive to capture evidence as soon as possible during the pandemic, when there was a backlog of trials, was a key factor in the increased use of evidence on commission. Scottish advocates were generally more positive, with prosecutors now routinely making applications on behalf of adult complainers, and the judiciary generally being receptive to them (BAC5). However, one judge suggested that acceptance among defence advocates has been motivated by less altruistic concerns.

> I think some [defence advocates] think that anything that makes it easier for a witness must be banned because they want it to be as uncomfortable as possible for witnesses, because they want them to be traumatised, they want them to not be able to give evidence. I think that is a view, I don't think many people would say that on a recording, but I suspect that, you know, in their hearts that's what some defence people feel. I think others calculate there might be an advantage in the evidence being in this limited form. And that their client might get an advantage in the trial if he comes across well, if he gives evidence. I think a lot of the defence calculations are not altruistic. (BAJ1)

The impact of remote evidence

Research since the 1970s has explored whether forms of remote testimony, as opposed to live evidence, are less impactful for juries. This research has largely involved mock juries, and, until recently, there was no consistent or compelling proof that digital evidence affected trial outcomes (Ellison and Munro, 2014; Munro, 2018). However, recent research conducted as part of University College London's 'Jury Project', which analysed Crown Court verdicts across England and Wales from 2016 to 2024, uncovered a correlation between the use of section 28 recordings and lower conviction rates. Unlike the international evidence reviewed by Munro (2018), this study is based on hard data from actual cases.

In written evidence to the House of Commons Justice Select Committee, Thomas (2024) claimed that the jury conviction rate was almost 10 percentage points lower when section 28 evidence was used (61 per cent) compared with when it was not used (70 per cent). The differential was even more pronounced in rape cases, with a 20 percentage point lower conviction rate when complainants' cross-examination was pre-recorded compared with when it was not. The project is ongoing and aims to explore further factors that might explain this divergence.

While understanding the impact of remote evidence on decision makers was not an objective of our project, the issue was touched upon by a number of judicial interviewees. One felt that the loss of impact was an exaggerated concern, commenting that while counsel often feared 'there is a sense of detachment that you're watching a video or film rather than real people' and 'because it's not in real time, the authenticity of it is lost', she herself didn't find it any less authentic, but rather 'efficient and useful' (ABJ1). Another was more dubious, commenting that '[i]t's just less powerful' (BAJ3). Some judges were more uncertain in their view, 'whether it makes any difference, whether it's done live or whether it's done in a pre-recorded hearing, I've got no idea' (ABJ2), but the same judge also felt that any detriment could be offset through an appropriate direction to the jury.

Some mentioned the lack of any impact on conviction rates as an indication that pre-recordings were no less impactful or persuasive, referring to it as a 'small risk' (ACJ2); 'it's made no difference' (ACJ3). As one Scottish judge explained:

> I suspect that a lot of people have a hunch that it has less impact than having a live witness in the courtroom, in front of them. I believe that there is research that shows that that effect isn't real, doesn't exist … It seems a bit counter-intuitive and certainly I can imagine that if you had a very charismatic accused person giving live evidence in the trial countering recorded evidence, he might conceivably get an advantage. (BAJ1)

At that point in time, however, judges would not have been aware of the correlation noted earlier between pre-recorded evidence and conviction rates.

The majority of counsel leaned towards a more adverse perspective. Many alluded to the relevance of demeanour and lack of immediacy as factors which were likely to make the evidence less compelling: 'I think juries want them to really give evidence … I think they want to see somebody give evidence and be cross-examined' (ACC4).

In Scotland, some judges and advocates expressed similar views, with questions arising as to who is best placed to discuss the pros and cons of both live and recorded evidence given prosecutors' professional interests in maximising the strength of their case:

> What is the best way as a prosecutor I could present this case? It would be to have the witness in court in front of the jury and they could see the reaction of the witness, the demeanour of the witness, the content of the evidence in the presence of the accused … I'm not suggesting we don't [use remote testimony] but as an observation, yes, I think it can diminish the evidence. (BAC1)

> I'm never sure that witnesses have explained to them the whole package, which is 'this makes it easier for you but it may also mean that you don't have the same impact' … I don't want to sound too cynical but for a prosecutor to have a distressed witness, reliving or recounting something of significant distress to him or her and for the jury to react to that. We see jurors themselves perhaps weeping or aghast. (BAC5)

However, some felt that even if televised testimony is less impactful (thereby potentially lowering conviction rates), that is nonetheless an acceptable consequence in any cost/benefit analysis given the moral imperative of easing the burden on vulnerable witnesses.

> I favour evidence on commission because it minimises the re-traumatisation and my own sort of calculation is if there's a slight lowering of the chance of a conviction, well so be it. (BAJ1)

> [You've] got to balance off [the risk of less impactful evidence] against that of the interests of the witnesses themselves … If you have a witness on a commission who's able to give their evidence in a coherent and relaxed manner, then that's always going to be better than a nervous witness, who's given their evidence in a poor way live in front of a jury. (BAC3)

Some interviewees acknowledged wider societal use of screens which may also influence jurors' more ready acceptance of televised testimony (BAJ1) while another felt that such criticisms tended to be a product of professional resistance to change (BAC2).

Ground rules hearings

As inferred earlier, the parameters for pre-recorded cross-examination are usually determined through a GRH. A GRH is a specific type of pre-trial hearing designed to allow the trial judge and advocates to plan necessary adaptations to questioning or the conduct of the hearing to facilitate the evidence of a vulnerable person (Judicial College, 2024: 48, §139). As noted in the previous chapter, GRHs evolved from informal meetings convened on an ad hoc basis to become a formal lynchpin of judicial management in England and Wales, despite lacking statutory footing. They were first endorsed by the Court of Appeal in *R v Wills* and subsequently confirmed in *R v Lubemba; JP* [2015] 1 WLR 1579:

> We would expect a ground rules hearing in every case involving a vulnerable witness, save in very exceptional circumstances ... The ground rules hearing should cover, amongst other matters, the general care of the witness, if, when and where the witness is to be shown their video interview, when, where and how the parties (and the judge if identified) intend to introduce themselves to the witness, the length of questioning and frequency of breaks and the nature of the questions to be asked. ([42]–[43])

Following *R v Jonas* ([2015] EWCA Crim 562), consideration must be given to holding a GRH in all cases involving vulnerable witnesses: '[t]he greater the level of vulnerability the more important it will be to hold such a hearing'.[7] The Advocate's Gateway Toolkit (The Advocate's Gateway, 2024) outlines best practices for GRHs and includes a checklist to help practitioners identify vulnerability among witnesses and defendants, as well as key issues to consider at the GRH. The Judicial College (2024: 54, §141) also recommends arranging GRHs in all cases involving child witnesses and other cases with vulnerable witnesses or defendants who have communication needs.[8]

Although intermediaries do not participate in Scottish criminal proceedings, there is a statutory requirement in Scotland that a GRH must take place when the evidence is taken on commission, though the GRH may be conjoined with another hearing (in practice usually the preliminary hearing).[9] Additionally, the commissioner may require written questions to be submitted in advance for review: 'to the extent that the commissioner considers it appropriate to do so, [the commissioner must] decide on the form and wording of the questions that are to be asked of the vulnerable witness'.[10]

7 Ibid [6.1.4].
8 See also *R v PMH* [2018] EWCA Crim 2452.
9 Section 271I (1ZA–1ZB) of the 1995 Act, as inserted by s 5 of the Vulnerable Witnesses (Criminal Evidence) (Scotland) Act 2019.
10 Section 271 of the 1995 Act, subsection (1ZD).

Practice Note (No 1 of 2019) provides guidance on when written questions should be requested: for any child under 12 years of age and witnesses with significant communication or comprehension difficulties; written questions may also be required for children aged 12 or over, depending on their best interests and capability.[11]

GRHs became part of Northern Irish criminal procedure with the introduction of the registered intermediary (RI) scheme, piloted in 2013 and rolled out in 2016 (Doak et al, 2021: §6.2.7). No explicit provision for their use in Crown Court Rules was made until the Gillen Review recommended GRHs for every case involving a child or vulnerable witness (Gillen Review, 2019: 319). As noted in Chapter 2, subsequently two protocols were attached to Practice Direction No 2/2019, *Case Management in the Crown Court including Protocols for Vulnerable Witnesses and Defendants*: Annex A (Vulnerable Witnesses) and Annex B (Vulnerable Defendants). Both protocols (A5.1 and B5.1) direct that GRHs should ordinarily be held in hearings involving vulnerable complainants and may be held in hearings involving vulnerable defendants; they must be arranged where the witness or defendant is a child, or where a RI has been appointed.

Until very recently, there was no formal intermediary scheme in Ireland, and, accordingly, no provision for the use of GRHs. Indeed, until the implementation of section 6(1) of the Criminal Procedure Act 2021 in 2022, there was no legislative provision for any type of preliminary hearing. However, Irish courts had occasionally used their inherent jurisdiction to conduct preliminary hearings to discuss how vulnerable witnesses might be questioned (Doak et al, 2021: §7.3.2). One counsel in this research spoke of his involvement in a 2015 case where the judge held the equivalent of a GRH and in *DPP v VE* ([2021] ICEA 122) the Court of Appeal held that although there is no statutory obligation for trial judges to convene a GRH, it seemed to be good practice. Section 6(1) of the 2021 Act now gives statutory authority for ground rules discussions to take place before trial, but these are conducted under the auspices of the pre-trial hearing and are neither labelled nor convened as GRHs. However, guidance recently issued to all newly qualified registered intermediaries (Courts Service of Ireland, 2024: 15) has adopted the terminology, stating that a GRH should be held to appoint the intermediary and set the ground rules for the trial. The judge may also order that the RI review the questions that the prosecution and/or defence plan to ask the witness and provide advice on their suitability.

11 High Court of Justiciary, Practice Note (No 1 of 2019) Vulnerable and Child Witnesses: written questions.

Purpose and function

Practitioners across England and Wales, Scotland, and Northern Ireland generally agree on the purpose of GRHs: to establish measures in advance of the trial to ensure effective cross-examination of a vulnerable witness or defendant. One judge described the GRH as 'an elaborate directions hearing … with its own protocol' (AAJ3). Others noted that GRHs help ensure fairness (ABJ1), smooth trial proceedings, and maximise participation (BAC3).

As discussed in Chapter 4, when intermediaries are involved, their role at a GRH may include reviewing and making recommendations on counsel's proposed questions and suggesting other forms of non-linguistic support. Even without an intermediary, GRHs can still be beneficial: 'sometimes a witness may still be vulnerable and require certain steps and measures in place, may be disabled, may be anxious, etcetera … a ground rules hearing will be useful to flesh out those issues' (ABJ1). These matters should be led by the judge, or commissioner in Scotland, though some judges believe a pre-trial hearing for non-linguistic issues is unnecessary (see further discussion in the next chapter). One judge stated that 'wigs and gowns, breaks, sitting hours and so on … should all be dealt with by the trial judge on the day of the trial' (ABJ2), while another remarked, 'we know what the intermediary would say, "get them on early, get them away quickly, don't repeat things, keep it all clear" … Well … I think we've got that' (ACJ2). Intermediaries, however, view GRHs as 'a vital piece of the jigsaw' to ensure 'all the foundations are there' (AAR1).

As GRHs have become standard practice, judges noted that much of the work between counsel and intermediaries in reviewing written questions takes place before the GRH. Intermediaries and many judges prefer that written questions be provided to the intermediary in advance so the judge can review the questions and consider the intermediary's input at the GRH. If there is a dispute or if the defence wishes to put the case more forcefully than the intermediary deems appropriate, the judge intervenes and makes the final decision (AAJ2). While submitting questions in advance is common practice, sometimes questions are produced at the GRH for the intermediary to review later (ACJ3). This is often due to the barrister's workload rather than a reluctance to engage with intermediaries (AAR3).

There was general agreement that counsel and intermediaries usually reach a consensus on the format and phrasing of questions, rarely needing the judge to resolve disputes: 'there's very rarely any fisticuffs, it's usually kind of agreed' (AAC3). Although 'occasionally you might get a bit of push-back from counsel and a little bit of conflict between counsel and the intermediary' (AAJ3), this collaborative approach seems to stem from the new framework for vulnerable witnesses and the understanding that this approach is now standard practice:

> It's the combination of the Gateway, the Toolkit, and the intermediary because the fact that we've been trained on these things, that we know that if the intermediary is saying a certain type of question or a certain topic or concept is beyond the witness, the defence advocate knows ... given the fact judges have been trained, there's no point in trying to win it or trying to crowbar something in when it's in writing because they're never going to win that argument. (AAC3)

Where there is no intermediary (or in Scotland, where intermediaries are not used), a judge or commissioner may still direct written questions, and the responsibility for reviewing the questions also falls to them. In either case, whether there is an intermediary or not, the judge is 'still the final arbiter of how the questions are going to be put' (AAJ1). However, judicial management of questions extends beyond appropriate construction to a broader consideration of what constitutes an appropriate way to cross-examine vulnerable witnesses, a matter which is properly for the judge and not the intermediary:

> I've been through it as a judge many times, taking them to the Advocate's Gateway and saying ... 'why are you asking this ... this is established in the evidence-in-chief, why do you want to ask it again?' (BAJ1)

> [GRHs] allow me to lay down a marker, that when it comes to this witness this is what I expect. I will say things about Advocate's Gateway ... [With] young witnesses, particularly vulnerable witnesses, what is it that you're seeking to achieve? How are you going to go about that? (CAJ2)

In Ireland it was clear that written questions were very rarely shared; here practitioners seemed more interested in other forms of accommodation. Requiring advocates to reveal in advance their line of questioning is a radical break from tradition and from both judges and counsel there was some resistance to the routine use of written questions, with one counsel saying, 'I just wouldn't like this to become the thin end of the wedge and this to become an established protocol whereby, by default, questions have to be submitted in advance' (DAC4).

Added value

There was a general consensus that the primary advantage of a GRH is that it allows for an agreement to be reached in advance of the trial regarding the needs of the witness and how best to support them, thereby enabling the best evidence to be given. As one intermediary noted, 'I feel really, barring disaster, that the child's got the best chance then. Our work's virtually done at that point really' (AAR1). One counsel added that the GRH 'causes you to engage and think about the process early on, to take onboard the difficulties that the witness has and to adapt yourself to them' (ABC2), and a judge asserted that it also ensures that 'the judge has ticked and crossed everybody's homework before you've even gone into court' (ABJ2).

GRHs can ensure that the questions asked are at a linguistic level that facilitates communication and provide an opportunity to discuss how the court environment can best be adapted to assist the witness in giving evidence. For example, they may include arrangements for entering the court building, for counsel and the judge to meet the witness before they give evidence, the use of first names, the time of day for cross-examination, required breaks, whether legal professionals should stand or sit in the presence of the witness, the use of special measures, and how the intermediary may intervene during questioning. Intermediaries provided examples where the GRH made the difference between the witness giving evidence or not, such as agreeing that a witness gives evidence first thing in the morning to avoid waiting all day (AXR1) or deciding to screen the defendant's view of the television screens when the witness indicated she would not provide evidence if she thought the defendant could see her (AAR3).

However, intermediaries reported that the quality of GRHs varies significantly depending on the judge's approach, with one describing it as a 'postcode lottery … and when I say postcode, same building, two different judges' (AXR1). The distinction appears to be between merely paying lip service to the discussion of ground rules and a pertinent, serious consideration of the needs of the witness or defendant. Some judges will go through the process step by step, ensuring everything is agreed or discussed, while others prefer a quicker approach, assuming everyone agrees without thorough discussion (AAR3).

Perfunctory discussions of ground rules are particularly concerning to intermediaries because 'having that opportunity to explain the recommendations to the court generates a greater awareness … and the value of them' (DAR1). More importantly, it reduces the risk of the witness's evidence being disrupted at court. Worse still is when intermediaries are not permitted to engage with or speak at the GRH (CAR1, DAR2, ABR1, ABR3, AXR1). The key for many intermediaries and counsel is creating the opportunity for full engagement with the issues: 'A ground rules hearing where it's really collaborative and really open and everyone got a really good problem-solving attitude, those hearings are really productive' (ABR1).

The requirement to hold a GRH when evidence is taken on commission, where cross-examination is pre-recorded, or where an intermediary is appointed seems to have been universally accepted into practice. However, more variability was reported in terms of the scheduling of the GRH. In Scotland, where the GRH is almost always conjoined with the preliminary hearing, few concerns were expressed about the timing of that hearing in relation to the trial. In England and Wales, local court centre protocols exist to require GRHs for vulnerable witnesses to be scheduled a week before the trial date or pre-recorded cross-examination hearing date.

However, practicalities often frustrate policy. Intermediaries reported that this schedule is not reliably applied, and in trial observations GRHs were often held just before the trial or just before a witness gave their evidence. One counsel noted that 'sometimes the ground rules, because you can't fit it in and nobody's available, happen on the morning of the trial, which isn't terribly satisfactory' and 'a lot of that is to do with the pressure on the system, funding of the system, and listing difficulties' (ACC1). Some interviewees even reported an advantage to holding the GRH on the first day of trial because 'trying to get everyone together [earlier] doesn't always work' (ABC1). Intermediaries also expressed some degree of disquiet surrounding the scheduling of GRHs: sometimes these were held on the morning of the trial, sometimes two weeks before and latterly they could be 'all over the place' (AAR1), a view echoed by an intermediary in Ireland, where GRHs are a recent innovation, potentially because scheduling protocols have yet to be established (DAR2). However, most interviewees recognised the risk that holding a GRH on the morning of the trial 'may disrupt the trial timetable, which is a very important factor if you've scheduled the vulnerable witness to attend … it may throw up things that haven't been expected … and if you have it on the morning of the hearing, you can't always cope with that' (ABJ3).

Intermediaries in England and Wales also disliked GRHs on the first day of trial, particularly when they had not previously been given counsel's questions to review: 'Sometimes as you're walking into court to have the ground rules hearing you're handed a list of questions which could be ten pages long and they say, "can you review these?", and you're like, "not effectively, no"' (ABR1). Intermediaries also felt that the GRH should be held after the court familiarisation visit, as the intermediary can then provide relevant feedback on how the witness coped with being asked questions over the video link (AAR3). In Northern Ireland, one judge mentioned that they had 'never had to conduct a ground rules hearing because they're almost always agreed before they get [put on]' (CAJ1), though this was not an experience reported in other jurisdictions.

Management of written questions

Advocates across the jurisdictions (with the exception of Ireland) now generally accept that written questions are necessary in cases involving very vulnerable witnesses. However, some expressed reservations about writing questions 'word for word' due to the need to react to unexpected answers (BAC1). Others suggested that judges are willing to permit further questions based on how the written questions are answered and are not 'so hamstrung with the actual order of the questions' as to disallow a supplementary question if an unexpected answer arises (BAC2).

Concerns linger among some advocates about whether it is appropriate to share written questions with the opposing party due to the risk that they might be discussed with the witness. Some judges expressed sympathy with this view:

> The basic principle is that the defendant's barrister is entitled to share everything with their client, whereas the prosecuting barrister is not representing or acting for the complainant or any other witness. What the defence barrister knows, they know on behalf of their client and need to share that. (ABJ3)

However, most judges did not see this risk as a valid concern, as counsel are aware of the basic rules and that passing questions to a witness would be viewed as coaching (ABC1, ABJ3). Others pointed to principles of open justice:

> If you're going to have a ground rules hearing at which these questions are discussed then the prosecution … have to see them to be able to participate in the hearing. You can't have a hearing at which there's a conversation between the judge and the defence about a document that the prosecution haven't seen. It's an open justice issue. (ACJ3)

A Scottish judge contextualised this within broader judicial management obligations:

> People are less reluctant to show their hand now … The Crown always had obligations of disclosure … [and] since 2005, we have preliminary hearings and we deal with matters that can be dealt with before a trial … You have to lodge a defence statement … So, in the last 15 or more years, we've all become a little more open about what's actually in dispute here? There's also an obligation now in statute on parties to agree what can be agreed … And I remind people of this from time to time. (BAJ4)

Vulnerable defendants

While GRHs are commonplace for vulnerable witnesses, especially young child witnesses, our research suggests they are much less commonly held for vulnerable defendants. This is largely because the driver for a GRH is often (though not exclusively) the appointment of an intermediary, which, as we will see in Chapter 4, is rare for a vulnerable defendant. Additionally, the use of pre-recorded cross-examination or evidence on commission is not available under statute for vulnerable defendants. However, intermediaries in England and Wales indicated that where they are appointed to support a vulnerable defendant, GRHs are becoming more frequent. One intermediary noted, 'I do generally manage to have a ground rules hearing, but typically it is the first morning of the trial' (AXR3). Indeed, a GRH on the first day of trial appears to be the norm for vulnerable defendants, largely because it is unclear before trial whether the vulnerable defendant will give evidence (ABJ4). In Scotland, a judge indicated that GRH discussions for vulnerable defendants are more likely to be deferred until after the defence has indicated that the defendant will be called to give evidence (BAJ2).

The Advocate's Gateway GRH checklist (2024) has recommended that consideration should be afforded to holding a GRH for vulnerable defendants before the trial and, if the defendant later elects to give evidence, a second GRH should be arranged specifically to discuss how questioning should be conducted (see further Cooper and Norton, 2017: 399). Judges and intermediaries tended to agree that best practice required holding two GRHs for a vulnerable defendant, one upfront for practical and environmental issues and another just before they give evidence for support measures during testimony:

> It falls into two parts. One part is obviously the nuts and bolts of the trial. 'Do they need a break? Should they sit in the dock or sit with their legal team? Do they need extra time to take instructions and give advice?' And then in terms of giving evidence it's probably best done just before they give evidence when you've got a feel for what measures are likely to help them and what's really going to make the difference. (AAJ2)

However, such best practice did not appear to be widespread. The general view, particularly among intermediaries, is that even when a GRH is held, the ground rules for a defendant are not addressed with the same level of seriousness: 'The recommendations which are accepted and adhered to aren't the same as when you're a "prosecution" intermediary … Sometimes they haven't even read the report' (AAR2). Another intermediary noted that for defendants, GRHs are often confined to deciding 'whether to consent to having an intermediary' (AXR1) rather than a serious review of the recommendations for that individual.

There was some indication of a more robust approach from some counsel, who, for example, indicated that they would seek intermediary advice on the prosecution questions to be put when cross-examining the defendant:

> You're not in the same way restricted, you don't have to submit them for analysis or anything like that, but what I have done is I've said to the judge, 'I've got various areas that I want to cross-examine about, I want half an hour with the intermediary now to ask the intermediary can I ask these sort of questions?' And I will go and have a word with the intermediary. (AAC2)

However, intermediaries reported that this is an exception to the norm, where requests for written questions are often rejected on the grounds that 'the barristers are suitably skilled to question' the defendant (ABR1). Another intermediary mentioned that prosecution barristers are 'a breed apart' when it comes to providing their written questions and that they have yet to fully understand and accept the use of defence intermediaries: 'I have only once had a prosecution barrister run their questions by me' (ABR2).

There also seem to be mixed approaches taken by judges. One judge stated that the same approach applies for vulnerable defendants as for vulnerable witnesses, with the prosecution required to draft questions in advance to be reviewed and accepted at the GRH (AAJ1). However, another judge raised concerns about the defence barrister seeing prosecution questions in advance but not being able to share them with their client (ABJ3). This scenario is avoided if the review of questions is delayed until after the defendant has given evidence-in-chief. Intermediaries reinforced this approach to ensure the prosecution's confidence that questions would not be shared, though they noted that even this approach met with some resistance (AAR2).

Conclusion

This chapter has focused on two of the most pronounced departures from the adversarial norm, pre-recorded cross-examination and GRHs. While the former undercuts the principle of orality, the latter erodes the principle of party control over the questions to be asked. On paper at least, England and Wales would seem to be something of a trail-blazer in this respect, with the pace and success of innovation being partly attributable to a series of important Court of Appeal decisions during the 2010s outlined in the previous chapter. Many practitioners, particularly judges and commissioners, acknowledged the evidential benefits of pre-recorded cross-examination/evidence on commission; evidence was likely to be more reliable and vulnerable witnesses would be spared the ordeal of giving live evidence. Judges emphasised the evidential benefits and the benefit for vulnerable witnesses in hearing their evidence in advance of the trial without a jury and relieving them of the trauma of giving evidence at trial. But concerns remain about plans to expand the mechanism to include a wider range of adult witnesses due to persistent problems relating to infrastructure and unreliable technology, and to increased workloads. These operational factors have dampened enthusiasm in England and Wales, but were not raised to the same degree by interviewees in Scotland.

GRHs have been generally welcomed and are now ingrained within all the surveyed jurisdictions, except for Ireland, where they continue to evolve at a nascent stage. There was a general consensus that the advantage of GRHs for witnesses is that, with everything approved in advance, they are better positioned to give their best evidence. GRHs ensure that the questions asked are at a linguistic level that witnesses can understand and respond to, and they provide an opportunity to discuss how the court environment can be adapted to assist the witness in giving evidence. The introduction of directions on how witnesses should be questioned, along with the increasing use of intermediaries to mediate the way questions are put, represents a significant change to the traditional 'advocacy' model of cross-examination.

Although GRHs vary considerably in their nature and form, perhaps the most innovative aspect is the requirement that, for some witnesses at least, counsel must prepare and furnish a draft list of proposed cross-examination questions for consideration by the judge, who will in turn invite representations from prosecuting counsel and the intermediary and make any directions accordingly. This constitutes a radical break from tradition as advocates are required to reveal in advance their line of questioning and, in the case of young children and witnesses with learning difficulties, to have the questions approved by a judge beforehand.

4

Shaping Cross-Examination through Intermediaries

An intermediary is an impartial communication specialist who works within the criminal justice system to assist vulnerable witnesses in giving evidence to the police and courts in criminal trials.[1] Their use is one of a range of special measures available by statute in England and Wales,[2] Northern Ireland,[3] and Ireland[4] to support vulnerable witnesses and, in some cases, vulnerable defendants. Scotland is noticeable among the jurisdictions included in the research as having chosen not to implement intermediary support for any type of vulnerable witness.

In England and Wales and in Northern Ireland, intermediary support is available to children under the age of 18 and to adult witnesses whose quality of evidence is likely to be affected by a mental disorder or impairment of intelligence and social functioning and those with a physical disorder or disability.[5] In Ireland, the measure is available to children under the age of 17 and adults with a 'mental disorder' testifying through a live television link,[6] though if the witness is not the victim of the offence, there is an additional offence gateway: the witness must be testifying in a relation to a sexual or violent offence. Provision for intermediary support for vulnerable defendants

---

1 https://www.gov.uk/guidance/ministry-of-justice-witness-intermediary-scheme. The role of the intermediary in assisting police officers when interviewing vulnerable witness pre-charge is not considered in this chapter, which focuses on the impact that intermediaries have on the cross-examination process.

2 Youth Justice and Criminal Evidence Act 1999, s 29.

3 Criminal Evidence (Northern Ireland) Order 1999, s 17.

4 Criminal Evidence Act 1992, s 14(1).

5 Youth Justice and Criminal Evidence Act 1999, ss 16 and 18(1); Criminal Evidence (Northern Ireland) Order 1999, ss 4 and 6(1).

6 Criminal Evidence Act 1992, s 14(1).

is more muted. In England and Wales, the relevant statutory provision[7] has never been brought into force and instead judges exercise their inherent jurisdiction to ensure fairness in proceedings to appoint intermediaries for defendants in appropriate cases (Criminal Practice Directions, 2023: 6.2.4). In Ireland, legislation authorising the use of intermediaries refers only to 'witnesses'. Strikingly, it is only in Northern Ireland that defendant access to intermediary support is underpinned by statute.[8] Notably, however, in both the implemented Northern Irish and unimplemented English legislation, there is a higher threshold for vulnerable defendant access to the intermediary measure. Unlike vulnerable witnesses, youth or a mental disorder/impairment of intelligence or social function is, of itself, insufficient to qualify for intermediary support. In addition, the vulnerable accused must demonstrate that as a result they are unable to participate effectively in the proceedings.[9]

The intermediary concept was first proposed by the Pigot Committee (Home Office, 1989) which recommended that counsels' questions to child witnesses should be relayed through a 'paediatrician, child psychiatrist, social worker or person who enjoys the child's confidence'. Pigot's proposal was met with significant opposition on the grounds that it might pose a fundamental challenge to the freedom of counsel under the adversarial model (Hoyano, 2000). The power of the intermediary to reword questions potentially disrupted well-established cross-examination techniques, leading to fears of a loss of meaning or emphasis, which might alter the substance of the question. This, in turn, raised concerns that judges would be required to adjudicate disputes between the questioner and the intermediary (Hoyano, 2000). However, in *Speaking Up for Justice* (Home Office, 1998: §8.73) the government accepted a similar, though wider, recommendation that where a witness, child or adult, requires it, an accredited intermediary should be available to 'explain questions which are put to the witness by counsel who use complex language'. As noted in the previous chapter, pre-recorded cross-examination and intermediaries were considered the most controversial special measures, both radically disrupting adversarial tradition. Intermediary use, for the first time, provided for someone other than the judge or opposing counsel to interrupt and query counsel's examination in a criminal trial (Henderson, 2015c).

7 Coroners and Justice Act 2009, s 104 inserting 33BA into the Youth Justice and Criminal Evidence Act 1999.

8 Criminal Evidence (Northern Ireland) Order 1999, s 21BA as amended by s 12 of the Justice Act (Northern Ireland) 2011. The provision was brought into force on 26 April 2013 by s 11 of the Criminal Justice Act (Northern Ireland) 2013.

9 Criminal Evidence (Northern Ireland) Order 1999, s 21BA(5) and (6); Youth Justice and Criminal Evidence Act 1999, s 33BA(5) and (6).

Despite this initial opposition, and as with pre-recorded cross-examination, evidence on commission (in Scotland), and the evolution of ground rules hearings (GRHs), we have increasingly seen criminal justice professionals accepting this disruption to their traditional ways of questioning, at least for the most vulnerable witnesses. The use of intermediaries has grown incrementally in England and Wales and in Northern Ireland, and has been rolled out on a gradual basis more recently in Ireland. Having emerged in the early 2000s on an ad hoc basis in England and Wales, they were formally phased in from 2007 and rolled out nationally in 2008 (Henderson, 2015c; Taggart, 2021). Similarly, in Northern Ireland they were rolled out across the country in 2016,[10] following pilots in 2013 and 2015. At the time of the research there was no formal scheme in Ireland,[11] though since 2019 some, limited, ad hoc use had been made of experienced intermediaries trained in Northern Ireland (Jackson et al, 2024: 46).

All three jurisdictions have accredited schemes of approved intermediaries providing a single point of access for criminal justice professionals seeking their services. In England and Wales, there are two separate schemes: a Ministry of Justice scheme to provide registered intermediaries (RIs) for prosecution witnesses and a HM Courts and Tribunals Service scheme to provide HM Courts and Tribunal Service (HMCTS) appointed intermediaries for defendants (Taggart, 2022; Fairclough et al, 2023). In Northern Ireland, the Department of Justice runs a Registered Intermediary Scheme, which is a unitary system providing intermediaries for both witnesses and defendants (Taggart, 2021). Similarly in Ireland, qualified intermediaries are placed on a panel and may work for both vulnerable witnesses and defendants (Delahunt, 2024). Intermediaries come from a variety of professional backgrounds, including speech and language therapy, psychology, social work, or education.[12] The common qualification is that each has specific expertise and skills in facilitating communication with children and/or adults with communication impairments (Cooper and Mattison, 2017).

This chapter examines how the role of the intermediary has impacted on the style and nature of cross-examination. We first examine the scope and extent of the intermediary role before considering how intermediaries contribute to facilitating a vulnerable witness's best evidence. We then turn to two of the most significant contemporary debates on intermediary use: overuse for vulnerable witnesses and underuse for vulnerable defendants. We conclude with some observations on the degree to which the intermediary has become embedded as another criminal justice professional with a recognised and valued skill set.

---

[10] www.justice-ni.gov.uk/ri.

[11] Though a Professional Diploma in Intermediary Studies was launched in 2022 at the University of Limerick.

[12] https://www.gov.uk/guidance/ministry-of-justice-witness-intermediary-scheme

The nature and extent of the intermediary role

The legislation in the three jurisdictions which allow for intermediaries is worded in similar terms. In England and Wales[13] and in Northern Ireland[14] the relevant provisions are identical:

> The function of an intermediary is to communicate –
> (a) to the witness, questions put to the witness, and
> (b) to any person asking such questions, the answers given by the witness in reply to them, and to explain such questions or answers so far as necessary to enable them to be understood by the witness or person in question.

And in Ireland,[15] the legislation states:

> Questions put to a witness through an intermediary under this section shall be either in the words used by the questioner or so as to convey to the witness in a way which is appropriate to his age and mental condition the meaning of the questions being asked.

The statutory wording implies an 'interpreter'-type role which narrowly focuses on understanding questions and answers exchanged during cross-examination. Yet from the outset intermediaries were trained to adopt a wider, 'facilitator'-type role in ensuring effective communication between the witness and criminal justice professionals which depended in large part on a specific understanding of the witness's communication needs and difficulties (Cooper and Mattison, 2017). Registered Intermediaries were also trained to consider and make recommendations on other special measures and adjustments which would support the vulnerable witness to give their best evidence (Cooper and Mattison, 2017). Intermediaries in the research emphasised this wider role in easing the trial-based challenges vulnerable witnesses face, with one describing their role as 'to assess and advise … on the communication of an individual and give advice on how things need to be altered to optimise that person's communication' (AAR3). Others conceptualised their role in terms of ensuring participation:

> I'm interested in the person being able to effectively participate, either as a witness or a defendant in a case. And that covers a huge

13 Youth Justice and Criminal Evidence Act 1999, s 29.

14 Criminal Evidence (Northern Ireland) Order 1999, s 17.

15 Criminal Justice Act 1992, s 14(2).

> range of things from whether they with their special needs need accommodations and adaptations in the court and whether they need adaptations and accommodations when they're giving their evidence. (AXR1)

Interviewees frequently described intermediaries as officers of the court, reinforcing statutory and official guidance (The Advocate's Gateway, 2019: §2.5; Criminal Practice Directions, 2023: §6.2.1; Ministry of Justice, 2023: 6; Judicial College, 2024: Ch 2, §96) on the neutrality of the role (see also Fairclough et al, 2023).

> The registered intermediary … [is] an expert in communication, they're impartial. They're not partial to the witness at all. (AAJ2)

> You're accountable to neither prosecution nor defence, and you really are aware of that. (ABR2)

> Your role is a neutral role … That is one of the things I'm quite passionate about, the neutrality of the role. (DAR 1)

As we shall see in Chapter 7, acceptance of the intermediary role by judges and counsel is steadily increasing and very few interviewees questioned the legitimacy of the role, with most now recognising the value intermediaries demonstrably add to the process of securing best evidence. In the next section, therefore, we examine how intermediary practice contributes to that project.

The added value of an intermediary

As we have seen, the legislation on its face suggests that the primary function of the intermediary is, in real time, to simplify and render understandable 'law-speak' (ACJ1), but it is clear that this is only a small part of the role as implemented in all of the jurisdictions in the research. This research confirms that intermediaries in practice play a significant role pre-trial in planning for witnesses' full and effective testimonial participation, and at trial they are less likely to 'interpret questions' as they are put and more likely to 'police' counsel's cross-examination to ensure that questions are linguistically and developmentally appropriate. Their involvement can be considered at three different stages of the criminal proceedings: pre-trial assessment of the witness's abilities and needs leading to a report for court; participation in ground rules hearings, giving advice on support needs and advising on the format and phrasing of questions; and appearing at trial to ensure questions are properly put during cross-examination.

Pre-trial assessment

The purpose of the pre-trial assessment is to assess the witness's communication skills for the purposes of giving evidence in a criminal trial. Following the assessment, the intermediary provides a written report to the court, based on a standard template, which advises on how best to communicate with the witness and which should shape discussion at the ground rules hearing on the directions necessary to support the witness during their testimony (The Advocate's Gateway, 2019: §9.1; Ministry of Justice, 2023: Part 4).

Assessment practice is not standardised; rather it is considered to be within the scope of the intermediary's professional practice (Cooper and Mattison, 2017: 358). However, best practice indicates that it should explore:

1. Receptive communication (ability to understand language and question forms);
2. Expressive language (ability to use language to inform, describe and clarify);
3. Ability to refute inaccurate suggestions;
4. Ability to shift perspective (comprehension of other people's thoughts and beliefs and feelings);
5. Ability to concentrate and attend to tasks, and to manage his/her own arousal and anxiety;
6. Use of external aids to support communication, such as drawing and 'cue cards'. (Cooper and Mattison, 2017: 358)

Interviewees confirmed that their assessment processes covered these matters and gave numerous examples of how they evaluate witnesses' communication abilities in order to 'get a notion of their expressive and receptive language' (ABR2) and to determine whether they have 'a linguistic or an emotional or a developmental reason that says that they can or can't cope with different aspects of the case being put to them' (AAR3). Intermediaries told us that they 'need to know if they can do a narrative … if they know positional, words, prepositions' (AXR3). They explained how they determine the witness's ability to give 'an account of something':

> What's their language like? What's their vocabulary like? … Their understanding … I give them a really long, complex sentence, 'We're going to play a game now, can you clap your hands before you jump up and down and shout?' … How much of an instruction can they follow? Because that would help us know what length of sentences to give? Can they respond to tagged questions … At the same time you're looking at their use of gesture, their use of eye contact. How they respond if I swap around from subject to subject very quickly?

> Do they get confused? What's their attention like? Can they maintain a conversation with me just face to face? (AAR1)

> If the case [is going to be] put to them, I will have given them some really silly examples but we will have practised the idea of a question that is, 'This is an assertion' and then a, 'Is this true?' We'll have practised some of those questions. (ABR2)

They also spoke about determining the ability to refute suggestion: 'I'm probably looking more specifically at things like comprehension monitoring … the ability to say, "I don't know", "I don't understand", "you're wrong", that kind of thing' (AAR3). And beyond linguistic capabilities, they described assessing the witness's 'understanding of the process … how it's going to work' (ABR2) and their 'anxieties, their wishes and needs' (AAR3). Another intermediary noted how children responded differently with or without toys at hand:

> It's not just the language, you're also assessing quite a lot else as well. I mean, little ones will perhaps chat happily whilst they're playing. Then when I move all the toys out of the way and just carry on talking, you get a very, very different response, and that's useful to know because you know they're not able to do questions and answers over a period of time without toys and things like that. (AAR1)

As part of the pre-trial assessment, the intermediary may also consider non-linguistic adjustments to normal court procedure to facilitate the witness's best evidence (The Advocate's Gateway, 2019). Intermediaries gave many examples of matters that may be relevant: how and when memory refreshing will take place; whether a fixed time for the witness to give evidence is required to avoid extended waiting periods; whether props or topic cards should be used to both support evidence giving and relieve anxiety; how the witness should meet the judge and counsel; whether formal court attire should be worn; whether counsel should sit or stand when asking questions; whether counsel should ask questions from the courtroom or move to the live link room; whether it is acceptable for the witness to write down answers for the intermediary to read out; whether regular breaks are helpful or distracting and, if required, at what frequency.

The following discussion features the first of a number of excerpts based on our observations and transcript analysis. For brevity and clarity, we have abbreviated the central actors as follows: judge (J); prosecution counsel (PC); defence counsel (DC); intermediary (IM); witness (W). On occasion, some cases may involve more than one witness, and these are labelled as defence witness (DW1, 2, and so on) or prosecution witness (PW1, 2, and so on).

Case A031 reflects a conversation which took place between the judge and the intermediary in the GRH which illustrates some of the non-linguistic issues that may impinge on the quality of the evidence of an adult witness with intellectual disabilities.

Case A031

J: Can you help us, I have seen in your report that we shouldn't wear wigs or gowns. That is not a problem. We wouldn't be wearing ties which I know she has a fear of. How would she react to us wearing a stiff collar and bands?

IM: When I saw her on Wednesday, it was the first thing she mentioned. Wigs and gowns. She made it very clear that wigs and gowns are something that petrifies her. There has been no mention of stiff collar.

J: You say she doesn't like strange things and things that are new. So, to err on the side of caution maybe we should just wear a shirt.

...

J: I was going to ask for some help of how I should speak to her. I was going to ask her if what she told the police was true, if she doesn't remember then she should just say. But I don't know if she will follow that?

IM: Those were the words I used on Wednesday, I told her to remember that she is coming to court to tell the truth and if she doesn't know something then not to make it up. I told her I have checked the questions and they are worded so that she could understand but if she doesn't just to say.

J: That is very helpful, thank you. Taking the oath, can she read? Or should I ask you to read it and have her repeat it.

IM: We discussed that, and she would prefer it read and repeat it.

...

J: Will anyone else be in the room?

IM: She had some support staff that wanted to be in the room, but the officer in the case and myself said no. They will be in the next room.

...

J: Talk me through your thinking that neither should be in the room?

IM: In the sense that we didn't want them to have any access to evidence and therefore not discuss it with her between Wednesday and when she gives evidence. I also didn't want her to be asked a question then looking to [X] for support. I want her answer to be her answer and not influenced.

...

J: Does she understand what a judge is?

IM: Yes, I went through all the roles with her and who can speak during live evidence and who can't speak. She asked what happens if he speaks during live evidence and I told her that the judge will stop him because he can't speak when she is giving the live evidence because the judge will stop him. I said that the judge is the boss, and we all have to do what the judge says. I think she understood that.

Therefore, while there may be a limited range of factors to be considered, the court's decisions turn on the individual circumstances of the witness's vulnerability, and as such the intermediary's personalised assessment is critical in ensuring reasonable adjustments are made to normal court procedures. Although some interviewees voiced criticism of the standardised nature of some of the reports, many more also commented on the additional focus on vulnerability that an intermediary's report can provide:

> You think about hidden disability which I think is very important because we tend to ignore hidden disabilities, cognitive disabilities, dyslexia, dyspraxia, all of those things and I think anything that reminds the judge trying a case that this [witness] ... may not have the same ability to follow the questioning and the evidence I think is a good thing. (AAJ3)

> An intermediary report saying, you know, 'X is a very lively child, bright as a bulb and completely clued in' or 'X is very subdued and quiet and isn't very forthcoming' is very helpful ... [It] gives you a good steer and then you can go in and you're not blundering around in that respect ... I think that's very helpful. And then of course just making sure that you're not operating on a level that's beyond where the child is ... is very easy to do. (AAC4)

And that this indeed may be a more important contribution than intervening at trial: 'In a proper case with a bespoke report telling us about the vulnerabilities of a witness, often I think that's all that is necessary ... because the intermediaries' involvement thereafter is actually very limited' (AAJ3).

Participation in ground rules hearings

While the previous chapter offered insights into the role and purpose of GRHs, this section seeks to provide a more focused understanding of the role of the intermediary within those hearings, particularly in relation to how their inputs may enhance the clarity and comprehensibility of questions originally devised by counsel. Unless the court directs otherwise, when a special measures direction for an intermediary has been made, the intermediary must attend to 'actively assist the court in setting ground rules and giving directions' (Criminal Procedure Rules, 2020: 3.9.2; Criminal Practice Directions, 2023: 6.2.10).[16] While the prime function of the intermediary at this pre-trial phase is to review and make recommendations on counsel's proposed questions for cross-examination, they also, as we have seen, make wider recommendations on other, non-linguistic, support measures.

Since Henderson's study on the value of intermediaries (Henderson, 2015c), there has been a proliferation of detailed best practice guidance on the questioning of vulnerable witnesses (see Chapter 3). Yet the value of the intermediary's specialist contribution in shaping questions pre-trial persists and was widely praised by many judges and counsel, with one judge highlighting that intermediaries bring with them 'an understanding of how people … under a certain age or with certain vulnerabilities don't interpret language in the same way':

> Using an intermediary … That was the first time I discovered what the problem was with a tagged question … I recall defence counsel who didn't put anything in an overly aggressive fashion but essentially said to [the vulnerable witness], 'Well X didn't take you into the woods did he?' and she said 'no', and so he said, 'This didn't happen, did it?', 'No', and all we got was 'No', 'No'. And I later discovered, having spoken to the intermediary … that that might have meant 'No, I don't agree with you', because that witness may not have understood the tagged questions. (AAJ1)

This judge concluded, 'counsel, they're doing their best, but they don't always understand what's gone wrong, and without an intermediary, that would be a problem'. Counsel too acknowledged that some of their colleagues need more assistance in crafting questions than others (see further Chapter 6), with one describing intermediary advice as a 'necessary evil, because … there are lot of advocates who haven't quite yet grasped how to ask the question' (ABC1). Particularly apposite is the intermediary's ability, based on their assessment, to foresee the difficulties that certain question constructs will cause. Judges gave examples of how useful they found this, one telling us 'they can explain that the witness may have difficulty in following this question because it uses a figure of speech and the witness has autism and will treat the figure of speech in a very literal sense' (ABJ3). Another said, 'I

[16] At the time of the research study, Criminal Practice Directions 2015 3F.12.

think that one of the things that intermediaries do encourage is the thought processes in relation to whether you're asking too many closed questions or not enough open questions' (AAJ1). A third recalled a witness who:

> Had real difficulties remembering names and places and getting things in order. The intermediary came up with a really useful timeline which showed where she'd lived and what she looked like when she was in school and [suggested questions such as] 'what did you look like when this was going on?' It was really helpful. (ACJ2)

Intermediaries nevertheless did not paint an entirely bleak picture of counsel's questioning abilities:

> It used to be that each question [would] be a paragraph … [Now] they're more likely to ask individual questions. So they might say, 'Now, I'm going to ask you about the time in the park', so they'll be grouped into a theme but nice, short, clear, concise questions with basic language. Whereas previously, you'd get these big, long, drawn-out paragraphs with lots of legal devices in them such as 'I put it to you', or, 'I'm going to suggest to you', but you don't see that hardly ever anymore in intermediary cases. (ABR3)

This suggests that certainly where an intermediary is involved, the push towards establishing more appropriate questioning is becoming less arduous. However, this same intermediary was also able to provide recent examples of the challenge some counsel face in resiling from their natural intuitive use of language likely to be unfamiliar to many vulnerable witnesses:

> I had an example … where this counsel was asking about the words 'sachets' and I was like, 'Oh, I don't think she'll know what sachets mean … Just use the word packet'. Or they might say just simple words like 'bathe'. I mean, common everyday people don't say that. (ABR3)

Even where The Advocate's Gateway Toolkits provide guidance on how to structure the questioning of a vulnerable witness, such as grouping questions into topics to demonstrate a clear navigation path through the evidence (The Advocate's Gateway, 2015a: §5.4), counsel praised the intermediary's added value in tailoring that general advice to the specific case:

> She gave me ways of putting [my case] in a way that shouldn't be so threatening … also [exploring] her actual evidence without being contradictory or confusing her. And we did it by breaking down

> into topics and doing the challenge at the end … She was very good. (AAC5)
>
> There's not a one-size fits all solution. Some children with a certain age can cope with a double negative in a question perfectly well while others can't. And the complexity of the language has got to be tailored to the individual which is what the intermediaries par excellence help to do. (ACJ1)

Intermediaries strongly believed that their individualised advice on counsel's questions makes a significant contribution to the quest for best evidence:

> For example, if an intermediary had been involved from the beginning and had done an assessment, that would have indicated that a witness really didn't understand time and that they were likely to give unreliable or inconsistent answers if asked questions about time. (AAR3)
>
> Somebody asked a man I was with, how far away something was. Often in court what they do with those questions is they say, well, I'm standing here, and the judge is over there. My clients can't conceptualise like that. I said, 'he's a window cleaner … ask him how many houses along was it?' (AXR1)
>
> I kept saying, 'if you're going to put the case … do it at the end so that you've got all the other bit first, and then if he walks out and he can't sustain that or isn't fit to continue, at least you've got everything else first'. (AXR4)

And as one judge pointed out, the advice of an independent specialist can be key to securing agreement between opposing counsel: 'If you don't have an intermediary, trying to arrive at a set of acceptable questions is a much more arduous business than if you've got this person to whom everyone can refer and it's a much, much slicker process' (ACJ3).

Assisting at trial

Many intermediaries spoke of their aspiration to play a minimal role at court: 'hopefully, if the questions have been put in the right way, then that minimises the number of interventions' (AAR3). One suggested that their mere presence has a positive influence: 'One police officer … said to me that even the presence of an intermediary "puts manners on them" … I think the fact that an intermediary has actually been appointed to the case changes the way in which counsel plan and direct their questions to the witness' (DAR1). But even if that influence is not discernible, the hope is that because the intermediary has 'done all the work beforehand' others will think they are 'just sitting there like a spare part' because 'nobody sees all the hours of work that you do before you get to that point' (AXR3). What is more, intermediaries are aware that interventions interrupt the flow of cross-examination for both counsel and, 'more importantly, for the witness because they have an increasing sense with every intervention ... that they're failing ... this is really difficult and I'm not able to answer that question' (AXR3). Nevertheless, almost all intermediaries reported that intervening at trial is a routine part of their job, either because counsel deviate from the ground rules agreements or because it is not possible to 'script every last question' (ACJ1) and there are occasions when intermediaries need to react in real time to questions arising from a witness's previous answer. Thus, intermediaries' interventions at trial can contribute significantly to the quest for 'best evidence', with one judge describing intermediaries at trial as 'absolutely vital' (ACJ1), and a barrister who opined that 'the good ones are the most fantastic facilitators of a fair trial, and the good ones don't ever stand in the way of a topic being explored but they support counsel to explore that topic' (ACC1).

In three of the six observed cases involving intermediaries there were minimal interventions at trial (A006, A007, and A031), with counsel using seemingly appropriate language. For example, defence counsel in case A006 made extensive use of signposting to indicate a change of topic, clearly provided background information in advance of a question, and repeatedly assured the witness that it was okay to say that they could not remember. Questions were short, direct, and simply structured:

Case A006

DC: Another thing I'm going to do is I'm going to tell you what topic I want to ask you about before I ask the questions, and I'll try and give you a reminder of what was happening at the time in case it helps you to remember to answer the questions, okay. So, I'm going to ask you questions in four different topics ... The topics are ...

...

DC: All right, I'm going to move on from Facebook now. That's the end of Facebook. I now want to ask you about Snapchat. Back in 2018, did you have a Snapchat account called [X]?

...

DC: In your first interview, you told the police that this chase happened just before Christmas. Do you remember saying that?

W: Yeah.
DC: Yes, are you sure that that's when it happened, just before Christmas 2018?
W: It was somewhere around there.
DC: Okay, whose house was it that you went to?
W: Z's.

As a result, there was no intermediary intervention during cross-examination. Similarly in case A007, the few comments that the intermediary made at trial appeared to be connected to procedural and comfort issues and did not relate to questions posed in cross-examination. Counsel again showed clear signposting of topics and simple sentence structures. In this case counsel 'put the defence case' to the ten-year-old witness, who was able to understand and respond to the questions put.

Case A007

DC: M, you told the police that B asked you to put your mouth on his willy. B says that he has never asked you to do that. Are you sure that he asked you to do that?
W: Absolutely certain.
DC: You told the police that B asked you to take your clothes off. B says he never asked you to do that. Are you sure that he asked you to take your clothes off?
W: I'm absolutely certain.
DC: You told the police that B made you watch videos of naked girls. B says he didn't. Are you sure he made you watch videos of naked girls?
W: I'm absolutely certain.
DC: B says he has never put his willy on you. Are you sure that he put his willy on you?
W: Yes.
DC: B says he never put his willy near you. Are you sure he put his willy near you?
W: Yes, I am certain.
DC: B says that you're telling lies about him, M. Are you telling lies?
W: No, I'm not telling a lie.

We might assume in these cases that the intermediary influenced the style and structure of counsel's questions, either through the soft influence of their involvement with the case or more directly through pre-trial advice, though we cannot rule out the possibility that counsel would, of their own volition, have made adaptations to their normal cross-examination technique.

In the remaining three observed cases (A004, A034, and D008), intermediaries made varying degrees of intervention. For example, in case A004 involving a vulnerable defendant, prosecution counsel signalled the use of topics but immediately strung together a number of matters and did not give the defendant the opportunity to respond to any of the three separate 'do you understand' questions. Numerous subsequent questions were then structured as a statement with a tag, which attracted comment from both the intermediary and the judge:

Case A004

PC: May it please your Honour. The intermediary, who sits just by you, has suggested it would be helpful if I split my questions up into different topics, do you understand, and I'm going to try and do that. Even though it sounds a bit odd, I'm going to try and say to you, 'I'm now moving on to this topic'. Do you understand? If I forget to do it, I'm sure she will, politely, correct me, but I'm going to do my best to remember, all right. As you've been told more than once, if you need a break or, of course, if the intermediary thinks you need a break, either you or she only need to indicate. Do you understand? The first thing is the topic of lies. Do you understand? I suggest that you've told a lot of lies in your interview and, also, today. What do you say about that?
J: There's a difficulty with that.
IM: Sorry, [PC] could you just ask the question in simple terms?
PC: I've put tag on the end, haven't I?
IM: Yes.
PC: Thank you.
...
PC: You filmed it so you could show people what you'd done. Yes?
J: I think [D] you're being asked –
D: No.
J: Can you help us as to why you filmed it? Why did you film it?
D: I don't know.
PC: Just so she's not ignored, the intermediary put her hand up. Has the issue been dealt with now or not?
IM: Sorry, I think you made a statement question.
PC: Sorry.
IM: I just wanted you to ask it as a question.
PC: No, you're right. I'm going to move on because the judge's question dealt with the same point.

The observed cases reinforce the views of most interviewees that intermediaries' interventions, either pre-trial or at trial, are a significant factor in ensuring that questions are appropriately put to and understood by the witness.

As important as intermediaries' judgements about counsel's language and sentence structures is their ability to pick up on 'the more subtle clues a witness might give about not understanding something or just pleasing somebody by giving an answer' (ACC1); 'they are very effective, very effective, at picking up when a witness is struggling and isn't understanding' (AAC2). In response, intermediaries:

> Might interject and say, 'Do you understand', or, 'I can see that you're not quite following this, should we ask the barrister to ask the question again?' Whereas in the past I don't suppose many barristers or judges would've said that to a witness. (ABC2)

> Are able to unpick that a bit, and to stand in the gap of … lack of communication, which is sometimes because we don't … know that witness very well, and sometimes because the technology makes things a bit more difficult. (ACC1)

And one intermediary highlighted how, in order to make the witness feel more comfortable, they would use a conversational tone that is 'probably more familiar for the child' and address counsel by their first name in asking 'could we just have that question again?' (AAR3).

We saw in the observed cases examples of an intermediary intervening to ask counsel to rephrase questions when she sensed a lack of understanding. For example:

Case D008

DC: D tells me he can't remember from the time you were kissing to that fella injecting himself. He says that's a period of time he does not remember. His next memory is you on his lap.
IM: I'm not sure from [witness's] facial expression that she's following–
…
DC: D told me his next memory is you sitting on his lap, with his penis out, and that it wasn't hard.
W: I wasn't sitting on him.
IM: I'm not sure [witness] is following all that information. Could you break it down?

Intermediaries and counsel also spoke about the value of the props that intermediaries create and use at trial, ranging from visual timelines along which were plotted text message screenshots (ABR1) or Post-it notes denoting key events (AAC5) to dolls labelled with the names of key persons in the cases (ABC1), anxiety-reducing toys (as observed in case A031), and cards which witnesses can use to represent a response they find difficult to verbalise (ABR1). Indeed, counsel reported being sufficiently approving as to adopt some of these techniques themselves, with one barrister describing an intermediary who had been so useful that:

> When I had a case where an intermediary had been refused, wrongly … I actually rang her and said, 'Could I have some of the visual aids that you used?' … We got some of these things that they could point to, to say, 'I need a break' or 'I don't know', just to make it simpler for them. And I did a timeline myself … so, I almost stepped into [the gap]. (AAC5)

A particular benefit at trial which stems from the intermediary's detailed pre-trial assessment is the degree of familiarity with the witness which is unavailable to any other criminal justice professional: 'If you get a child whom … I've met briefly, I don't know what their difficulties are, I don't know how that affects them. And I can't work all that out very quickly' (AAC4). Many judges and counsel recognised therefore that intermediaries uniquely have an insight into the witness's capabilities (ACJ1), 'their level of understanding, and their comprehension, or their ability to concentrate … there's a value to that' (ACC4). Counsel also acknowledged the rapport the intermediary has established with the witness (ACC1) and their in-depth understanding of the difficulties the witness is likely to face when testifying (ABC2). As a result, and having 'been through communication exercises with them', the child is likely to be 'confident in communicating with the intermediary' (AAC3). The extent to which this familiarity then puts the witness at ease during their testimony was highlighted by some judges and counsel as one of the most significant consequences of intermediary use.

> It reassures the witness there's somebody there that will make sure … that people don't talk posh to them or don't treat them as stupid. That reassures them at an early stage … Giving evidence is a big thing for anybody. But giving evidence … when they have intellectual challenges, with communication difficulties, is an even bigger thing, it's hugely intimidating … but to know that, at an early stage, there will be somebody there to help if needs be … Helping people into the process is I think the most important aspect of it. (ACJ1)

> They give the witness the confidence that they can deal with whatever is coming at them because they've got somebody … they have an

> intermediary, somebody through whom it comes, who can moderate it for them … They behave towards the witness in such a way that the witness feels as though there's a professional ally in the room, not a friend, but somebody who's got their back and who will assist in making sure that things are done fairly. (ACC1)

Intermediaries also spoke of their role in alleviating the stress of giving evidence, where witnesses look for reassurance and encouragement (AAR3) and 'feel listened to … can communicate at their level … they've been in a comfortable safe place where they feel that they're not overwhelmed, and they can actually take part' (AXR3).

> When I'm assisting a victim … it'll all be nice and calm, all the questions will be agreed, I know the sequence of the questions, I know the topics, I've even got my visual aids, whether I've got a body map board or a timetable, and it's all in order by my leg in that room. Everyone's calm. (AAR2)

This calming, stress-relieving effect may be critical in facilitating a witness's evidence; it 'sometimes can be the difference between whether a person can give evidence or not' (ABR1). The ability of witnesses to remain focused is also crucial for navigating cross-examination. One intermediary who supports younger children said, 'for this age group you'd have to intervene for their attention levels, the fact that they've got fed up and they're now distracted by the pipes that are making a noise under the table, that sort of thing' (AAR1). Judges and counsel also pointed to the intermediary's contribution as 'another pair of eyes and ears' in the courtroom who may detect inattention (ACJ2).

> Very often, they'll gauge whether you've got the witness' attention as well and can help to stop the witness drifting, if I can just put it that way. They will just turn and they'll say, 'John, now, the man is asking a question here'. And we'll get the attention back. (ACJ1)

> Sometimes rather than intervention … it will be encouragement, getting the child or vulnerable person that's less likely to come up with an answer, to get them communicating, to direct attention back towards the camera or, if they get being distracted, to give them the fiddle toy … If they've got something to do with their hands, they're more likely to remain engaged … You often see that happening off the screen … the intermediary kind of coaching the child into giving an answer. (AAC3)

And we observed the intermediary in this role in case A031, where the vulnerable witness fled from the live TV link, and the intermediary, at the judge's request, successfully persuaded them to return and complete their evidence.

A point which emerges, then when looking at the wider role of the intermediary is whether, in creating the conditions in which the witness can effectively participate and give their best evidence, the intermediary is the criminal justice professional who most explicitly applies their mind to the witness's best interests during the trial process.

> So, you've done little bit of work with witness care, you've maybe had a visit with the person, you've got there early and made sure everything's okay for them. You've done the memory refresh, so you know they've watched their ABE. You've done a little bit of prep work, 'remember this is how it's going to be, this is what I'm going to do to help you, this is where we're going to sit'. You assist them to meet advocates and the judge possibly before you go in … You've introduced them to the usher, and then when your usher comes, you go, 'okay, say bye to whoever came with you, it's all going to be good. When we come back from here, it's going to be done'. (AXR3)

In this, we might see the intermediary as plugging an 'advocacy' gap left open by other criminal justice professionals who, while having a degree of responsibility for the witness's testimonial experience, have other demanding professional responsibilities which compete to weaken their focus on the witness's needs. Advocacy in this context does not refer to the advancement of a particular case. Rather it points to the possibility that part of the professional role of the intermediary is to ensure that the witness can find and use their voice in the criminal trial process. Whether the intermediary role can and should adapt to this wider function is also alluded to the next chapter and is briefly discussed in Chapter 8, where the tensions it raises with the impartiality of the role are mentioned.

Concerns around overuse

Having considered the contribution that intermediaries are able to make towards the effective participation of vulnerable witnesses in criminal trials, we now turn to a concern expressed by a meaningful minority of judges and counsel in the research who seemed to lack full commitment to the intermediary as a new criminal justice actor: overuse. Previous research has pointed to an enduring belief among lawyers and judges that the extent of inappropriate questioning of vulnerable witnesses is overplayed and that when it occurs it is easily controlled and corrected by the trial judge (Henderson, 2015a). Henderson reported increased awareness among criminal justice professionals of the potential of conventional cross-examination to obfuscate the evidence of vulnerable witnesses and a more sophisticated understanding of the linguistic devices that cause most problems. She also detected an increased motivation to improve practice (Henderson 2015a: 676). However, 'a significant minority, whilst theoretically committed to improving practice, nonetheless disputed the extent of the problem as defined by researchers and the appellate courts' (Henderson 2015a: 668). We too saw that such views, though on the decline, persist. This translated, at the one extreme, into the view that intermediary assistance is simply unnecessary because judges and counsel have the requisite skills to question appropriately.

> Frankly, I question how many witnesses ever do need the assistance of an intermediary. Rather how many witnesses need a patient, sensitive advocate guided by a judge dealing with the case properly to ensure that they are looked after and having support. I've rarely seen cases where intermediaries have made any real difference to the cross-examination in a trial that I've been presiding over. (ABJ1)

> [An intermediary] is just another ingredient to the trial. It's another unnecessary complexity and it can be dead wood. There's a degree of fashionability about these things, I think. And it's very difficult to argue against … because of course who's going to say or argue that it's a bad thing or a wrong thing to have somebody helping a vulnerable witness? (AAJ3)

Interviewees in this research voiced similar opinions on the overuse of intermediaries to those expressed in Henderson's 2013 study, which spoke of the use of intermediaries in 'appropriate cases only' or in 'extreme cases' (Henderson 2015a: 669). In our research, even those judges and counsel who accepted the potential contribution of an intermediary expressed reservations that 'we've just got to a point where almost any vulnerability will lead to an intermediary' (AAC4). The concern is that, particularly for children, intermediary provision has become a blanket rule that overlooks the specific communication capabilities of the child (ABJ3).

> For a witness who is young, an intelligent nine- or ten-year-old, or … whose learning issues are fairly modest, then they are managed simply by ensuring that the questions are short, focused and don't use very complicated words. And I don't think you need an intermediary to tell you that. (ABJ3)

> When you've got someone … who is 22, says they've got ADHD … and has limited educational skills, are not very good at reading and

> writing, or they don't know how to use long words and they wouldn't understand certain words, they don't need an intermediary on the whole ... They need a good advocate and a good judge [who] will make sure that the questions are broken down. (ABJ1)

> If we've got a witness from the age of nine upwards who is broadly intelligent ... We will probably have an intermediary report [but] none of us really need it. What you're going to be told is that they need breaks, don't [use] tag questions ... You know, headlining and all that sort of thing. (ACJ2)

Such views focus entirely on developmental criteria and overlook the impact of the environment on a vulnerable witness's ability to attain what might be expected to be their ordinary communication abilities. This point is clearly illustrated in intermediaries' criticisms of judges' and counsel's tendency to draw what intermediaries see as simplistic conclusions on the necessity for an intermediary at court if one had not previously been used during an Achieving Best Evidence interview:

> One of the big problems we have is that both judges and defence barristers believe that that witness, if they managed to do an ABE without assistance, can come to court without assistance. And that's an enormous hurdle ... they have no understanding of ... the impact of communication environment on the way we talk. (AXR1)

Intermediaries highlighted the clearly different language demand when speaking with a police officer 'in an interview suite where nobody is challenging you' (AXR1) and a barrister in court where, 'you're focusing on different demands of communication' (ABR3). Indeed, one counsel also pointed out that 'there's a very different dynamic because the police officer's just eliciting information, there's no challenge' (ACC1). And it is these wider aspects of communicative challenge that intermediaries believed some judges and counsel continue to overlook.

It is intriguing, therefore, that a significant number of judges and counsel believed improved training and resources, together with learning from previous experience, would render them sufficiently skilled to appropriately word questions without assistance or review, at least for vulnerable witnesses with less complex communication needs: 'I think ... we're getting towards a point where judges and The Advocate's Gateway and the Judicial College are sufficiently well-informed to be able to deal with some cases without an intermediary' (ACJ3); 'We've kind of learned how to do it as advocates and judges, and so we do it without the intermediary having to be there and get involved' (ACC3). Although a point made more explicitly in relation to intermediaries appointed to support defendants (see later in the chapter), we also detected a sense that, given the financial pressures within the criminal justicc system, only the very needy should be eligible for support by, so it is perceived, another professional who is 'ferociously expensive' (ACC4) and 'often the best paid person in the room' (AAJ3), because, as one judge told us, 'one does have to have regard to the public purse in all this' (ABJ3).

There was no evidence of overuse in this research study. Although we must be wary about drawing conclusions from a limited number of cases, as can be seen in Table 4.1, intermediaries appeared in six of the 40 trials observed and, in each, observers considered whether their use was appropriate.

Table 4.1: The use of intermediaries

Case	Witness eligibility criteria
A004	Child defendant (16-year-old) with ADHD charged with a grave offence and so appearing in the Crown Court.
A006	Child complainant (15-year-old) in rape and other sexual offences case involving multiple defendants.
A007	Child complainant (10-year-old) in rape and other sexual offences case.
A031	Adult complainant in sexual assault case with acute vulnerabilities, mental health issues, and anxiety.
A034	Child complaint (13-year-old) in rape and other sexual offences case.
D008	Adult complainant with intellectual disabilities in sexual offences case.

Three of the observed cases (A002, A020, and A027) raise the potential for underuse. Case A002 involved an eight-year-old complainant in a sexual offences case who appeared able to understand and answer defence counsel's questions, which largely followed The Advocate's Gateway guidelines and attracted no judicial intervention. Nevertheless, the young age of the vulnerable witness raises questions over whether an intermediary would have been appropriate. In both A020 and A027, which involved respectively 14- and 13-year-old complainants to sexual offences, both the judge (and in A020, the Independent Sexual Violence Adviser) intervened during defence counsel's cross-examination to suggest that the witness did not understand the question put. In A027, the judge intervened on successive occasions, telling counsel, 'that's too complicated a question', 'that's not an appropriate question', and seeking to clarify for the witness the meaning of counsel's question. Following several apparently frustrating exchanges between the judge and counsel, he sent the jury out to allow further discussion on counsel's questioning style. These two cases would therefore seem to be examples where pre-trial review of questions by the intermediary could have better shaped the cross-examination experience, resulting in less interruptions to the flow of questions.

Intermediaries on the whole disagreed with the suggestion that they are overused, though there were some exceptions. One agreed that youth alone is an insufficient justification for intermediary support, giving the example of 'a teenager, you know 14, 15 years old, typically developing, so no learning difficulties, no mental health difficulties, just a normal teenager … there's no communication impairment' (ABR1). Another conceded that potential overuse is a valid concern.

> There is a tendency in the RI world, partly because the RIs come from therapeutic backgrounds, to say everybody needs an intermediary and that doesn't do us any favours. Because then you have a judge who says, 'Well, I've never seen a report that says somebody doesn't need an intermediary'. (AXR1)

Most intermediaries tended to the view that some, though not all, judges and barristers continued to fail to grasp the extent of some witnesses' vulnerabilities or had a misplaced confidence in their own abilities to communicate appropriately with them, or potentially both (see further Chapter 6). Central to this is a failure among legally qualified professionals, who have 'a certain way' of behaving and 'a certain level that they speak at' (AXR3), to recognise the intermediary as a highly qualified professional with a distinctive skill set (see also Fairclough et al, 2023: 453). One pointed to her 'master's degree, 20 years' worth of clinical practice and 20 years of CPD [continuing professional development]' as the reason why criminal justice professionals are 'never going to understand linguistic processes in the way that a speech therapist would' (ABR1). Another echoed this sentiment: 'Unless they get convinced that we have a separate set of skills, they think they know the same as us. They really do … They don't know enough about communication. They never will. And they think they can make those judgements' (AXR1).

What emerged, therefore, was a divide between advocates who see the increased use of intermediaries as an implicit criticism of their competence to question a vulnerable witness and advocates who see intermediaries as making an additional, specialist, contribution to that task. In the next section we consider a further aspect of this debate: the continued challenge to arguments in favour of intermediary support for vulnerable defendants.

Asymmetrical provision for vulnerable defendants

We saw earlier that statutory provision for intermediary support for vulnerable defendants is more restricted than for vulnerable witnesses. Legal policy, at least in England and Wales, is that access should be the exception rather than the rule (Hoyano and Rafferty, 2017). Judges must use their inherent jurisdiction to appoint intermediaries for defendants, and it was held in *Rashid* that it would be a 'rare case where the threshold of disability is crossed such that an intermediary is required when the defendant gives his evidence' and 'cases in which an order will be made for an intermediary to be present for the whole trial will be very rare'.[17] The Court has, however, recognised the need to appoint an intermediary 'when necessary' (*R* v *Grant Murray and Others* [2017] EWCA Crim 1225, [225]) where 'there are compelling reasons for taking this step, it being clear that all other adaptations to the trial process will not sufficiently meet the defendant's needs to ensure he or she can effectively participate in the trial' (*R* v *Dean Thomas* [2020] EWCA Crim 117 [37]). There are signs that a less restrictive approach is now being taken to the appointment of defence intermediaries. Criminal Practice Directions handed down in 2023[18] no longer refer to the appointment of defence intermediaries as a rarity and state more neutrally that the court may appoint an intermediary, 'when giving evidence or for the entire trial'. However, *Rashid* remains good law, and it remains to be seen whether the new, more neutrally worded,[19] Practice Direction will result in a change to judicial practice.

The provision for vulnerable defendants in Northern Ireland is less contentious; intermediary use is still evolving and policy explicitly recognises that equality of arms considerations require equality of intermediary provision for both witnesses and defendants (Taggart, 2021: 143). Intermediary support is available by statute (Delahunt, 2024) and the Protocol for Vulnerable Defendants (Lord Chief Justice's Office, 2019) emphasises that vulnerable defendants must be able 'to understand and participate in the proceedings and engage fully with their defence'. The protocol adopts identical criteria for when vulnerable witnesses and defendants should be assessed by an

[17] *R v Yahya Rashid* [2017] EWCA Crim 2, per Lord Thomas CJ at [84]. Approved in *R v Biddle* [2019] EWCA Crim 86.

[18] Seemingly following criticism by the High Court as to the manner in which it was being interpreted: *TI* v *Bromley Youth Court* [2020] EWHC 1204 (Admin) [2020] Crim LR 951. Dame Sharp considered that the reference to appointments being 'rare' referred to all cases coming before courts. 'In that context most cases will involve defendants who do not require the assistance of an intermediary. Therefore, the appointment of an intermediary will be rare. It does not follow that there is a high hurdle to overcome for the appointment of an intermediary if one is necessary for the effective participation of a defendant in the trial process' [39].

[19] Para 6.2.4 states that the court may use its inherent powers to direct the appointment of a defence intermediary, 'there is however no presumption that a defendant will be so assisted and, even where an intermediary has the potential to improve the trial process, appointment is not mandatory'. Para 6.2.6 directs that the court may appoint an intermediary, 'when giving evidence or for the entire trial'.

intermediary.[20] In Ireland, intermediary use is very new and to date legislation has not extended their use to defendants. However, graduates from the recently established postgraduate professional Diploma in Intermediary Studies may be placed on a panel to work with both vulnerable witnesses and defendants (Delahunt, 2024), and judicial and counsel interviewees in Ireland were noticeably open to the idea that the defence may need an intermediary throughout the trial to allow vulnerable defendants to understand the issues and give instructions. Accordingly, our examination of the extent of defence intermediary provision will focus on the research findings in England and Wales because this is where their use is most firmly established.

In England and Wales, we found that the law's policy on limited intermediary support was reinforced by broadly held judicial perceptions of lack of need. The overwhelming sense from the interview data was that practice was faithful to case law and the Criminal Practice Directions which then applied (Criminal Practice Directions, 2015); it is difficult to secure an intermediary for a vulnerable defendant, and extremely rare for the intermediary to support the defendant throughout the whole trial. Differential access to intermediary support was reinforced by the separate schemes for Registered Intermediaries for vulnerable witnesses and HMCTS-approved intermediaries for defence intermediaries (see Fairclough et al, 2023).

The predominant view of intermediaries was that vulnerable defendants are not granted the same level of support as vulnerable witnesses:

> Defendants do not get the same treatment as complainants, regardless of their need. Vulnerability does not come into it … A complainant would get a registered intermediary who's an expert in communication, who's done additional training, who does a full and comprehensive assessment of this person and gives guided recommendations, The defendant, none of that. (ABR1)

> It's unusual for a defendant to have an intermediary … It is not at the point that witness assistance is yet, definitely not. (AXR3)

One intermediary described it in terms of 'inequity [of] provision for a defendant and a witness' (ABR2), and even a barrister who was in general sceptical of intermediaries recognised that 'if you're going to have them, then you should have fairness for defendants, which we don't have at the moment' (ACC4). Counsel were well aware of the

[20] Note, however, that unlike in England and Wales, intermediary involvement with defendants in Northern Ireland is limited to the duration of the defendant's oral testimony (see Taggart, 2021).

significant vulnerabilities that intermediaries could help address. One barrister described a recent case using a defence intermediary in which the defendant was 'so vulnerable that he couldn't even participate in the trial ... what little interaction I did have with him initially, was through an intermediary, but it was difficult' (ABC2).

And an intermediary described a case where:

> In a few weeks' time, I'm going to be travelling down to a defendant's house to an 86-year-old man who's a defendant in a trial and he's going to participate in this trial over [a remote live TV link] ... He is so frail he can't be transported up to [the court] ... I'm going to be sat next to him in his house ... and he will be cross-examined over this link ... [It's] pretty groundbreaking stuff ... at the minute I think there are some judges who are being very creative. (AAR2)

But the sense among interviewees is that 'there's a lot of work to be done with the judiciary recognising vulnerabilities in defendants' (AAR2).

> I think there's been a little bit of a push-back from the judiciary in terms of granting applications ... in cases of defendants. (AAJ3)

> If a defendant who is a vulnerable person requires an intermediary to assist with communication difficulties or is just vulnerable, the judge may well know that, but subconsciously may still have a prejudice. Not an open one, not even a known one, but a prejudice at the concept that defendants are able to have someone to help them communicate. (ABC3)

> There are some judges who are very open-minded and I would say support fair justice ... And there's the other side of the judiciary who are very prosecution-minded who think that intermediaries are bloody expensive. (AAR2)

Judges did accept that some vulnerable defendants have communication support needs that require an intermediary, though most focused on the defendant's testimonial experience when they, like other vulnerable witnesses, may be 'subjected to questioning or language that's inappropriate, or too oppressive, because the defendant requires a certain time for questioning, and not to, as it were, just capitulate and agree with everything that's said' (AAJ1). Nevertheless, judges appeared to set a higher benchmark for the appointment of intermediaries for vulnerable defendants than for other vulnerable witnesses. As we saw above, this higher threshold is indeed incorporated in the unimplemented, statutory provision for defendant intermediaries, which may have influenced judges when exercising their inherent jurisdiction. The following judge, while speaking in terms of equality, appeared in referring to a psychologist's report to set a higher level of qualification.

> There are far more applications for intermediaries for defendants now than there ever were. And in appropriate cases … a psychological report pointing out particular difficulties, particular concerns, and particular measures that might be put in place for a trial, we will do our best to accommodate all of that if it's an appropriate way of dealing with it. And to be fair, if a psychologist is telling you a defendant is vulnerable, they have difficulty in processing things and taking on board new information, then I think all judges would obviously follow that and take breaks and allow extra time for things to be explained and make sure they can participate properly. (AAJ2)

Similarly, another judge suggested that a defendant would need to have a significant communication issue to justify intermediary support, a seemingly higher level of need than for a vulnerable witness when ADHD is frequently cited as justification.

> Sometimes you get defendants who have quite significant problems … So yes, an intermediary would be necessary there. But for the kind of run of the mill defendant in the fairly low-level type of offending, who probably has ADHD and all sorts of emotional issues, addictions, and all the rest of it, you're not going to get an intermediary. (AAJ3)

This need for a psychologist's report was reinforced by counsel: 'I've called a psychologist to explain why my client might answer questions in a particular way' (ABC1); 'The psychiatrist said he was fit to stand trial only if he had assistance so I was able to get an intermediary, but it's pretty rare to get that' (ACC4).

A number of interviewees pointed to fiscal concerns as being the underlying reason for judicial reluctance to appoint defendant intermediaries, a factor which has been highlighted in other research which showed that intermediaries are perceived as expensive given the limited financial resources available (Fairclough et al, 2023: 443–5). Numerous judges and counsel made this point:

> The resistance is fiscal. (ACJ1)

> Let's not beat at the bush, the only reason they are trying to restrict them is intermediaries are expensive. (ABC2)

> The funding for defence intermediaries is problematic, and so you don't get so many. (ACJ3)

> There is a limited amount of financial budget to go round and we have to be careful with the money that there is. (ABC3)

In contrast, this concern has not led to call for limits on the use of intermediaries for vulnerable witnesses (Osuwu-Bempah, 2020: 625).

Like Fairclough et al (2023), we also detected a continuing sense among some counsel that in comparison to their own levels of remuneration intermediaries are overpaid: 'They're ferociously expensive. They're paid more than we are. So, they can sit there for an hour in a day, and they earn more than the barristers do who are there for the whole day' (ACC4). Intermediaries are aware of this view but believe it is mis-stated and a consequence of a failure among some, though not all, legally qualified criminal justice professionals to recognise the intermediary as a similarly highly qualified professional with a distinctive skill set: 'Nobody ever talks about the cost of an interpreter' (AXR1). Consequently, the view pervades that the legal representative is fully able to support their client in understanding proceedings: 'Of course, communication involves listening to what's happening when the defendant is not taking an active role in the trial, but the barrister ought to be able to ensure that the defendant is kept fully abreast of the hearing' (ABJ3).

But not all judges and lawyers share this confidence that barristers can fully ensure their clients' understanding of the case against them. Some are explicit that the legal representative has a different set of skills than the intermediary, and we have already seen in relation to vulnerable witnesses that a valued function of the intermediary is to render understandable 'law-speak' (ACJ1), which is not restricted to direct questioning of the defendant. A number of counsel expressed reservations about their ability to ensure a defendant's full understanding of proceedings:

> There is a belief that the legal system can be adapted to ensure that the defendant receives a fair trial. Sometimes that happens, but it is almost impossible from the perspective of a non-neurodiverse or disabled person to comprehend the thought processes of a disabled or neurodiverse person. There may be an unconscious bias working there, which is they'll be fine, we're very good, but I'm not sure that we always are. (ABC3)

> I understand that it is part of my job to communicate properly with my client but I'm not a speech and language therapist, and I'm not a child psychologist … I'm a barrister and however hard I try and

> communicate and however long I spend with my client, I may not have those skills. (ACC1)

> These are people who are trained in communicating with people with vulnerabilities and yes of course I can discuss the case with [the defendant] but I do wonder, and worry, how much of it goes in. People are not going to stand there often and say, I don't know what you're saying … People are embarrassed to say things like that. (ABC2)

And it is also a question of whether counsel have the capacity to ensure a client's understanding of proceedings, given their concurrent responsibility to present the client's case and challenge the prosecution's evidence:

> I worry about defendants who don't have an intermediary throughout the trial because … solicitors are almost never there [and] counsel don't have enough time during the course of an ordinary court day to ensure that a defendant has processed the evidence that's being given, and often they don't. (ABC3)

However, despite this challenge from within the Bar, the orthodox view that the legal representative can ensure their client's understanding of proceedings remains. Furthermore, concerns over costs generally and, significantly, that defendants are undeserving of the additional criminal justice spending that an intermediary entails (Fairclough et al, 2023: 445) combine to limit the period of appointment and thus the cost of a defence intermediary. 'Some judges will take the attitude that, you know, [XXX] in the dock, he was clever enough to commit the crime, he should be clever enough to listen to a trial. And they'll either say no intermediary at all or they'll say for evidence only' (AAR2).

There seems, therefore, to have been little movement from the accepted position that even where a defence intermediary is granted, permission to support the defendant throughout the entire trial will be rare. It was exceptional for a judge to take the opposing view that, 'whenever I can, I will fight to get an intermediary present for the whole of the trial' (ACJ1). The consensus among counsel was that 'the defendant is not entitled to an intermediary throughout the entire trial … you really do have to battle to get one for a defendant' (AAC2), and even those judges who recognise some need regard it as limited, with one telling us that they had appointed an intermediary for the whole trial on occasion for 'defendants with very low IQ or special educational needs', but even then the intermediary tends to be restricted to 'the beginning of the trial … maybe the prosecution opening, and then for a time in the lead-up to a defendant giving evidence so that the intermediary can take part in a conference with counsel' and then 'if the defendant decides to give evidence then I'll appoint the intermediary for that portion of the trial' (ABJ4).

Intermediaries, however, framed the debate around the defendant's participatory rights and access to and better understanding of the trial process. Indeed, in line with Osuwu-Bempah's (2020) notion of meaningful participation, intermediaries were more likely to take an expansive approach to facilitating understanding of the entire trial process rather than simply the questions put to the defendant:

> It's about people having a fair trial … it's about somebody, if they're a defendant, actually understanding the process. And, you know, even if they are guilty and they're found guilty, at least they can recognise that it was a fair process. (AAR2)

> There [are] very few defendants who only need help at evidence stage, very few … First of all, let's see it in terms of evidence. How are you going to answer questions about a case where you haven't understood what the prosecution evidence is? And many people don't. And second of all, if you have not understood the case … you are very likely to say no, you don't want to give evidence. (AXR1)

Several counsel echoed the view that a proper understanding of proceedings is vital to defendant engagement:

> I just think if what you're saying is a defendant cannot properly understand the proceedings and needs somebody to broker the communication between him and the process, I don't really see that they are any less useful during examination-in-chief of the complainant than they are during his own evidence. (ACC1)

> If you are 14 and you have autism and you're charged with murder, your engagement in the trial process lasts from the minute you come up on day one till the minute you go down on the last day. (ABC3)

Intermediaries gave several examples of how they add value in promoting the defendant's participatory rights, firstly when supporting the defendant in conference with their solicitor or barrister:

> [I am] constantly [saying], 'Did you understand? What did so and so say? What questions have you got?' … They'd be saying, 'I don't understand that', 'I don't know what that is', and I'm constantly writing down questions that they will then ask the solicitor … to assist them give them instructions to their solicitor. (AXR3)

And subsequently during the prosecution case: 'It's things like saying to them, "Now, I want you to concentrate hard because the witness is coming in … I'm going to make notes for you … so that I can go over it with you afterwards"' (AXR1).

In similar fashion to intermediary support for vulnerable witnesses who may struggle to maintain focus on the proceedings, defendant intermediaries can assist with that same difficulty, which, for a defendant at risk of conviction, is particularly important. One intermediary described how if a defendant 'is going offtrack, I can just say "focus now" and it just brings her back to be listening to what's happening' (AXR3), and gave an example of one such defendant who 'was unscrewing the seat in front, and I looked at her and she started screwing it back up … I do feel it is on me to make sure that they stay focused' (AXR3). Another told us that 'my job is to make sure that they are in the moment, concentrating, looking and listening to the person asking them questions, not distracted by anything else in the room' (AAR2).

However, despite this clear sense among intermediaries that there is a role for them to play in effecting meaningful defendant participation, this research confirmed the view of other commentators that the intermediary role is both conceived and executed differently for vulnerable witnesses and defendants. This raises the question, explored further in Chapters 7 and 8, whether 'best evidence' is, outside of the intermediary community, much less of a live issue for vulnerable defendants than it is for vulnerable witnesses.

Conclusion

Intermediaries are now an established participant in criminal justice proceedings in England and Wales and are increasingly becoming so in Northern Ireland and Ireland. Acceptance among their criminal justice peers has been steadily building over the past two decades, and this chapter examined the extent to which intermediaries feel that they are now fully embedded as a criminal justice actor with a recognised and valued skill set. We first looked at the scope and extent of intermediary involvement, paying particular attention to the value that intermediaries add to the cross-examination experience of vulnerable witnesses. We then considered the debate around overuse for vulnerable witnesses and the continued resistance to the use of defence intermediaries. The overuse argument persists and is largely underpinned by a narrow view of the intermediary's skill set, simplistic assumptions about witnesses' and defendants' abilities to communicate in the environment of the courtroom, and fiscal concerns over the increased costs of introducing an additional criminal justice professional into a system already under considerable financial pressure. Perceived tensions continue around overlaps with what is thought of as the proper domain of the barrister in how best to craft a question and how to ensure that defendants are properly able to participate in the proceedings. It is clear that some judges and counsel fail to recognise and value the expertise of intermediaries and remain sceptical on the question as to whether an intermediary's professional skills and experience can complement rather than challenge those of the barrister in the attempt to secure best evidence for vulnerable witnesses and defendants.

5

Cross-Examination at Trial

The previous two chapters have explored findings regarding practitioners' views on the use of pre-recorded evidence, ground rules hearings (GRHs), and intermediaries. These elements have significantly altered the traditional focus of cross-examination. This chapter shifts our attention to the trial itself, presenting key data and findings from trial observations undertaken in Crown Courts (or their equivalents in other jurisdictions) to gain first-hand insight into the conduct of cross-examination in practice.

Trial observations involved researchers sitting in courtrooms to watch proceedings as they unfolded. During COVID-19 restrictions, when physical presence was not possible, we observed trials remotely via the court's Cloud Video Platform (CVP), an internet-based video service. In both cases, once we identified a trial of interest, proceedings were observed in full, including legal arguments, rulings on procedural matters and points of law, GRHs, *voir dires*, informal discussions between counsel, and the general management of the case by the judge. The questions, answers, and any interjections in evidence-in-chief, cross-examination, and re-examination were noted by the observer, as well as the duration of questioning, with some exceptions.

This comprehensive approach, including some aspects of the process not seen by juries, allowed us to understand the nature, content, and conduct of cross-examination within the full evidential context of each case, and to examine differences in cross-examination practices between prosecution and defence counsel across different categories of witnesses and a range of offences. Our fieldnotes recorded everything we saw and heard in real time, as close to verbatim as our novice shorthand skills and the speed of proceedings allowed. For those trials identified for inclusion in the linguistics analysis in the next chapter, fieldnotes were supplemented by official transcripts.[1]

[1] In total we observed over 200 hours of testimony, amounting to 2,500 pages of typed data – excluding the official trial transcripts obtained for linguistic analysis discussed in the next chapter (see further Jackson et al, 2024).

Over a 16-month period, two members of the research team observed 40 criminal trials across five Crown Court centres in England and Wales, and one centre each of the High Court in Scotland, the Crown Court in Northern Ireland, and the Central Criminal Court in Ireland. The trials observed involved the prosecution of 43 defendants charged with 190 offences, including thefts, frauds, burglaries, death by dangerous driving, neglect, administering a noxious substance, grievous bodily harm (GBH), robbery, rape and other serious sexual offences (RASSOs), attempted murder, and murder. Across the trial sample, we observed the evidence of 194 witnesses, including lay, professional, and expert witnesses called by the prosecution (n = 150) and the defence (including defendants) (n = 44). Thirty-four defendants were called to give evidence. Using our working definition in Chapter 1, 50 prosecution witnesses were considered vulnerable, and three defence witnesses, two of whom were defendants.

We generally did not see verdicts being returned unless this happened the same day the jury was sent out, though we were often able to ascertain trial outcomes through contacts in listings offices or news outlets. We have outcomes for all but four of the 40 observed trials. Twenty trials (50 per cent) resulted in guilty verdicts, with a further case resulting in convictions when the defendant changed his plea during trial. Fifty-three per cent of the trial sample therefore resulted in convictions. Eleven trials (28 per cent) resulted in defendants being acquitted of all charges, three had hung juries (7.5 per cent), and one resulted in a mistrial. In line with national data and statistics reported elsewhere (Thomas, 2023), juries in the trial sample convicted more than they acquitted. Similarly, in the 25 RASSO cases observed, 14 trials (56 per cent) resulted in convictions, seven (28 per cent) resulted in not guilty verdicts, the jury could not agree on a verdict in one case, and a mistrial was declared in another. The outcomes in two RASSO trials are unknown. Again, these outcomes broadly align with statistical findings elsewhere (Thomas, 2023).

Modes of testimony

Not every witness whose evidence is adduced at trial will testify in person. In addition to the 194 witnesses observed testifying in our trial sample, the statements of a further 78 witnesses were read into evidence. The reading of a witness's evidence may occur for various reasons, including where the evidence is uncontested, or where witnesses are deceased or otherwise unavailable. Indeed, vulnerable witnesses were sometimes among those whose statements were read rather than being required to testify in person. In A024, for example, the defendant (D) was on trial for nine counts of theft and five of fraud. All nine of D's victims were elderly patients in geriatric wards in several hospitals. None testified at trial. Instead, by agreement among the parties, six of their witness statements were read into evidence, along with statements from nine other prosecution witnesses with relevant first-hand knowledge. The prosecution in this case proved its allegations against the defendant through other independent evidence, including CCTV footage, mobile phone data placing the defendant at relevant locations, identification evidence from police officers, and evidence of (a raft of) previous convictions for similar offences. The only prosecution witnesses called to testify were three police officers, from different forces, who had identified D in images circulated nationally by investigators.

Certainly counsel's efforts to (drastically) reduce the number of witnesses attending court in A024 reflected in large part the heightened COVID-19 restrictions in place at the time. However, this was not an isolated case. We saw other instances in less restrictive times where, rather than relying on the testimony of an ostensibly significant witness, the prosecution proved its case via other evidence. While significant vulnerable witnesses will typically be called to testify in criminal trials, this is not invariably the case. And a witness who is not called, vulnerable or otherwise, will not be subject to cross-examination.

Moreover, of those witnesses that *are* called to testify at trial, not all of them will undergo cross-examination. Although comparatively rare, seven witnesses in the trial sample were not cross-examined by opposing counsel. These included police officers testifying to the authenticity of exhibits and other witnesses whose testimony was uncontentious. Of those witnesses who were cross-examined, it was unexpectedly brief: 46 witnesses were cross-examined for 10 minutes or less and 23 for 5 minutes or less, with six undergoing just 1 minute of cross-examination (which was the smallest unit of measurement used in our observations). The brevity of cross-examination and, indeed, the short duration of a witness's entire testimonial evidence was perhaps the most unanticipated and certainly one of the most striking findings from the trial observations.

Duration

Testifying in a Crown Court criminal trial was shorter than we had initially anticipated given the severity of the cases, averaging about an hour per witness, encompassing their evidence-in-chief, cross-examination, and any re-examination. Of the 194 witnesses observed testifying across the trial sample, we have complete and accurate timings for 163. In total, these 163 witnesses spent 164 hours and 25 minutes giving evidence equating to witnesses' combined evidence-in-chief, cross-examination, and any re-examination, lasting 1 hour (60.5 minutes) on average. This is a noteworthy finding in and of itself. However, as shown in Table 5.1, there are striking differences in the duration and distribution of testimony among different categories of witness.

Table 5.1: Average duration of testimony by witness type and vulnerability status (in minutes)

Witness type	Evidence-in-chief	Cross-examination	Re-examination	Total
Prosecution				
All witnesses	35	22	2	59
Vulnerable witnesses	55	40	3	98
Defence				
All witnesses	31	38	2	71
Vulnerable witnesses*	47	86	4	137

*Note: Data for vulnerable defence witnesses should be interpreted with caution due to the small sample size (n = 3) and significant individual variation.

Prosecution witnesses spent an average of 59 minutes giving evidence. In contrast, defence witnesses, most of whom were defendants, spent an average of 71 minutes in the witness box. While prosecution witnesses generally spent more time in evidence-in-chief than cross-examination, the opposite pattern was true for defence witnesses, who spent the largest proportion of their time in cross-examination. These distinct patterns between prosecution and defence witnesses held regardless of their vulnerability.

Whether a witness for the prosecution or the defence, vulnerability significantly extended testimony duration. This was a clearly discernible pattern in the trial data. Compared with other witnesses, vulnerable witnesses spent longer on average giving evidence: their evidence-in-chief was longer, as was their cross-examination. Nevertheless, the overall pattern of prosecution witnesses spending more time in evidence-in-chief while defence witnesses spent more time in cross-examination held true.

There are several factors which may, singularly or in combination, explain this. First, guidance on questioning vulnerable witnesses emphasises short, uncomplicated questions using simple language. What might be presented to a non-vulnerable witness as a single complex question will thus be broken down into multiple shorter, simpler questions for vulnerable witnesses. While this approach better enables vulnerable witnesses to engage with and respond effectively to forensic questioning, it is almost inevitable that it will take more time.

Second, vulnerable witnesses' testimony is often emotionally charged, particularly vulnerable prosecution witnesses, and especially in RASSO cases where complainants are recounting traumatic events. A witness's individual vulnerabilities may, by their very nature, exacerbate the already stressful experience of testifying. Across the board, vulnerable witnesses were observed to be more likely than non-vulnerable witnesses to become visibly distressed, agitated, angry, confrontational, or reluctant to answer certain questions, requiring judicial intervention to explain the necessity of responding to properly put questions. Vulnerable witnesses were significantly more likely to be offered breaks during their testimony; offers that, although frequently made, were rarely accepted, with witnesses generally expressing a preference to 'get it over with'. In addition, vulnerable witnesses, again, particularly those in RASSO cases, may be so quietly spoken that they are regularly asked to repeat themselves. These natural pauses, interventions, interjections, and clarifications all contribute to longer testimony duration.

Third, a sizeable proportion of the vulnerable prosecution witnesses in our sample were complainants in RASSO cases, who are classified as intimidated (and thus, for our purposes, vulnerable) witnesses under section 17 Youth Justice and Criminal Evidence Act (YJCEA) 1999. Evidentially, RASSO cases are typically heavily reliant on complainant testimony as incidents often occur in private or secluded settings without – or at least with limited – CCTV, eyewitnesses, or other independent evidence to prove essential matters (Saunders, 2018). In addition, many of the RASSO trials observed involved complainants making multiple allegations against an accused, requiring witnesses to testify about numerous separate incidents, which inevitably extends the duration of their testimony.

Unsurprisingly, then, and as shown in Table 5.2, complainants in RASSO cases spent longer testifying, on average, than any other type of prosecution witnesses. RASSO complainants spent an average of 50 minutes in evidence-in-chief and 46 minutes in cross-examination, while defendants in these same cases spent 48 minutes in evidence-in-chief and 57 minutes in cross-examination. The prevalence of RASSO complainants in our sample thus substantially inflates the average timings for vulnerable prosecution witnesses overall. If we exclude RASSO trials, vulnerable prosecution witnesses spent an average of 33 minutes in evidence-in-chief, 31 minutes in cross-examination, and 2 minutes in re-examination.

While acknowledging the size of the trial sample, there was no relationship between the duration of significant witnesses' evidence and verdict. This was

Table 5.2: RASSO cases: average duration of complainant and defendant testimony (in minutes)

Witness type	Evidence-in-chief	Cross-examination	Re-examination	Total
Complainant	50	46	4	100
Defendant	48	57	3	108

the case whether the witness was called by the prosecution or the defence, was vulnerable or non-vulnerable, or testifying in a RASSO or non-RASSO trial. This indicates that case outcomes hinge on the substance of witness testimony rather than its duration; what matters is the content and credibility of what witnesses say, not how long they take to say it. The brevity of the process of testifying is, nevertheless, an important and revelatory finding.

Special measures

Identifying vulnerable witnesses presents methodological challenges for researchers. Beyond the offence-based criteria outlined in section 17(4) YJCEA, the attributes or characteristics that determine eligibility for special measures are often not apparent to observers or explicitly stated in open court. As such, our count of 50 vulnerable prosecution witnesses and three vulnerable defence witnesses is based solely on official recognition through special measures applications and directions. While this serves as a practical proxy for witness vulnerability, it is not without limitations, as it may underestimate the actual number of vulnerable witnesses in the trial sample. The process is not always straightforward: in some cases, it is clear that a special measures direction has been given; in others, it is not. Similarly, the reasons for granting a special measures direction are sometimes apparent, but not always. Crucially, there is no procedural requirement to disclose a witness's vulnerability or lack thereof when special measures have not been requested or granted.

We drew on special measures applications and directions as indicators to assess the prevalence of witness vulnerability within the sample, rather than focusing on the actual implementation of these measures. Not all witnesses known to be subject to a special measures direction used the measures directed. Six witnesses explicitly declined the measures directed, electing instead to give their evidence live in court, and with no additional measures in place. In A022, for example, the defendant was a young woman charged with murdering her child. The defendant's mother and father – grandparents of the deceased – were the first two witnesses in the prosecution's case. Prior to calling his first witness, D's father and, in the absence of the jury, the prosecutor informed the judge: 'I have seen the witnesses, [PW1] and [PW2], and they are understandably distressed and upset. No special measures that have been offered have been accepted. They wish to come into court as it is.'

Similarly, in A028, a burglary trial, the homeowner, C, was a lady in her late 70s. For reasons that were not stated, C had carers who came in to help her at home and was described as having 'memory issues'. A special measures direction provided for C's evidence-in-chief to be given by means of a video interview with police, made at her home closer to the time of the offence. On the day of trial, prosecuting counsel told the trial judge that he had intended to put in a special measures application that morning requesting additional special measures, specifically, the use of a video link for C's cross-examination to avoid her having to come to court. However, according to the prosecutor, C was 'demanding her day in court', without *any* special measures. After some persuasion by prosecuting counsel, she agreed her pre-recorded evidence-in-chief should be played but insisted she did not want special measures during cross-examination: 'She wants live cross examination, and she doesn't want to be behind a screen or in a separate room appearing on a link. The only thing she needs, she says, is for understanding that she might need longer to answer questions.' This was accepted by the judge, who reiterated that the previously directed requirement that questions be put to C one at a time must be strictly followed.

Given these complexities and contingencies, we took a necessarily pragmatic approach to identifying vulnerable witnesses in the trial sample. Based on special measures applications and directions, we identified 53 vulnerable witnesses across the 40 trials observed: 50 prosecution witnesses and three defence witnesses. Special measures featured in 32 of the 40 trials observed. These prevalence rates reflect our sampling strategy, which deliberately prioritised cases involving vulnerable witnesses and special measures. The figures reported here merely describe our achieved sample while acknowledging its limitations. They should not be interpreted as representative of the prevalence of vulnerable witnesses in Crown Court trials more broadly.

Our observations clearly demonstrate that special measures directions do not always result in the actual use of those measures. This can be attributed to several factors. For instance, some witnesses may choose to decline the measures they are entitled to, opting instead to give evidence without them. Others may express a preference for alternative special measures rather than those directed or choose to accept certain measures while rejecting others. Additionally, there are instances where special measures, despite being both directed by the court and preferred by the witness, cannot be implemented due to technical failures or resource constraints. For example, in A020, special measures directions were issued for two prosecution witnesses to give evidence via video link. However, when called upon, the video link was unavailable. The absence of a screen in the courtroom meant that no alternative special measure could be provided. This highlights an important finding from our observations: variability in witness preferences and the practical availability of special measures, rather than their legal eligibility alone, plays a significant role. Bearing these limitations and caveats in mind, we now turn to our analysis of the use of special measures observed during the trials.

Pre-recorded evidence, live video links, and screens

From the outset, it is important to clarify that this section does not offer an exhaustive analysis of individual directions for all eligible witnesses in the observed trials or their practical implementation. Instead, the focus is on identifying key patterns in the combinations of special measures most commonly granted. This analysis is limited to vulnerable prosecution witnesses, as there were only three vulnerable defence witnesses observed – two of whom were defendants. Both defendants testified live in court, with one receiving assistance from an intermediary. Beyond these basic empirical observations, the available data is insufficient to conduct a detailed examination of the provision of special measures for vulnerable defendants in practice.

In contrast, the observations of vulnerable prosecution witnesses yielded robust and richly detailed data, revealing significant patterns and offering valuable insights into the practical application of special measures in modern criminal trials. A prominent finding from these observations is that special measures for vulnerable prosecution witnesses are both widely accessible and regularly utilised during proceedings. Excluding the use of intermediaries – which is addressed separately later – the special measures applied during evidence-in-chief and cross-examination of these witnesses encompassed those shown in Table 5.3.

Overall, the most commonly observed combination of special measures involved the use of screens during both evidence-in-chief and cross-examination. This approach was adopted by 16 vulnerable prosecution

Table 5.3: Special measures combinations for vulnerable prosecution witnesses

Special measures used		**Number of witnesses**
Evidence-in-chief	**Cross-examination**	
Screen	Screen	16
Pre-recorded (ABE or equivalent)	Video link	11
Pre-recorded (ABE or equivalent)	Screen	9
Pre-recorded (ABE or equivalent)	No special measures used	3
Pre-recorded (ABE or equivalent/evidence on commission)	Pre-recorded (s 28/ evidence-on-commission)	3
Video link	Video link	3
No special measures used	No special measures used	5
Total		50

witnesses, representing 32 per cent of those observed. However, this was not the predominant method by which vulnerable witnesses gave evidence. Instead, just over half (n = 26, or 52 per cent) of vulnerable witnesses provided pre-recorded video evidence for their evidence-in-chief, with cross-examination conducted either via live video link (n = 11) or in court, behind a screen (n = 9).

Distinct and more meaningful patterns emerged when differentiating between categories of vulnerable witnesses and types of cases. The first distinction lies between vulnerable adults and children. All 16 vulnerable witnesses who used the screen + screen combination were adults. Conversely, every child witness in the sample (n = 9) had their evidence-in-chief pre-recorded. Following this, five of these child witnesses underwent cross-examination via video link, while three were cross-examined in court. Of these, two declined all special measures offered, opting to testify without any, while one declined the video link and instead testified behind a screen. The ninth child witness's cross-examination was pre-recorded. In accordance with the 'primary rule' in section 21 YJCEA, the only child witnesses who physically entered the courtroom for cross-examination were those who had explicitly requested to do so.

Variation primarily occurred among vulnerable adult witnesses. Here, clearer patterns emerged based on the type of case rather than witness categories. Specifically, there was a noticeable distinction between RASSO cases and non-RASSO cases, the latter encompassing a range of offences, from theft to homicide. In non-RASSO cases, the screen + screen combination of special measures was predominant, with 11 adult witnesses (almost 70 per cent) in these cases giving their evidence-in-chief and undergoing cross-examination in court using this method. In contrast, pre-recorded evidence-in-chief is a dominant feature in RASSO cases, reflecting statutory provisions and presumptions.[2] Outside of Scotland, the admission of the complainant's 'Achieving Best Evidence' (ABE) is standard practice. In all observed RASSO trials across England and Wales, Northern Ireland, and Ireland, only one complainant's evidence-in-chief was not pre-recorded. This appeared to result from the absence of an ABE process. The greatest variation in RASSO trials was found in the special measures employed during cross-examination. Among RASSO complainants, 12 underwent cross-examination via video link, while another 12 did so in court using a screen. Three complainants' cross-examinations were pre-recorded, and two chose to undergo cross-examination in court without any special measures.

---

2 See eg Youth Justice and Criminal Evidence Act 1999, s 22A.

Age also emerged as a significant factor influencing these patterns. Of the six child RASSO complainants, four underwent cross-examination via video link, one testified behind a screen in court, and one's cross-examination was pre-recorded. For adult RASSO complainants, 11 opted for cross-examination with a screen, eight used the video link as directed, two declined all special measures, and two underwent pre-recorded cross-examinations.

In summary, the trial observations indicate that vulnerable witnesses are routinely provided – or, at least, directed to receive – special measures. For child witnesses and complainants in RASSO trials, irrespective of age, the standard direction remains ABE + video link. In practice, however, the combinations of special measures employed reflect not only the age of the witness and the nature of the alleged offence but also the preferences expressed by the witness on the day of testimony.

Whether physically present but shielded from public or defendant view via a screen or testifying remotely through a video link, these special measures are integral to enhancing the witness's experience of giving evidence at trial. Beyond physical arrangements, these measures offer additional critical support mechanisms for witnesses facing particular challenges. Notably, no witnesses across the trial sample received aids to communication under section 30 YJCEA. However, several trials included intermediaries assisting witnesses. The role and impact of intermediaries are explored in the following section.

Intermediaries

As discussed in the previous chapter, intermediaries are widely used for child witnesses and individuals with communication difficulties, and their role is generally viewed positively by other criminal justice professionals. However, intermediaries were observed in only six trials across the sample. In five RASSO trials (four in England and Wales and one in Ireland), intermediaries assisted the complainants. Additionally, an intermediary supported the defendant in A004 – a child with ADHD and other complex needs – who was on trial for GBH with intent. In another case, A005, an intermediary assisted one of two child RASSO victims during the investigative stage. However, since the prosecution did not call either child's evidence, no intermediary was required at trial.

These findings reveal a notable disparity between how often intermediaries were anticipated and how often they were actually observed. The reasons for providing – or not providing – an intermediary were sometimes unclear. Age, for instance, was not a decisive factor. In three separate trials involving child RASSO complainants aged 8, 11, and 13 years, no intermediary was provided. By contrast, in A034, a 14-year-old RASSO complainant described by the prosecutor as 'a troubled child with plenty of issues', and in A006, a 15-year-old complainant with no apparent triggers beyond her age, both received intermediary support. These observations support the findings our interview data discussed in Chapter 4, namely that while there is little evidence of overuse, there is some evidence of underuse.

A005 involved two young victims aged seven and nine years old respectively. The seven-year-old complainant, C1, was not assisted by an intermediary during her police interview. Her nine-year-old brother, C2, was. The different approaches taken by police to these two young witnesses was discussed by the Investigating Officer (PW1) during her cross-examination at trial:

PW1: Although [W1] was younger, she was educationally more advanced than [W2]. [W2] has some learning difficulties. I wanted to assess his abilities as best I could and work out who would be the best person to ask questions and the best setting.
DC: He [W2] was happy to talk to you?
PW1: Yes.
DC: He understood who you were?
PW1: Yes.
DC: A more formal video recorded interview with [W2] was arranged for [date] … [DC describes and explains the ABE suite which PW1 agrees]. An intermediary was present?
PW1: Yes. So that they can make sure he understood the questions and facilitate his answers back.
DC: You were satisfied that was appropriate?
PW1: Absolutely, yes.
DC: Appropriate for his needs and to obtain the best evidence?
PW1: Yes. We didn't want to ask him questions that he didn't understand.
DC: He was interviewed for 50 minutes, with breaks? Is that right?
PW1: Yes.
DC: During that interview, he did not disclose any offences committed by [D] against him?
PW1: No.
DC: Thank you, that is all my questions.

In contrast, the adult RASSO complainant in D008 was provided with an intermediary due to behavioural and emotional challenges, as well as cognitive difficulties. During her pre-trial assessment to the court, the intermediary described the complainant as having 'the understanding of a five-year-old – five years and 11 months to be exact'. While age is only one factor in determining a witness's communication ability, this comparison raises a critical question regarding the criteria for intermediary provision: if having the comprehension level of a young child justifies the appointment of an intermediary, why does being a young child not automatically warrant the same support?

Case A005, however, highlights a deeper and more fundamental paradox, not only in the provision of intermediaries but in the application of special measures as a whole. As demonstrated in the exchange, defence counsel's questioning of the investigating officer emphasised the extent to which police had gone to facilitate this victim's ability to provide their 'best evidence'. Yet, despite these measures, C2's 'best evidence', like that of his younger sister, was that he had not been sexually victimised by D. Evidence retrieved from the defendant's digital devices, however, proved otherwise, leading to D's conviction for offences against both children, C1 and C2.

On one level, it is almost self-evident that measures intended to enhance a witness's ability to provide an account do not guarantee the account's accuracy or truthfulness. Yet, on another level, there is an undeniable paradox in referring to these accounts as 'best evidence' when 'best' clearly does not equate to being reliable or accurate – or, to put it simply, true. In this instance, C2's 'best evidence' was demonstrably flawed, as he denied acts that were later proven to have occurred.

Case A005 highlights the conceptual ambiguity surrounding the definition of 'best evidence'. If the primary objective is to enable a witness to provide the clearest, most complete, and coherent account possible, the resulting evidence may not always align with the prosecution's case and could even be subject to reliability concerns (see further Chapter 8). Alternatively, if 'best evidence' is understood simply as testimony that ensures a witness can communicate effectively, without distortion or misrepresentation, this raises a further concern that, on occasion, judicial control over cross-examination may restrict the rigorous testing of that evidence, as illustrated in D008, particularly where inconsistencies cannot be appropriately explored.

In case D008, defence counsel challenged the application for pre-recorded evidence-in-chief, video link cross-examination, and the appointment of an intermediary. He argued that the combination of these measures was unnecessary and unfair, stating that the complainant had 'coped' during her ABE interview without an intermediary. He further contended that the measures would present the complainant's account as more coherent and reliable than it truly was, remarking, 'When the prosecutor asks for the play button to be pressed, the prosecution is avoiding all the problems and issues of calling [C] as a witness'. Despite these objections, the court approved all the requested special measures.

The defence's argument highlights a broader tension: while special measures are designed to support vulnerable witnesses in providing their best possible testimony, concerns remain about whether restrictions on cross-examination can inadvertently limit the effective scrutiny of that testimony. As the judge observed, inconsistencies in the complainant's various accounts 'may be the forensic implications of not having special measures earlier in the process. An intermediary at special interview, and possibly even at the time of initial disclosure, might have resolved what [defence counsel] is now presenting as evidence of confusion, lack of clarity, and inconsistency in [C]'s testimony'. This suggests that rather than distorting evidence, special measures may actually serve to improve clarity and coherence when implemented at an early stage.

An additional significant issue regarding intermediaries, identified through trial observations and discussed by interviewees (see Chapter 4), relates to the boundaries of their role. In two RASSO cases, D008 (discussed earlier) and A031, vulnerable adult witnesses underwent cross-examination via video link with intermediary support. Both witnesses became increasingly distressed during cross-examination, each stating, 'I can't do this. I don't want to do this'. In A031, the complainant even fled the room at one point. In both instances, the video links were temporarily suspended while intermediaries calmed the witnesses and persuaded them to resume their testimony.

Although the judges in both cases were satisfied that the respective intermediaries had not discussed their evidence with the witness, encouraging clearly reluctant witnesses to give their evidence rather than merely assisting them to do so raises fundamental questions about the boundaries of the intermediary role. While intermediaries may be essential in helping vulnerable witnesses understand the questions put to them and articulate their answers, they are neither trained nor intended to provide emotional support or encouragement to testify. In Chapter 4, we saw that there are arguments for giving intermediaries a more expansive role in relieving stress and providing encouragement and reassurance to witnesses. But no matter how well-intended, attempts to do so may compromise both the impartiality of the intermediary's role and the integrity of the evidence-giving process. Chapter 8 revisits this issue alongside alternative roles such as witness supporters or Independent Sexual Violence Advisers (ISVAs).

Finally, one might assume that the involvement of intermediaries – who may request rephrasing of questions – would lengthen cross-examinations. However, trial observations revealed the opposite in RASSO cases, where cross-examinations involving intermediaries lasted an average of 36 minutes. This correlates with our findings in the previous chapter that witnesses with communicative impairments may benefit from the input of an intermediary at trial.

Witness supporters

Aside from intermediaries and interpreters, witness supporters in criminal trials play crucial roles in ensuring that witnesses feel supported and are equipped to give their best evidence. These may include family and friends,

Witness Service volunteers, as well as specialist roles such as ISVAs, Children and Young People's Independent Sexual Violence Advisers (CHISVAs), and Independent Domestic Violence Advisers (IDVAs). Supporters help witnesses navigate the court process, providing information about court proceedings and accompanying them if needed.

Supporters were observed in 11 trials: nine in England and Wales and two in Northern Ireland. In these cases, the jury was generally informed that the witness had a supporter with them. However, it was not always clear in what capacity the supporter was attending (whether they were family/ friends, volunteers, or in one of the more specialised roles). One witness was clearly observed to be accompanied by an ISVA in the witness box (A039), while an ISVA was present in court but not in the witness box in A033. A CHISVA accompanied the complainant during cross-examination via video link in A020. Whether seated alongside the complainant or elsewhere in the courtroom, the role of the witness supporter was limited to simply being present while the witness gave their evidence.

In contrast to professional witness supporters, family and friends might be more of a distraction than a quiet, reassuring presence. For example, in A034, the complainant's sister (CS) attended court to support her at trial. During the complainant's cross-examination, conducted in the courtroom from behind a screen, her sister was seated in the public gallery. According to the dock officer, she was seen silently mouthing 'rapist' and 'you are a rapist' to the accused during the complainant's evidence. This was not brought to the judge's attention until later in the day, after she had been released as a witness. In the absence of the jury, the judge warned the public gallery:

> I'm just going to stress this, I'm not suggesting for one moment there's any truth in the suggestion; I am entirely neutral on the topic. But it is important that any personal feelings or attitudes are kept private in order to see that justice is done fairly and to both sides. In the event that inappropriate conduct is witnessed again by anybody and reported to me, I will have no choice but to clear the public gallery and the person responsible, whomsoever that might be, would find themselves, potentially, in a contempt of court direction.

The following day, while her sister attended court, the complainant did not. When court rose for lunch, an usher informed the Officer in the Case that the complainant's sister appeared to have been recording the morning's proceedings on her mobile telephone. The Officer immediately sought out and confronted CS, demanding that any such recordings be deleted, whereupon CS immediately left the court building. The Officer was then admonished by the judge for not having retained the material and letting the court exercise its powers in dealing with it.

Concerns around the potentially disruptive impact of family and friends supporting the complainant caused some consternation in another rape case, A034. These concerns were pre-emptively addressed by the judge, prosecuting counsel, and the intermediary during a special measures discussion involving all parties (including DC) on the morning C was due to be cross-examined:

J: … okay. Let's take it as read then, thank you. And you've introduced yourself? Wigs and gowns off, we understand. Meeting of parties?

IM: We hadn't actually got as far as discussing meeting because she was deciding between giving her evidence on the live link and coming into court, and she's got rather a … she's got a lot of people there with her so things were getting a little bit tricky to discuss.

J: Yes.

IM: So, we have – the Officer in the Case has spoken to her separately just to make sure the coming into the courtroom is, is definitely her decision and that is what she would like to do. She's very keen to get it, to just, to just go ahead and do it. I don't think any more waiting time would be beneficial.

J: Alright, well, we ought probably just to check, specifically, whether a meeting is required, what her preference is. I don't suppose it'll take too long to check.

IM: No.

J: Perhaps that could be done through the Officer and without too much of a, an assembly around her.

IM: Yes.

J: Although obviously, if she wants somebody to be there, then she should. But I, I think we ought to know that.

IM: Okay.

PC: Your Honour, I know that one of the issues that's been troubling all of us is the question of what to do with the entourage, if I can call it that way. She's got her mum here, grandmother …

J: Mother, Mr [PC].

PC: Mother, sorry, grandmother, aunt and a number of other associates and, I think it's fair to say, I don't want to be unkind to anyone, but I think it's fair to say that they're, they're obviously supporting her, but there is a risk that they will perhaps become a distraction rather than a support and we've been, we discussed with the intermediary whether it would be best if they were in the upper gallery where they couldn't be heard, which – I think, there's a risk that then they might be tempted to interject and

nobody wants that. If they were in the upper gallery, they couldn't be heard.
J: Well, it wouldn't happen more than once.
PC: I'm sorry?
J: It wouldn't happen more than once.
PC: No, I'm sure. The trouble with being up there, of course, is they're in her line of sight and –
J: Well, exactly and if they're in the public gallery they won't be.
PC: Yes.
J: So, that seems to be better. I can't close the court to any interested parties.
PC: No, of course not, no.
J: And that's obviously not what you're asking me to do.
PC: No, it's not.
J: So, I would've thought better in the public gallery, as per usual.
PC: So be it.
J: The one downstairs, that is, and if there were to be any interjection, if it's thought sensible to mention it in advance, from the public gallery, anybody doing so would be removed immediately.
PC: Yes, could I suggest it isn't put in quite those terms at the outset, just because one wouldn't want to –
J: Well, I might, if I were doing it, which I'm not, couch it in slightly more diplomatic terms but the message should be clear.

Of course, regardless of its general brevity, cross-examination will likely be a distressing and traumatic experience for the witnesses involved. We turn, therefore, to the conduct of cross-examination as it was observed in the RASSO trials, specifically, its manner and tone.

The tone and manner of cross-examination

By and large, cross-examination was not the protracted, combative, and aggressive confrontation that is sometimes portrayed in earlier literature (see, for example, Victim Support, 1996; Davies and Seymour, 1998; Ellison, 2001; see also Chapter 2). This does not mean we did not see witnesses being mocked and derided as liars or incompetents in gruelling, fast-paced, quick-fire cross-examinations, but those on the receiving end tended to be either police officers or defendants.

Beyond these witnesses, the tone of cross-examination was generally observed to be courteous and professional. There were, of course, differences between individual counsel. Some were perfunctory and concise in their manner. Others appeared more compassionate, even gentle, especially when the witness was vulnerable or intimidated. Questions were frequently, but not uniformly, grouped by topic, with witnesses signposted to new topics as cross-examination progressed. The pace of questioning was generally (and, again, unexpectedly) slow. If the pace quickened, judges would interject.

The fact that the trial judge takes detailed notes of a witness's evidence serves as a natural brake on the pace of cross-examination. Judges regularly asked counsel to pause while they caught up on their notes. Questioning also temporarily halted if a witness became upset, with the judge or defence counsel asking if the witness required a break. Typically, the witness would decline, wanting to 'get it over with'. In such cases, the witness would be given a few moments to regain composure before continuing. This may partly explain why cross-examination is, on average, longer for key prosecution witnesses in RASSO cases than for those in other offence categories.

Questioning that deviated from the considerate and polite tone was conspicuously noticeable, as the observer recorded in her fieldnotes for one RASSO case (A011):

> At around 50 minutes, this was one of the longer cross-examinations I've observed. But it's difficult to comment on: I was struck by the apparent disdain on DC's face while he questioned C; he constantly looked like he had a bad smell under his nose, but then, he looked like that throughout the prosecution's case. And he [DC] turned away from C after every question, like he was refusing to look at him, which appeared very dismissive. Then again, the court wants witnesses to talk to the jury, not to counsel, and maybe the fact that I'd got a camera traced on DC's face made this look like more of a big deal than it was. So, it is difficult to draw any firm conclusions but, impressionistically, this counsel's 'tone' stands out in comparison to other trials observed so far. Questions in cross were slow and deliberate ... it wasn't a brutal cross by any measure and, I didn't think, was particularly effective. Given that the jury couldn't reach even a majority verdict (of either guilty or not guilty), we might conclude that it persuaded at least some jurors.

Cross-examination in this case was flagged not so much as an example of 'bad practice', but to the observer it fell short of 'best' practice. This assessment was based less on what was said than how it was said. Conversely, good practice was exemplified by the careful, gentle, and compassionate manner in which searching cross-examination was conducted in A035 and led the observers to flag it for inclusion in the linguistic analysis (see Chapter 6).

When it comes to cross-examination, nonverbal communication speaks volumes. This is neither a novel nor a prosaic finding. Mehrabian (1972) set out his still much-cited thesis that, in judging the attitude of a speaker, we tend to rely on nonverbal signals: 55 per cent of this assessment is based on the speaker's body language; 38 per cent on tone of voice; and 7 per cent on the words they use. This is where the mixed methodology combining real-time observation of cross-examination with detailed linguistic analysis of official transcripts comes into its own. We know *what* was asked in cross-examination, and, crucially, we know *how* it was asked. For the most part, it was reassuring to find that cross-examination of RASSO complainants was careful, considerate, courteous, and professional.

As we shall see in Chapters 7 and 8, some criminal practitioners expressed the view that subjecting witnesses – particularly vulnerable and intimidated witnesses – to harsh, humiliating, or insensitive treatment in cross-examination is counterproductive. The judge in D008 (discussed earlier) warned DC of precisely this when, contrary to the reports and recommendations before the court, he sought leave to ask the complainant tagged and leading questions:

J: I must interrupt. I have seen witnesses questioned with tagged questions or leading questions and answered in monotone. The jury can see what's happening. It does the defence no good and, in fact, can do harm. I have been in your situation with a complainant with borderline mental disorder. A much more powerful tool is to get someone to agree with you in these circumstances, rather than when the jury can see a vulnerable witness struggle. You will lose the jury.

An extreme, though hopefully rare, example of a jury's reaction to challenging cross-examination was observed in case A025. The defendant faced five charges of robbery, one of rape, and one of possession of a firearm with intent. The five complainants, all sex workers operating out of a city centre hotel, had been robbed – and one also raped – by the defendant during pre-arranged meetings for paid sex in their hotel rooms. While some complainants remained calm and composed throughout their testimony, others were visibly upset during cross-examination, prompting audible reactions from the jurors. During a break in the evidence, the judge addressed the jury directly: 'This is a typical case in that it involves two diametrically opposed accounts, and it is entirely normal for the witness to be challenged. A challenge that is robust but done compassionately is the only way.' He further explained that different witnesses respond differently, some become very upset, while others appear stronger. When the jury went for a break, the judge turned to DC:

J: Juror #10 has been reacting in a physical way, hence my direction. I wanted to explain that everything is being done properly. The witnesses acted very differently. We know that

> is normal, but the jury may not. I didn't see anything of great concern, but I will keep an eye on it.

When the judge rose, the court clerk and DC discussed what had happened. It transpired that Juror #10's physical reaction had apparently been an attempt to climb out of his seat and get to defence counsel: 'I thought he was going to swing at you at one stage', said the clerk.

In sum, while we regularly saw distressed and upset witnesses during cross-examination in RASSO cases, we did not observe counsel deliberately setting out to make witnesses cry, trip them up, or tie them up in evidential knots. This is not to say that witnesses' evidence was not subject to challenge, and in the eyes of the observers such challenges were generally unobjectionable.

Case A002 provides a compelling illustration. The case concerned an eight-year-old complainant whose 13-minute cross-examination was strictly limited by the judge in terms of both its duration and content. Defence counsel was permitted to ask only a series of pre-approved questions, all following the same basic structure: 'In your interview, you told the police X happened. Are you really sure X happened?' Upon the complainant confirming her certainty, counsel was required to move on to the next question, leaving inconsistencies in her account unexamined. In a case that both prosecution and defence counsel described in their closing speeches as one in which the jury had to decide whom they believed, the jury returned a verdict of acquittal.

This case highlights two closely linked issues. First, when independent evidence is scarce, juries may view cross-examination that fails to address glaring inconsistencies in a witness's testimony with scepticism. Overly restrictive cross-examination, intended to 'protect' vulnerable witnesses, may inadvertently disadvantage them by denying opportunities to clarify or explain, which could strengthen their evidence. As discussed in Chapters 7 and 8, juries may be wary of accounts they perceive as insufficiently tested during cross-examination.

Second, as highlighted in Chapter 2, restricting defendants from robustly challenging the evidence against them risks undermining fair trial rights. The challenge, therefore, lies not solely in reducing the trauma of cross-examination for vulnerable witnesses but in finding methods that achieve this without compromising either the complainant's ability to provide their best evidence or the defendant's right to meaningfully test it. While this case is an isolated example, it reinforces the findings in Chapters 7 and 8 that juries tend to be sceptical of accounts they perceive as inadequately scrutinised through cross-examination.

Conclusion

This chapter has presented detailed findings from our observations of cross-examination practices across multiple research sites, with a particular focus on proceedings involving vulnerable witnesses. Several key patterns emerged from the data. The brevity of testimony was striking, with cross-examination being shorter than suggested by existing scholarly literature. Defence witnesses were typically subject to longer questioning than prosecution witnesses, and RASSO complainants faced more scrutiny compared to other prosecution witnesses. The use of special measures – such as screens, video links, and pre-recorded evidence-in-chief – has become standard practice for vulnerable witnesses. Our observations revealed significant flexibility in how these measures are implemented, with witness preferences playing a crucial role in determining their use. Many witnesses opted to decline certain accommodations despite formal directions. Notably, while pre-recorded cross-examination and intermediary assistance are on the rise, they featured less commonly than anticipated. Inconsistencies in the provision of intermediaries were particularly evident and warrant further exploration.

The tone and manner of cross-examination observed largely challenge traditional portrayals of the process as inherently aggressive or adversarial. Cross-examination of vulnerable witnesses was predominantly conducted with professionalism and courtesy. However, the widespread use of special measures and the constraints placed on cross-examination give rise to inevitable tensions. These tensions lie between supporting vulnerable witnesses to provide their 'best evidence' and upholding defendants' rights to challenge effectively evidence presented against them, which is a key component of their overarching right to a fair trial. We revisit this theme in Chapter 7, exploring how the nuances of cross-examination can be better understood within the broader context of evolving professional cultures, shifting social attitudes, and an international trend towards harmonisation.

6

The Language of Cross-Examination

Following the discussion in the previous chapter relating to the tone and manner of cross-examination, this chapter sharpens our focus on the specific nature of the language used by advocates during questioning. This chapter presents an empirical corpus-assisted linguistic analysis of trial transcripts which provides a quantitative overview of the main features of cross-examination as exhibited in our dataset. The analysis focuses on elements of cross-examination that emerged from our interviews with practitioners, and those which have been identified as potentially problematic in case law and professional best practice guidelines. Several extracts are presented from the transcripts to show the features under discussion in use in trials.

The complete dataset contains transcripts from 22 out of the 40 trials that we observed across five Crown Court centres in England and Wales, one in Northern Ireland, and in the Central Criminal Court in Ireland. We also obtained and analysed an official transcript of one trial that was not observed. Official trial transcripts are generally considered to be accurate accounts of what was said and provide reliable data for linguistic analysis (Tkačuková, 2015: 151). Our dataset includes transcripts of 56 cross-examinations, and includes complainants (n = 29), defendants (n = 18), prosecution witnesses (n = 8), and defence witnesses (n = 1). There are 37 cross-examinations from defence counsel and 19 from prosecution counsel. Crucially, there are cross-examinations of 34 vulnerable witnesses and 22 'non-vulnerable' witnesses. There are 40 advocates represented in the data, most of whom (n = 28) appear only once. Nine advocates appear in two cross-examinations, two cross-examine three witnesses, and one cross-examines four. The majority of vulnerable witnesses in our sample are complainants (29/34), with three prosecution witnesses and two vulnerable defendants. In terms of the 'types' of vulnerabilities represented in the transcripts, there are cross-examinations of children under 18, witnesses whose quality of evidence is likely to be diminished because of a mental health disorder or significant impairment of social functioning (eligible under section 16 of the Youth Justice and Criminal Evidence Act); complainants and their relatives in violent offences or rape and serious sexual offences (RASSO) cases, and elderly witnesses (eligible under section 17).

Although this study focuses primarily on vulnerable witnesses, a sample of cross-examinations of non-vulnerable witnesses was also included to provide a valuable comparison set against which the questioning of vulnerable witnesses can be contrasted. The non-vulnerable witness dataset contains the cross-examination of 16 defendants, five prosecution witnesses (including one police officer), and one defence witness. All but one of the 16 non-vulnerable defendants were defendants in the trials in our sample that included vulnerable complainants. It is the case, then, that when we make comparisons between the cross-examinations of vulnerable witnesses with non-vulnerable witnesses, we are largely comparing vulnerable complainants with non-vulnerable defendants. This should be kept in mind when interpreting the findings of comparisons made later. In particular, it may make even more stark those instances where the comparative results reflect an unfavourable reality for vulnerable witnesses.

With this sample of trial transcripts, the linguistic analysis presented does not claim to be representative of all trials and no reliable claims can be made about cross-examination generally. However, the analysis is based on a substantial corpus of data, and the comparison of cross-examinations of both vulnerable and non-vulnerable witnesses allows us to offer a snapshot of the patterns, similarities, and differences in the questioning practices that we observed. Empirical evidence from cross-examinations allows us to observe the extent to which practice is reflecting perceptions and expectations of how vulnerable witnesses are questioned. The analysis focuses on the following issues: the number of questions put to witnesses, the length and complexity of questions, the use of open/closed questions, statements/comments-as-questions, the signposting of topics, tag questions, and direct challenges. Where relevant, evidence of these features in our data will be compared with advice given in the various professional best practice guidelines such as the *20 Principles of Questioning* and The Advocate's Gateway Toolkits. Where relevant, we also incorporate insights on the use of language from the practitioners we interviewed.

Number of questions

One of the most readily observable differences between the cross-examination of vulnerable and non-vulnerable witnesses in our data is that, on average, vulnerable witnesses were asked fewer questions during cross-examination than non-vulnerable witnesses (see also corresponding section on the duration of questioning in the previous chapter). The corpus analysis

Table 6.1: Number of questions put to witnesses in our sample of transcripts

	Vulnerable witnesses	Non-vulnerable witnesses
Shortest cross-examination	20 questions	29 questions
Longest cross-examination	693 questions	544 questions
Median length of cross-examination	115 questions	158 questions

revealed that vulnerable witnesses were asked on average 42 (or 31 per cent) fewer questions than non-vulnerable witnesses (Table 6.1).

The shortest cross-examination in our transcript sample was of a 12-year-old complainant in a rape and sexual abuse case in Ireland, who was asked 20 questions. However, it should be added that this particular child was cross-examined by five different defence counsel and was asked a total of 369 questions across all three of those cross-examinations combined. The shortest single cross-examination of a vulnerable witness therefore comprised 23 questions asked of a complainant in a sexual assault trial. The longest single cross-examination, in terms of number of questions asked, was also of a vulnerable witness – a vulnerable adult defendant in a murder trial for whom no special measures were in place. This defendant was asked 693 questions. In this particular case, from England and Wales, defence counsel objected to how long the cross-examination was taking:

Extract 1: *Extract from the longest cross-examination in our transcript data. A cross-examination of a vulnerable adult defendant in a murder trial (case A022)*

DC: My Lord, it does trouble me, what has happened I've stayed mercifully silent because my learned friend knows how vulnerable this young lady is. She knows that I didn't ask for a ground rules hearing, although I was going to, because of the medical reports as to the nature of cross-examination and whether it could be dealt with succinctly and pointedly rather than, I'm afraid – I don't like to criticise, but this has been one of the slowest cross-examinations I've seen.
J: Well, I think you are now into criticism.
DC: I am now, and I don't apologise for it. In the circumstances of how vulnerable this lady is – and the medical situation, which my learned friend knows well about – one would have expected things to have gone a little bit more apace. I was assured yesterday that my learned friend would get her speech in today. Yes, my Lord may raise an eyebrow. I'm raising –

J: I don't think I did, actually; I was just looking at the computer. Thank you.

DC: Forgive me, but this has gone on long enough. For my learned friend to say, in answer to my Lord's question, 'Well, I think I have actually got a little bit more', or whatever the expression was, didn't sound from this side of the bench to be much of a speeding up. So I am putting down a marker that there has to be care taken when someone is vulnerable and unwell, and none has been.

J: Well, [DC name], I disagree with that. I think there has been a tremendous amount of care taken so far, which is why I asked whether there was very much left. I'm sure there has now been covered most, if not all, of the matters, and I suspect there's going to be very little left tomorrow.

DC: One can only hope, my Lord. There are, of course, several factors which influence the number of questions that are put to a witnesses and to ignore that would oversimplify the picture.

The discussion presented in Extract 1 between counsel and the judge reflects the fact that there is no objective measure of how long is 'too long' when it comes to cross-examination, and there is clearly a disagreement here. Whether or not too many questions are being put to a vulnerable witness is contested, but ultimately, discretion is with the judge to manage this (see also Chapter 3).

Much of the case law on length of cross-examination relates specifically to child witnesses. *R v Barker* ([2010] EWCA Crim 4, at [42]) stipulates that:

> Notwithstanding some of the difficulties, when all is said and done, the witness whose cross-examination is in contemplation is a child, sometimes very young, and it should not take very lengthy cross-examination to demonstrate, when it is the case, that the child may indeed be fabricating, or fantasising, or imagining, or reciting a well-rehearsed untruthful script, learned by rote, or simply just suggestible, or contaminated by or in collusion with others to make false allegations, or making assertions in language which is beyond his or her level of comprehension, and therefore likely to be derived from another source.

This is also reflected in the perceptions of change reported by practitioners in our interviews. One judge said that in the case of young children, cross-examination is now in most cases 5–15 minutes and 'it's a list of questions which are contained on one side of A4' (AAJ3). Indeed, as far as our sample is concerned, children were asked on average fewer questions in

Figure 6.1: Number of questions put to different groups of witnesses during cross-examination

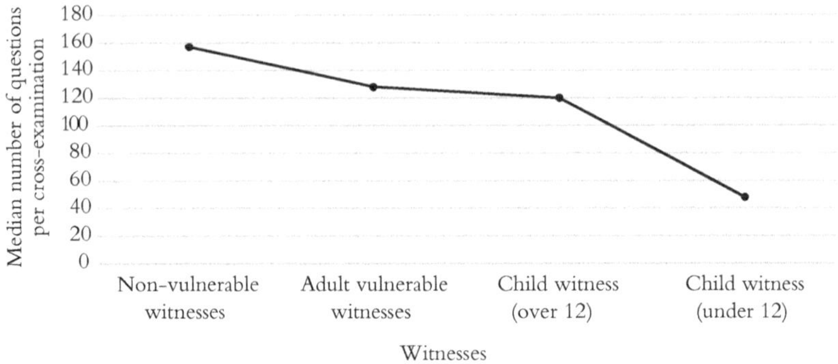

cross-examination than adult vulnerable witnesses (Figure 6.1). However, while younger children (under the age of 12) are spared lengthy cross-examination – being asked on average 48 questions – there seem to be fewer accommodations made for older children (over the age of 12), who were asked only eight questions fewer (120) than vulnerable adults (128). In one concerning example of a cross-examination of a 12-year-old complainant, counsel began by promising: 'So, I'm going to ask you a few questions and I hope it won't take very long; is that okay?' After that, 89 questions were put to the child before questioning was eventually interrupted by the child's intermediary, who requested a short break. Following the break, counsel asked an additional 30 questions, before concluding with an apology: 'thanks very much for answering my questions. It's been nice to talk to you and sorry I kept you so long, I know I promised you I'd be quicker'.

Furthermore, as we have observed elsewhere (Cooper et al, 2024), there is an inequity in the treatment of vulnerable defendants and vulnerable non-defendant witnesses in cross-examination. We have already seen in Extract 1 that the one vulnerable adult defendant that we have in our sample is asked the most questions of any witness in the data. Further to this point, it is significant that, as a group in our data, child witnesses are asked on average 108 questions per cross-examination, while the child defendant (over 12) is asked 265 questions (157 per cent more). This is not only more than the average for child non-defendant witnesses but is more than the average for non-vulnerable witnesses. Overall, our sample seems to reflect an awareness or a desire to limit the number of questions put to vulnerable witnesses, at least in comparison to non-vulnerable witnesses. This is driven particularly by the short(er) cross-examinations of young children; there is by contrast very little difference in the number of questions asked to older children and adult vulnerable witnesses. This suggests that any change, accommodation, or adaptation to the witness is not being felt by older children to the same degree as younger children. Starker still is the finding that vulnerable defendants, both adult and child, are asked far more questions than vulnerable non-defendants and indeed more than all other witnesses.

Length and complexity of questions

In our interviews, practitioners commented on the need to avoid long questions and on making questions shorter and more concise: 'no more I think than seven, eight words, and possibly even five or six' (ABC2). The same practitioner noted: 'We've had to learn to substantially reduce the length and complexity of the question and keep it as short as possible, which is no bad thing really, we should've probably done that anyway' (ABC2). The perception tended towards a feeling that 'the general standard of questioning has improved vastly', resulting in a 'more simple cross-examination, a more understandable cross-examination across the board' (ACJ1). In particular, it was recognised that there has been a move away from multi-part questions, or, as ACJ3 pointed out, 'the question that was three questions in one'. One judge commented: 'The style of cross-examination now is much more uniform … Your linguist, if she or he looked at historical transcripts, would probably see a very significant difference in the length of a question, the number of clauses in the question, the complexity of a question' (AAJ3).

The *20 Principles of Questioning* is also clear that 'concise' questions are 'simpler and easier for children and vulnerable people to process and to understand' (Inns of Court College of Advocacy, 2022: 17).

One way of measuring the complexity of a question is the number of words that it contains. In this analysis, this measure was applied broadly, and the number of words were counted for every speaking turn taken by an advocate. The results show that the average length of question (measured by words per question) was actually longer in the cross-examination of vulnerable witnesses than it was for non-vulnerable witnesses (Table 6.2). The difference is small; questions put to vulnerable witnesses included on average one word more than those put to non-vulnerable witnesses. The shortest average question length for vulnerable and non-vulnerable witnesses was ten words. At the longest end of the spectrum, the cross-examination of one non-vulnerable witness saw counsel having very long 'turns', or questions, at an average of 34.49 words per question, much longer than anything that we saw in the questioning of vulnerable witnesses. Extract 2 shows a rape complainant, who had a first language other than English, being asked a question that is 80 words long.

Table 6.2: Average question length (words per question) in cross-examinations in our sample

Witness type	Median question length (words per question)	Cross-examination with the longest average question length	Cross-examination with the shortest average question length
All vulnerable	18.47	28.17	10.49
Adult vulnerable	18.77	28.17	13.21
Child (under 12)	18.86	22.43	12.77
Child (over 12)	18.16	26.95	10.49
Non-vulnerable	17.22	34.49	10.29

Extract 2: *An 80-word question being put to an adult rape complainant during cross-examination (case A013)*

DC: So, at the beginning of my question today, you said no you didn't speak to him via any other communication. When I suggested Snapchat, you said you couldn't think and you couldn't remember and you weren't sure. So, I want to be fair to you; because we're coming up to lunch, maybe over lunch you can check. But so no one is in any doubt, what I suggest is that you did communicate with [name] via Snapchat yesterday. Didn't you?

W: I can't remember.

Nor did there appear to be any specific accommodations made for child witnesses. Child witnesses (both under and over 12 years old) were asked questions of the same average length as adult vulnerable witnesses, and slightly longer questions than non-vulnerable witnesses. Long questions are notoriously difficult for children to monitor and answer accurately (Andrews and Lamb, 2018: 190). The Advocate's Gateway (2015a: 27) recommends that advocates 'keep questions short because in order to answer accurately, the child needs to be able to remember and process the whole question'. Extract 3 shows a 50-word question being put to a child witness, which contains as many as six clauses, quoting and reformulating the child's previous testimony, and that of the defendant, before eventually ending with a 'do you remember' question, which are also advised against in best practice (Inns of Court College of Advocacy, 2022: 12). This example clearly contravenes the desire to keep questions short and simple:

Extract 3: *A 50-word question being put to a child complainant (over 12) (case D010)*

DC: And in relation to another thing that you said to the gardaí, you said … people touching your privates and you listed [name] as one of those people [who] had touched your privates and again [name], when she spoke to the gardaí, she said she didn't do that and do you remember?

W: I think I might have made a mistake on that.

DC: Okay. That it wasn't [name]?

W: No, I don't know that I'm remembering more I don't think [name] was doing it, all that … I don't think she was that much involved in it.

The structural complexity of a question is not just measured by the number of words per question, but is also determined by components such as average word length, number of phrases, clauses, sentences, and number of false starts (Andrews and Lamb, 2017). In fact, words-per-question turn can be a rather blunt instrument for measuring complexity and it can lead to overgeneralisation and over-inflating the length of questions. For instance, some questions may include a lengthy preamble, presumably in place to aid or support the witness, before a question (that may well be short and simple) is subsequently asked. However, as shown in Extract 4, taken from the cross-examination of a child complainant, it is not always easy to determine where the preamble ends and the question begins:

Extract 4: *A question put to a child complainant (over 12) (case D010)*

DC: Now, one thing I should say, [complainant], and people have said it to you already, but I'm going to repeat it. You're not under any pressure. You're under no – there's no trouble. No one's saying anything about you. This is simply questions we're obliged to ask, we have to ask. And I'm going to ask you a question, and I'm not asking you to name anybody, so you can keep names out of it, but I'm going to ask you. You said [name] said something to you. Do you remember that? At the soccer field? Sorry, [intermediary's] hand.

IM: I'm just asking, just wondering, if it's possible, could that be made more specific?

DC: Very well. You said yesterday, [complainant], that at that soccer field [name] said something to you. Do you remember saying that?

W: Yes.

DC: And I'm saying to you, I'm asking you, was it not somebody else? Never mind – sorry, the hand is up again. Sorry, [intermediary].

IM: I'm afraid that's a very complex formulation. I wonder if you could break it down for [complainant], please.

In this exchange, the child witness was asked a question by defence counsel which was 99 words long and which prompted the intermediary in the case to request that the question be made more specific. However, we see that after counsel attempted to reformulate the question, the intermediary was still of the opinion that the question was too complex a formulation for the child and requested that the question be broken down into shorter, simpler parts. A lengthy preamble, then, risks padding questions out with redundancies (Plotnikoff and Woolfson, 2015: 194).

At the same time, questions do not necessarily need to contain a large number of words to be complex, or multi-part 'compound' questions. Hanna and Henderson (2018: 418) found that while lawyers can readily identify multiple questions when they appear in lengthy utterances, intermediaries also pick up on 'less obvious examples appearing in shorter questions'. This can be observed in Extract 5. The initial question put to the witness contained only 20 words – far fewer than those in previous extracts – yet the intermediary intervened and requested that the question be rephrased in smaller chunks. Counsel subsequently proceeded to break the question down into four questions, which range between four and 14 words. In examples such as this, length is not a sufficient proxy for complexity. Even short questions can be complex and contain multiple propositions that require answers from witnesses.

Extract 5*: A short but multi-part question put to a child complainant (over 12) (case D010)*

DC: That's absolutely fine. Did you ever tell [name] or [name] that your parents contacted you by telephone when you knew that wasn't true?

W: Yes.

IM: I was just going to say that was quite a long question. Maybe could rephrase to shorter chunks, please.

DC: Thanks, [intermediary name]. Okay. And why did you do that, [complainant name]?

A: I don't know.

IM: I'm unsure if [complainant name] actually understood what you were asking him in that question.

DC: I'll go back and start again.

IM: Yes.
DC: Did you once tell [name] or [name] that your parents contacted you by phone?
W: Yes.
DC: And was that true?
W: Yes.
DC: Are you sure it was true?
W: Yes.
DC: Did you ever tell them that when it wasn't true?
W: I can't remember.

'Open' versus 'closed' questions

Open questions are 'information-seeking' (Maley, 1994: 36), in that they invite a longer narrative response from the witness. Closed questions, by contrast, are 'confirmation-seeking' and constrain the response options available to the witness, usually to 'yes' or 'no' (for example, Heffer, 2005: 112). When put to some vulnerable witnesses, such as people with an intellectual disability, responses to open questions tend to have a higher rate of accuracy than closed questions (Kebbell et al, 2004). Similarly, when children are asked open, free-recall questions, they can 'provide accounts with accuracy rates broadly similar to the general population' (The Advocate's Gateway, 2015a: §5.3.1). The *20 Principles of Questioning* holds that 'open-ended questions are better for all people, including those who are young or otherwise vulnerable' (Inns of Court College of Advocacy, 2022: 15). One judge we interviewed stated:

> The general standard of questioning has improved vastly, who, what, where, when, how and did? And these very simple techniques create a great, great dividend and carry through into more simple cross-examination, a more understandable cross-examination across the board in my experience. (ACJ1)

Despite the general consensus on the benefit of open over closed questions, in our sample vulnerable witnesses were asked fewer 'WH-' questions (*who, what, where, when, how*) than non-vulnerable witnesses (Table 6.3).

Non-vulnerable witnesses are asked more of all types of WH- question, with the exception of *who* questions. It appears here that practice on the ground is not strictly following professional guidance, or reflecting the practitioner perception. Breaking down different types of vulnerable witnesses, children over 12 were asked more WH- questions (n = 146, 9.31 per cent of all questions) than children under 12 (n = 19, 7.85 per cent). Complainants in sex cases were asked almost an identical proportion of

Table 6.3: Frequency of WH- questions in cross-examinations of vulnerable and non-vulnerable witnesses

Type	Examples	Vulnerable: frequency (%)		Non-vulnerable: frequency (%)	
Who	Who did you receive the phone call from? Who did you go there with?	47	(0.81)	33	(0.66)
What	What did you do with the bucket? What colour are the walls in your room?	204	(3.53)	368	(7.39)
Where	Where did this meeting take place? Where were you when that was happening?	53	(0.92)	51	(1.02)
When	When did you ask that question? When did you change your mind?	27	(0.47)	39	(0.78)
How	How could you tell you'd hurt him? How did you get on with her?	156	(2.70)	203	(4.08)
Total		487	(8.43)	694	(13.94)

WH- questions as older children (*n* = 237, 9.32 per cent). The disparity between the proportion of open questions being asked to younger and older children might be explained by an awareness among advocates that particularly young witnesses, or witnesses with intellectual disabilities, may be less able to deal with open narrative-inviting questions and can struggle to provide the factual information that the questions require (for example, Morrison et al, 2021: 235). This possibility is further supported by the frequency of *did* questions in our sample. Although the judge(ACJ1 in the quotation earlier) associates *did* questions with WH- questions, they are much more restrictive on the witness's response. Generally, rather than inviting a narrative from the witness, *did* questions are closed, and aim to elicit a yes/no response (Henry et al, 2021: 1394). Therefore, *did* questions are to be treated with caution in the cross-examination of vulnerable witnesses because a series of such questions can have the effect of being overly suggestive to witnesses and can lead to compliant but inaccurate answers (Inns of Court College of Advocacy, 2022: 15). In some instances, however, yes/no questions may be the only option available when a person is unable to respond to more open question types (The Advocate's Gateway, 2015a: 31). In our sample, *did* questions were more commonly asked to vulnerable witnesses (*n* = 636, 11.01 per cent of all questions) than non-vulnerable witnesses (*n* = 390, 7.83 per cent). Moreover, *did* questions were more commonly used with children under 12 (*n* = 65, 26.82 per cent of all questions) than children over 12 (*n* = 262, 16.70 per cent). Extract 6 shows a section of the cross-examination of a child complainant (under 12) in a sexual assault case.

Extract 6: *A sample of 'did' questions put to a child complainant (under 12) (case A002)*

DC: Okay. Now, I'm just going to remind you, you said that you pulled your clothes back on and you said that [defendant] touched you under your clothes, on your chest or boobies. And so my question is, are you really sure that [defendant] touched your chest or your boobies under your clothes?
W: Yes.
DC: Did [defendant] say anything to you when he did that?
W: No.
DC: And did you tell your mummy straight away when [defendant] did that?
W: No.
DC: So, [complainant name], I now want to ask you some questions about a separate day when you were in the kitchen at home getting an apple, is that okay?
W: Yes.
DC: And I'm just going to remind you what you said, so you said you went into the kitchen to get an apple and [defendant] came in and pulled your knickers down. And so my question is are you really sure that [defendant] pulled your knickers down in the kitchen?
W: Yes.
DC: And did [defendant] say anything to you in the kitchen when he pulled your knickers down?
W: No.

It may be the case that these *did* questions were used because the child would struggle to provide relevant factual details to more open questions. In that sense, they may be a helpful questioning device. However, our observation of this cross-examination noted that all of these questions had been pre-approved by the judge at a ground rules hearing (GRH), and that all of the questions were limited to 'in your interview, you said [X] happened. Are you really sure that [X] happened?' When the child responded 'yes', counsel had to move on to the next question, without any follow-up. The question arises through the observation of the trial and the analysis of the transcript as to whether this series of questions (and closed confirmation-seeking questions more broadly) properly constitutes 'testing the evidence'.

The fine line to be trod when using closed restrictive questions is clear if we compare this cross-examination with another in our sample. The questioning of a complainant in a sexual assault trial who had profound mental health issues (anxiety and depression) took place over live video link. Of the 23 questions put to the witness, 18 (78.26 per cent) were *did* questions. Despite having the possible intention of helping the witness provide relevant responses, while also potentially having the effect of stymying an effective challenge of the evidence, a series of *did* questions was also upsetting for the witness. During the cross-examination in Extract 7, the witness held a soft cuddly toy throughout the questioning. After ten minutes under questioning, she became progressively more agitated.

Extract 7: *Did questions in the cross-examination of a vulnerable complainant (case A031)*

DC: Thank you. [complainant name], would you and [defendant] go on [in-person game] together?
W: Just me and [defendant], or me and [defendant] and others.
DC: Did you and [defendant] become friends?
W: Yes.
DC: Did you enjoy going on [game] with [defendant]?
W: If he was there, yes, but he wasn't there for half of them.
DC: Would you and [defendant] joke with each other?
W: Not really, no.
DC: [Complainant name], I'm going to ask you about the [game] you went on with [defendant] in [date]. When you were on that [game], did you tell [defendant] that your bottom is squidgy?
W: No.
DC: Did [defendant] ask to touch your bottom?
W: No.
DC: Did [defendant] ask if he could feel what a squidgy bottom felt like?
W: No.
DC: Did you tell [defendant] to put his hand on your bottom?
W: No. (Several inaudible words).
IM: Your Honour –
J: Would you like a break?
IM: Yes. She's left the room. She said she can't do this.

At this point in the cross-examination, the court adjourned while the intermediary successfully convinced the complainant to come back and finish giving evidence. For the remainder of the cross-examination, the witness mostly answered by either shaking or nodding her head and having the intermediary reply either 'yes' or 'no' for her. Again, she got progressively more upset, she was visibly shaking and was hugging the soft toy tightly and burying her face in it. At the end of questioning, the judge said to the witness: 'Those are all the questions that [defence counsel] wanted to ask you. I'm sorry it's upset you, but it's all over and done with now'. This example, therefore, demonstrates the ways in which *did* questions and their content can still cause vulnerable witnesses distress.

One type of WH- question that is not included in Table 6.2 is *why* questions. Unlike the other WH- questions, *why* questions are 'potentially accusatory and can imply involvement, and thereby partial responsibility' and are therefore to be avoided in the cross-examination of vulnerable witnesses (Inns of Court College of Advocacy, 2022: 14). Based on our sample, it appears as though this advice is being heeded; *why* questions are more frequently asked to non-vulnerable witnesses (*n* = 269, 5.4 per cent of all questions) than vulnerable witnesses (*n* = 101, 1.75 per cent). However, of the 101 *why* questions put to vulnerable witnesses in our sample, 45 (44.55 per cent) were in cross-examinations of two vulnerable defendants. The rest were distributed across 16 other non-defendant witnesses. The accusatory properties of *why* questions can be seen in action in Extract 8. This extract is taken from the cross-examination of a 16-year-old defendant with ADHD in a GBH with intent case and shows counsel using a series of *why* questions to press the defendant on the issue of whether they intended to kick the complainant in the head:

Extract 8: *'Why' questions in the cross-examination of a child defendant (over 12) (case A039)*

DC: Did you punch him?
W: No.
DC: Why didn't you punch him?
W: I don't know.
DC: Did you want to hurt him?
W: (Pause). Not to the extent of the injuries, no.
DC: You've already said you wanted to hurt him.
W: Yes.
DC: Why not punch him then?
W: I don't know. It was the heat of the moment.
DC: If you kick someone in the head you can do a lot of harm. Have I got that right?
W: Yes.
DC: Say again.
W: Yes.

DC: Why did you choose his head?
W: I couldn't even remember it being his head. Like I said, it all happened so quick, and it was the heat of the moment.
DC: Did you choose his head?
W: No.
DC: Whose foot was it?
W: My foot.
DC: Whose head was it?
W: [Complainant]'s head.
DC: Why did you choose his head?
W: I didn't choose his head.
DC: Was it your foot choosing it?
W: (No audible response).

Our sample suggests, therefore, that *why* questions are generally being avoided with vulnerable witnesses, at least compared to their use with the non-vulnerable witnesses in our data. However, vulnerable defendants do not seem to be offered the same accommodations, and *why* questions remain a powerful strategy in the prosecution putting the case to the witness.

Statements/comments-as-questions

One of the judges whom we interviewed neatly characterised the changes that advocates have been required to confront in cross-examination questioning as follows: 'So, the interminable long question, the question with the tag on the end of it, the question that was three questions in one, the questions that jumped about, the questions that were too confrontational, the questions that made statements … all of that had to change' (ACJ3). Another added: 'The position now is the old, what will be regarded as the razz-matazz of the multi-part question and the comment dressed up in a question has now fallen away and judges universally insist upon a genuine question which is put in simple terms' (ACJ1).

In both of these interviews, judges pointed out that the statements or comments as questions are not features of the cross-examination of vulnerable witnesses. Counsel utterances that are statements or comments (albeit perhaps with rising intonation to indicate their questioning function) rather than questions are used to make assertions (Henry et al, 2021: 1394). According to Woodbury (1984: 28), such statements-as-questions carry a greater pragmatic load than typical yes/no questions as they 'allow the questioner to indicate to the jury what *he* believes the facts are and what answer *he* expects from the witness'. Statements posing as questions present an additional challenge because their leading nature can be underestimated by lawyers (Krähenbühl, 2011: 413). The *20 Principles of Questioning* advises advocates to avoid statements posed as questions when questioning vulnerable people and children:

> The traditional style of asking a question which only becomes a question as a result of a change of intonation is not appropriate for a vulnerable person or a child. Some children and vulnerable people may not recognise the expectation of an answer. For others, such 'questions' which involve implicit tags have the same effect on accuracy as explicit tags. (Inns of Court College of Advocacy, 2022: 12)

In this analysis, a binary distinction was drawn with regard to the 'form' that advocates' utterances take: they were either grammatically interrogatives (which usually perform the function of questions) or grammatically declaratives (which usually perform the function of statements). What we were looking for here were those turns by cross-examiners which are declaratives – statements – rather than interrogatives. Even with a rising intonation (which is not determinable by transcripts in any case), and even if they are intended to serve an eliciting function, a declarative is still a declarative in form and may cause confusion for vulnerable witnesses. In this section of the analysis, those questions where statements were followed by a tag were counted as questions (and are discussed in a separate section later in the chapter).

In our sample, statements-as-questions make up almost exactly the same proportion of counsel's turns in the cross-examination of vulnerable and non-vulnerable witnesses (Figure 6.2). Adult vulnerable witnesses are asked more statements-as-questions than non-vulnerable witnesses. The frequency of statements-as-questions in the cross-examination of adult vulnerable witnesses may reflect the fact that many such witnesses in

Figure 6.2: Proportion of statement-as-questions in the cross-examination of different types of witness

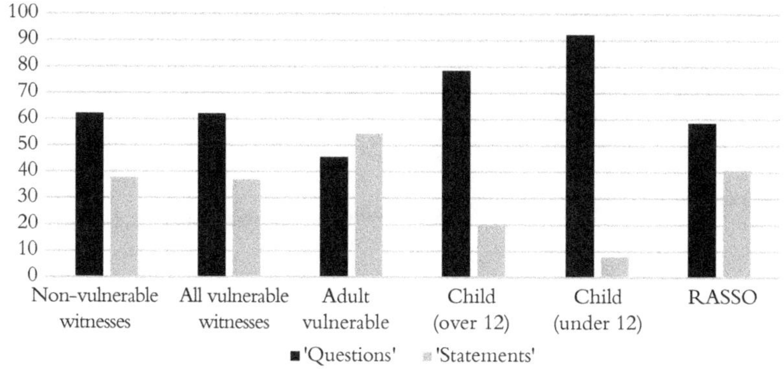

our data are vulnerable because of the nature of the offence in question rather than because they are a child or that they have some intellectual or communicative deficit. In which case, then, this type of 'question' is less developmentally problematic. The picture is different for child witnesses, however, and younger children (under 12) specifically; 92.15 per cent of all counsel turns were in interrogative form. In one cross-examination of a seven-year-old complainant, for instance, counsel took 48 turns, and 47 of those turns were interrogatives. Similarly, in one longer cross-examination of a ten-year-old rape complainant, 104 'questions' were put to the witness, of which 100 were interrogatives. Comments-as-questions were more common in the cross-examination of complainants in RASSO trials, with the balance between questions and comments being much more even. Extract 9 is taken from the transcript of the cross-examination of a complainant in a historical child sex abuse trial on their relationship with the defendant. In that cross-examination, defence counsel took 519 turns, 264 (50.87 per cent) of which were statements-as-questions (note: the transcripts with which we were provided often included question marks at the end of the turns, even though the utterance was not gramatically a question. Original transcripts are reproduced here):

Extract 9: *Statements-as-questions in the cross-examination of a complainant in a historical child sex abuse trial (case A039)*

DC: And you also say at points you implied perhaps a little aggressive with you but I'd like to talk to you about him generally. Was he generally kind to you?
W: He was generally one of the nicest adults that I had contact with at that time apart from my grandma.
DC: You enjoyed spending time with him?
W: Yes.
DC: You liked him?
W: Yes.
DC: And those feelings just from what we can see from your ABE [Achieving Best Evidence] developed into you falling in love with him?
W: Yes, I would say so.
DC: I would say he is not from your memory of him an uncaring unkind person at all?
W: That's a very difficult question because if I look back on how I felt about him then and I look back on how I should have felt about him now, there's two different prospectives on how I should feel about him.

DC: But focus on what you thought of him then when you were in school?
W: What I thought about him then I thought he was wonderful.

Indeed, some cross-examinations saw counsel making far more comments than questions. For example, in a cross-examination of a vulnerable complainant in a violent robbery case, 76 (70.37 per cent) of the 108 turns that counsel took were statements rather than questions. For example:

Extract 10: *Statements-as-questions in the cross-examination of a complainant in a robbery trial (A025)*

DC: So is that when you're on the floor you put your foot on the dressing table?
W: The dressing table was on the floor. Me foot was on the floor and put me foot on it and try to wiggle out.
DC: Trying to wiggle away.
W: Yes.
DC: So he's behind you on top of you with his arms around your neck?
W: His two arms around me neck.
DC: Restraining you?
W: Yes.
DC: I believe you said five to ten minutes. You think eight?
W: Yes.
DC: I think is what you said?
W: Yes. I didn't time everything.
DC: No, of course not. Of course not. Now, you then describe how you went from to that position in that part of the room, over to where you say the money was kept?
W: Yes.
DC: And you did that by crawling on your …
W: On me knees, like walking like this (indicated).
DC: And he still had his something around your neck?
W: Exactly. He wouldn't let go.
DC: And that was obviously quite an awkward thing to do, difficult thing to do?
W: Awkward? It was terrifying.

Therefore, although child witnesses are spared statements-as-questions in our sample, adult vulnerable witnesses often are not. Despite the perception that statements are more pragmatically ambiguous and restrictive than yes/no questions, it may not always be the case that they prevent vulnerable witnesses giving their best evidence, nor are they always challenging for witnesses. It depends on the nature of the vulnerability. If the witness is vulnerable because of their age, mental illness, or has a significant impairment of intelligence and social functioning then statements-as-questions should be avoided. But for RASSO complainants who do not have additional intellectual or communication needs, statements-as-comments may not present the same problems. Extract 9 contains nine statements from counsel, but the end result of this exchange could be interpreted as the successful mutual reconstruction of the complainant's evidence. For the most part the statements are seeking confirmation from the witness on earlier parts of their testimony that are, presumably, not disputed by the defence. This type of statement-as-question, therefore, is very different in nature from that in Extract 11, taken from the cross-examination of an 11-year-old complainant in a sexual assault trial.

Extract 11: *Statements-as-questions in the cross-examination of a child complainant in a sexual assault trial (under 12) (case A027)*

DC: I'm going to suggest that there was no improper contact by [defendant] to you at all.
W: That would be incorrect.
DC: I'm going to suggest there was certainly no touching of your bottom which lasted for about a minute.
J: Well, again, there are different ways to answer that. Are you saying there was no touching of the bottom?
DC: No, there was no touching at all –
J: Right.
DC: – and it didn't last for a minute.
J: Well, if there was no touching at all, it couldn't have lasted for a minute.
DC: Exactly so.
J: Right, so you're suggesting that there was no touching of the bottom.
DC: That's exactly right.
J: Well, then just suggest that.
DC: And he didn't say, 'Don't tell your friends about it'?
W: That would be incorrect.

It is evident that these statements-as-questions, used to challenge rather than reconstruct the complainant's version of events, are more problematic in nature. The child is resolute in their rebuttal of these 'suggestions' ('that would be incorrect'), showing that they *do* understand that a response is required to these statements. Rather, the difficulty with these examples is that they are used to directly challenge and undermine the testimony of the vulnerable witness and are indirect accusations of lying (more on such accusations below). Furthermore, this type of 'suggest' statements, used by barristers to project and assert a version of events that conflict with that of the witness (see Heffer, 2005: 138) are considered 'old-fashioned' and 'antiquated' by lawyers and are thought to be 'just legal verbiage which add nothing' (Hanna and Henderson, 2018: 415). *I suggest, I'm going to suggest* and *If I was to suggest* formulations appear in similar quantities in the cross-examination of vulnerable witnesses (98 questions, 1.7 per cent of all questions) and non-vulnerable witnesses (71, 1.43 per cent).

Signposting topics

Topic management and rapid topic changes can be used strategically by advocates in traditional cross-examination to exercise interactional power over the witness and to restrict the time that the jury has to process the details of an ongoing narrative (Aldridge and Luchjenbroers, 2007: 95). The *20 Principles of Questioning* and The Advocate's Gateway advise counsel to signpost new topics and changes of topic when questioning vulnerable witnesses (The Advocate's Gateway, 2015a, 2015b; Inns of Court College of Advocacy, 2022: 10). This advice is based on the suggestion that sudden switching from one topic to another can easily confuse and disorientate a vulnerable witness (Davies et al, 2010: 353) and that topic signposting helps witnesses keep their focus and gives them time to reorient to a new subject. There are various ways in which this can be performed by counsel, the most explicit perhaps being direct references to 'topic', for example:

Extract 12: *Signposting topic change in the cross-examination of a child defendant (over 12) (A004)*

DC: New topic, complete change of topic. Your history with [complainant], all right.
W: All right.

However, this particular type of signposting was rare in our sample, with the word 'topic' appearing only 26 times in the 34 cross-examinations of vulnerable witnesses. More commonly preferred were the signposts: 'I want to ask …' or 'I'm going to ask …' (and variations of these, such as 'I just want to ask you …'). For example:

Extract 13: *Cross-examination of a vulnerable complainant in a rape trial (A035)*

DC: I want to ask you a little bit about drugs.
W: Okay.

In our data, signposting sequences are more common in the questions to vulnerable witnesses than they are in the questions to non-vulnerable witnesses. There are 101 signposts in the 5,774 questions put to vulnerable witnesses (1.75 per cent of all questions) and only 41 in the 4,979 questions put to non-vulnerable witnesses (0.82 per cent of all questions). This indicates a recognition from advocates that they serve a particular function in helping vulnerable people during cross-examination and are in line with professional best practice guidelines. They are most prevalent in the cross-examination of young children (under 12), where they account for 24/242 questions (or 9.92 per cent). Extract 14 is an example from one cross-examination in which the advocate employed this technique consistently with a ten-year-old rape complainant.

Extract 14: *The signposting of topics in the cross-examination of a child complainant (under 12) (A007)*

DC: [Complainant], now I'm going to ask you about when you were living with your grandparents with mummy and [defendant], okay?
W: Okay.
DC: [Defendant] says that, when you all lived at your grandparents' house, he was never alone with you. Is that true?
W: Yes, that's true, but grandma would always be downstairs.
DC: [Complainant], I'm going to move on now to ask you about your father, okay?
W: All right.
DC: When you were living in [place], did you spend time with your father?
W: Yes, I would spend one or two days with him …
DC: I'm going to ask you now, [complainant], about when you moved to [place]. [Defendant] said that he did not look after you without mummy when you were in [place]. Is that true?
W: No, when my mum went out, he used to look after me.
DC: [Complainant], I'm now going to ask you about when you moved to [road name] in the [place], all right?
W: Okay.

However, signposting is not always successful in its aim to focus the witness's attention. In Extract 15, for example, defence counsel starts the cross-examination of a 12-year-old witness with a lengthy signposting sequence, in which they outline no fewer than four topics at once. Henderson (2014: 13) raises doubts over whether child witnesses derive 'any assistance whatsoever' from this sort of enumerating of topics:

Extract 15: *Cross-examination of a child complainant in a grooming case (over 12) (case A006)*

DC: Another thing I'm going to do is I'm going to tell you what topic I want to ask you about before I ask the questions, and I'll try and give you a reminder of what was happening at the time in case it helps you to remember to answer the questions, okay. So, I'm going to ask you questions in four different topics, and all of the questions are about things that happened in [year]. The topics are, firstly, how you and [defendant] met; secondly, a police chase; thirdly, a visit from your social worker; and then, finally, the contact that you had with [defendant], all right. Good. So, the first topic is how you and [defendant] met. So, think back –
W: It was in (Inaudible) –

In a lengthy turn such as this, outlining so many topics, there is a risk that counsel could confuse or overwhelm the young witness. It also appears in this extract that the child does not fully understand the signposting activity, and provides a response to the signpost, rather than a question. Elsewhere, the occurrence of ostensibly signposting sequences does not mean that genuine signposting is happening. For example, in Extract 16, the question that immediately follows the signpost is not related to the topic that had been signposted. This caused difficulty for the vulnerable witness in this instance and undermines the motivation for signposting in the first place – to avoid confusing the witness by rapidly shifting from one topic to the next.[1]

Extract 16: *Signposting in the cross-examination of a complainant in a rape case (case A035)*

DC: I'm going to ask you about leaving the club now.
W: Okay.
DC: Do you agree that there is a big difference between remembering something and consenting to something happening?
W: (Pause). I'm not – I'm not sure what you mean.

Tag questions

One type of question that has received near-universal criticism in the context of vulnerable witnesses is tag questions – statements with a 'question tag'

[1] For a greater in-depth analysis of topic signposting and the interactional issues that can arise from it during cross-examination, see Wright et al (forthcoming).

appended (for example, *you didn't see him, did you?*). Tag questions are often considered the most controlling and coercive question in the cross-examiner's toolkit (Woodbury, 1984: 205; Berk-Seligson, 1999: 36). The *20 Principles of Questioning* and The Advocate's Gateway both recommend that counsel be cautious about using tagged questions or avoid them altogether (Inns of Court College of Advocacy, 2022: 14; The Advocate's Gateway, 2015a: 30; 2015b: 21). The *Equal Treatment Bench Book* (Judicial College, 2024: 58) has this to say about tag questions:

> These are powerfully suggestive and complex: to respond accurately, the witness has to be able to judge whether the statement part of the question is true; understand that the tag expresses the advocate's point of view, and is not necessarily true; be able to counter that point of view; and (if the question combines both a positive and a negative) understand that a positive statement takes a negative tag and vice versa.

It is widely recognised, therefore, that tag questions are too challenging for certain types of vulnerable witness. In order to identify the type and frequency of tag questions in our sample, the corpus of transcripts was batch-queried for 196 question tag formations to compare their use in the cross-examination of vulnerable and non-vulnerable witnesses (for example, *did you, didn't you, is it, isn't it*, and so on). In our sample, vulnerable witnesses were asked fewer tag questions than non-vulnerable witnesses. A total of 831 (14.40 per cent) out of 5,774 questions put to

Figure 6.3: Proportion of tag questions put to vulnerable witnesses during cross-examination

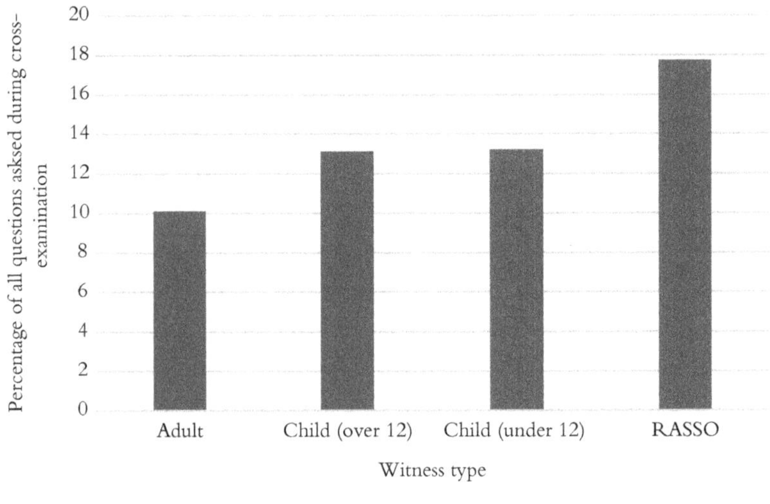

vulnerable witnesses were tag questions, compared with 909 (18.26 per cent) out of 4,979 questions for non-vulnerable witnesses. When it comes to different types of vulnerable witnesses, child witnesses are asked more tag questions than adult vulnerable witnesses, except for complainants in RASSO cases, who were asked the most tag questions of all vulnerable witnesses (Figure 6.3).

In terms of the types of tag questions present in the transcripts, there was a similar patterning across both sets of witnesses. The top ten most frequently used tags in the questioning of vulnerable and non-vulnerable witnesses are very similar. The tags *is that right*, *yes*, *isn't that right*, *isn't it*, *didn't you*, and *is it* are all among the most common for both types of witness (Table 6.4). Therefore, while it seems as though the *frequency* of tag questions was being reduced to accommodate vulnerable witnesses, it does not appear to be the case that the *types* of tags being used were being adapted to vulnerable witnesses. When vulnerable witnesses are asked tag questions, they are most often the same types of tag questions that are put to non-vulnerable witnesses. The exception to this seems to be the tag *okay*, which is much more prevalent in the questioning of vulnerable witnesses. In the questioning of child witnesses, it seems as though this particular tag can serve a facilitative, rather than controlling function, alongside topic signposts to check the child's comprehension (for example, 'I'm going to move on now to ask you about your father, okay?').

The overall numbers provide some evidence to suggest that the move away from tag questions in the cross-examination of vulnerable witnesses is at least

Table 6.4: The top ten most common question tags in the cross-examination of vulnerable and non-vulnerable witnesses

Vulnerable			**Non-vulnerable**		
Tag	**Freq**	**% of all tags**	**Tag**	**Freq**	**% of all tags**
is that right?	143	17.21	is that right?	184	20.24
yes?	86	10.35	yes?	89	9.79
okay?	76	9.15	didn't you?	82	9.02
isn't that right?	56	6.74	isn't it?	69	7.59
isn't it?	49	5.90	is it?	40	4.40
all right?	34	4.09	did you?	28	3.08
is that correct?	33	3.97	isn't that right?	26	2.86
didn't you?	24	2.89	wasn't it?	24	2.64
is it?	23	2.77	weren't you?	20	2.20
do you?	21	2.53	wouldn't you?	19	2.09

underway. However, they were far from being avoided completely; only two vulnerable witnesses were asked no tag questions at all, while in the cross-examination of another vulnerable witness, a 12-year-old rape complainant, 43 per cent of the questions asked were tagged questions (Extract 17). As is shown in the following extract, this repeated use of tag questions results in multiple interventions by the intermediary.

Extract 17: *Tag questions in the cross-examination of a child complainant in a rape case (over 12) (case D010)*

DC: All right. So, in terms of your own brothers and sisters, you have an older brother, [brother name1]; isn't that right?
W: Yes.
DC: Yes. I think he's 14 or thereabouts now, about 14; is that right?
W: I'm not quite sure.
DC: That's okay. And then obviously [brother name2], who's living with you with [name2] and [name3]; isn't that right?
W: Yes.
DC: And he'll be – I think he'll be 12 soon. Sorry, too fast?
IM: May I intervene? I wonder if we could avoid tag questions and questions posed as statements when it's evidential matters.
DC: So, if I start again, [intermediary name] stop me, okay, I don't mean to –
IM: I will, I know.
DC: So, [brother name2] is – I want to get just a sense of the family. Okay, so [brother name2] is living with the [family name] with you?
W: Yes.
DC: He will be 12 later, I think in July; is that right?
W: Yes.
DC: And then you have two younger brothers as well, [brother name3] and [brother name4]; isn't that right?
W: Yes.
DC: … question, sorry, [intermediary name] … and [brother name3] I think is aged nine now; is that right?
W: I'm not quite sure.
DC: Around that age I think?
W: Yes.
DC: So, he's a bit younger, he's the youngest of the boys and he's eight I think?
W: I think so.
DC: Great. Now, I don't want to be upsetting you, but I know that about five years ago now, in [date], you won't remember

the date, but five years ago you went to live with the [family name]; isn't that right?

W: Yes.

DC: In that house, living with you on a regular basis is Mum, which is [name 3]; is that right?

W: Yes.

DC: And yes, sorry, sorry.

IM: I wonder if we can avoid the tag questions if at all possible. They can be quite – 'when you say Mum was living at home, isn't that right'.

DC: Okay.

IM: Can you pose it as a question rather than as a statement, please?

Unlike some of the other features analysed in this chapter, tag questions were less frequently asked to vulnerable defendants (8.45 per cent) compared to non-defendant vulnerable witnesses (15.57 per cent). But as Figure 6.3 shows, complainants in rape and sexual assault trials in our sample are asked a disproportionately large number of tag questions compared with other vulnerable witnesses. In fact, the cross-examination of a vulnerable witness that had the highest absolute number of tag questions was of an adult rape complainant, which contained 106 tag questions out of a total of 516 questions put to the witness (20.54 per cent). For this vulnerable witness, one in five questions they were asked was a tag question. An extract from that cross-examination is in Extract 18.

Extract 18: *Tag questions in the cross-examination of an adult rape complainant (case A034)*

DC: Okay, you accept that what you have in your head about somebody forcing their penis into your mouth that night might not be true.

W: Yeah, I accept that.

DC: What I'm not suggesting to you is that you're telling a deliberate lie about that. Do you understand?

W: Yeah.

DC: I'm not saying you're a liar.

W: I – I'm aware that might not be the truth. I've stated that from the beginning.

DC: If it isn't a deliberate lie on your part but it's not true, then it's something else, isn't it?

W: Yeah.

DC: And what I'm saying is it's some sort of nightmarish fantasy. It's a bad trip, isn't it?

W: Potentially, but I remembered that when I wasn't high.

DC: Sure, but you don't know if it's true or not.
W: No, I don't.
DC: So, if it isn't true, then it's some sort of imagined horror story, isn't it?
W: Yes.

Although there is general recognition that tag questions should be avoided for certain types of vulnerable witness, there is also an acknowledgement that 'this does not mean that all tag questions have an adverse effect' (*R v Grant-Murray & Others* [2017] EWCA Crim 1228, [114–115]). On the basis of the transcript in Extract 17, and the fact that this witness faced a large number of tag questions, the tag questions would seem problematic. However, the notes from the observation of this trial give an account of a cross-examination that in other respects adhered to best practice:

> It [cross-examination] was challenging in that the gaps and issues with C's evidence were highlighted, and the defendant's case was put to her, as it must be. At the same time, however, counsel's tone and pace, the judge's interjections, were sensitive and measured. When C got distressed, counsel paused, the judge asked if she wanted a break, etc. DC was almost apologetic prior to putting D's case to her, forewarning her that there were some distressing questions coming and that he [DC] would be as quick as possible.

This observation sits uneasily alongside the manipulative or aggressive image of cross-examination in rape cases that is painted in much of the prevailing literature (Zydervelt et al, 2017; Smith, 2018; Booth et al, 2019). Each vulnerable witness will present with unique communication needs and abilities (Cooper et al, 2018: 397). It might be the case that tag questions, when used with care, can be facilitative and supportive in some contexts and with some witnesses, rather than being primarily or exclusively coercive or suggestive. As was suggested to be the case with statements-as-questions, for RASSO complainants who are not otherwise vulnerable due to their age or incapacity, tag questions may not present the same challenges. On the contrary, for such witnesses, tag questions may be an appropriate means of navigating difficult and traumatic testimony.

Direct challenges

One difficulty that arises for counsel in avoiding confrontation with vulnerable witnesses is when they need to challenge what the witness is saying, such as when they wish to put inconsistencies to the witness or are required to 'put their [client's] case' to the witness – that is, putting the defendant's version of the facts to the witness during cross-examination (see Chapter 2). As one judge whom we interviewed put it:

> Judges expect you to put your case. It is actually quite difficult and requires quite a lot of thought as to how you're going to do that in the way that we are, we now expect counsel to do it, because if the case is … this is all lies and you are not permitted to say to a child, 'Well you're telling lies aren't you?' or 'Have you told lies?', then it's difficult to put the case. So the two things don't sit well together, if you see what I mean. (AAJ1)

One counsel contrasted the way he would challenge 'normal witnesses', sometimes putting it baldly to them that they are lying, in contrast to child witnesses, where he does not put the emphasis on the child lying (ABC1). A judge said that she could not remember the last time a sexual offences complainant was accused of outright lying: 'That kind of language just isn't used anymore … And it's unnecessary, so … what's more likely to be put is, "The defendant says that he didn't do any of these things to you. Is he telling the truth or is he telling lies?"' (ABJ4).

In *R v E* ([2011] EWCA Crim 3028), the Court noted that 'direct challenges', such as accusations of lying, are unhelpful and risk confusion or capitulation for the child witness (at [28]). The Advocate's Gateway (2015a: 24) advises counsel to 'take care with questions suggesting the child is lying or confused because these question types are likely to have an adverse impact on concentration and accuracy'. One, albeit perhaps crude, way of identifying direct challenges of this kind in our sample is by isolating explicit mentions of lying and truthfulness in counsel's questions in which they suggested that the witness may be lying or may have lied at some earlier point (for example, in evidence-in-chief or police interview). Our analysis finds that generally, direct challenges and accusations of lying were rare overall in the cross-examinations in our sample. However, there were more direct challenges to the truthfulness of non-vulnerable witnesses' evidence than to that of vulnerable witnesses (Table 6.5).

Despite this general trend away from accusing vulnerable witnesses of lying, there were still several examples of vulnerable witnesses explicitly being accused of lying. In our data, almost half of the direct challenges of this kind (61/129, 47.29 per cent) were made to complainants in RASSO cases. In Extract 19, for example, counsel accused a rape complainant of lying about being sexually assaulted and raped. What compounds this particular example is that counsel not only accused the complainant of lying in this case, but also invoked allegations that the complainant had made in a previous case. This double accusation of untruthfulness is seen to cause confusion for the complainant, whose first language is not English.

Table 6.5: Frequency of words related to truth and lies in cross-examination

	Vulnerable witnesses		Non-vulnerable witnesses	
	Frequency	**Per 1,000 words**	**Frequency**	**Per 1,000 words**
lie	34	(0.34)	68	(0.76)
lied	7	(0.07)	12	(0.13)
lies	12	(0.12)	24	(0.27)
lying	3	(0.03)	11	(0.12)
true	36	(0.36)	41	(0.46)
truth	37	(0.37)	47	(0.53)
Total	129	(1.29)	203	(2.27)

Extract 19: *Direct accusations of lying put to a complainant in a rape case (case A013)*

DC: That is what the police wanted to interview you about, and that is ultimately what [defendant] has admitted doing, is it not?

W: Yes.

DC: And just like with [name1], when you were making your complaint, because you said that [name1] physically abused you as well, yes? [name1]?

W: Yes.

DC: (Question interpreted) Just in the same way when you told the police you did not just stick to the truth, did you? You exaggerated it and made up allegations of sexual assault and oral rape.

W: (Interpreted) Sorry, are we talking about the late, last case or the previous one, [name1]?

DC: (Question interpreted) We are talking about this case, but my point is you did the same thing to [defendant] as you did to [name1].

W: (Interpreted) Can you please repeat your question because I don't understand?

DC: (Question interpreted) Yes. We agree that [defendant] was despicable towards you. And he beat you to the point where you could not be beaten anymore.

W: Yes.

DC: (Question interpreted) Because who knows where it would have ended and what he would have done to you.

W: Yes.

DC: (Question interpreted) And you had the courage, and it really is courage to tell the police about this. And when the police were talking to you and you were telling them about the way he had been beating you up, during the course of that otherwise truthful account, you made up things that were not true about sexual assault, about oral rape. Those things which did not happen.

W: No. No.

It is important to reiterate that the linguistic analysis here draws from a smaller, hand-picked sub-sample of the 40 trial observations discussed in Chapter 5. The case highlighted in Extract 19, A013, was selected for inclusion in this smaller sample precisely because, in the context of the broader observational dataset, it provided a striking example of practice that had not, at that point, been encountered in other trials. Defence counsel's approach to cross-examination was notably more aggressive and confrontational than was typically observed across the trials. Moreover, defence counsel's introduction of unsubstantiated accusations about prior false allegations during cross-examination occurred without the court's leave and resulted in swift and scathing judicial admonishment. Crucially, defence counsel's efforts to persuade the jury that the complainant was neither a reliable nor a credible witness – that she was a liar – were clearly unsuccessful as the jury convicted. Ultimately, direct accusations by defence counsel that a prosecution witness – including complainants in RASSO cases – was lying were uncommon across the broader sample and is why, when such accusations were observed, the relevant trials were flagged up as potential candidates for the sub-sample analysed here.

Conclusions

The empirical linguistic analysis of the trial transcripts of cross-examination 'on-the-ground' presents a somewhat mixed picture and, perhaps, captures a change in progress in how vulnerable witnesses are cross-examined in criminal trials. There is evidence that vulnerable witnesses, and particularly young children, are spared some of the more challenging elements of traditional cross-examination, such as lengthy questioning, 'why' questions and statements-dressed-as-questions while also appearing to benefit from the signposting of topic changes during questioning. There were only two vulnerable defendants in our sample, but our results show that they were often not afforded the same accommodations to cross-examination as other, non-defendant, vulnerable witnesses, which is in line with our findings on the treatment of vulnerable defendants in trials more generally (Cooper et al, 2024). Similarly, some features of cross-examination, such as comments-as-questions and tag questions still proliferate in the questioning of complainants in RASSO trials (see Chapter 2 as to why these are problematic). In some cases, the cross-examination of vulnerable defendants and RASSO complainants included a greater number and range of challenging questioning techniques than that of non-vulnerable witnesses, suggesting that there is still more work to be done in redressing the balance for defendants and complainants in sex offence trials. At the same time, it has been argued here that particular types of questions may present difficulties for some (types of) vulnerable witnesses but not others.

The results have emphasised the fact that when it comes to guidance for best practice in relation to specific questioning techniques, there is no 'one size fits all'. Notwithstanding the different communicative needs for different types of vulnerability, some techniques that are challenging for one vulnerable witness may not be for another. Likewise, well-intentioned changes to traditional cross-examination can cause unforeseen interactional problems. For instance, the 'complexity' of a question does not always equate to its length. Open 'WH-' questions might be suitable for some vulnerable witnesses but not others, who might struggle to provide relevant responses. In such cases, closed 'did' questions can help, but they too can leave a vulnerable witness feeling distressed. Although comments-as-questions and tag questions are generally recognised as being confusing or overly suggestive for vulnerable witnesses, they can also be facilitative and supportive for a witness. Signposting of topics, while motivated by the need to focus the attention of the witness, can lead to long and complex question turns. Taken together, these findings suggest that continued efforts to develop appropriate methods of cross-examining vulnerable witnesses would benefit from guidance and training that are furnished with added nuance, contextual richness, and empirical linguistic evidence.

7

The Changing Culture of Cross-Examination

Systems theorists have long proclaimed that legal systems develop their own procedures and rules which can be highly resistant to pressure from society at large (see, for example, Teubner, 1992). Scholars have pointed out that this is nowhere more evident than when it comes to reform of proof at trial. Langbein (1978) has argued that nothing is quite so embedded in a legal system as the procedures for proof and trial, because most of what a legal system does is to decide matters of fact-finding and therefore reforms aimed at reconstructing fact-finding procedures disturb, at one level or another, virtually every vested interest. As a result, 'a legal system will do almost anything, tolerate almost anything, before it will admit the need for reform in its system of proof and trial' (19). As examples, he highlighted the use of torture for half a millennium in continental European systems and the 'evils' of plea bargaining that have long been entrenched in Anglo-American systems.

Another practice that has long been entrenched within Anglo-American systems is an adversarial procedure where trials become a gladiatorial contest conducted by lawyers and the questioning of witnesses is controlled by lawyers advocating on behalf of their clients. Henderson (2014: 94) has commented that when it comes to reform of cross-examination, judges and advocates are the last people one could expect to initiate significant changes as the legal professions would have extreme difficulty changing practices 'freighted with deep cultural significance'. In our study, however, we have seen that changes are being made to methods of cross-examination that have long been characteristic of adversarial procedure, with discernible differences in the ways in which vulnerable witnesses are cross-examined as opposed to other kinds of witnesses. Most notably, there was little evidence in the cross-examination of different kinds of vulnerable witnesses of the gladiatorial tendency to brow-beat and humiliate witnesses which has been one of the features long associated with traditional cross-examination. At the same time, as we saw in the last chapter, there was also considerable variation in the extent to which the principles of questioning associated with best practice were followed in practice.

This chapter examines the extent to which the adjustments that are being made to the way in which vulnerable witnesses are being cross-examined are heralding a changing culture of cross-examination away from its traditional focus on advocacy and towards achieving best evidence. We will first examine the degree of acceptance we found on the ground for the changes to cross-examination across the jurisdictions examined and the challenges these have brought to bear on practice. We then consider what has done most to drive cultural change across the jurisdictions. Finally, we assess the extent to which changes affecting the cross-examination of vulnerable witnesses are also spilling over more generally into the cross-examination of other witnesses and whether a new cultural paradigm of 'best practice' is emerging from the changes.

Acceptance of change

There was widespread acceptance among interviewees across the jurisdictions of the need to change the approach to the cross-examination of vulnerable witnesses within the legal profession in order to achieve better evidence and to benefit vulnerable witnesses. Judges were wholeheartedly in favour of the new approaches to questioning vulnerable witnesses as they increased the chance of best evidence being taken from a witness and therefore the chance of justice being done and, very importantly, they reduced the chance of re-traumatisation of the witness: 'A win, win, win for the interests of justice and the interests of witnesses', according to one judge (BAJ1).

Some advocates also spoke highly about the benefits that a more witness-centred approach had achieved:

> Asking a defendant who doesn't understand it, what's the point? But if he quite clearly understands what you're driving at, and you can see that he understands it, then his answers are worthwhile then. (AAC1)

> Without any shadow of a doubt, [the changes have] made it easier for vulnerable witnesses to give their account. (AAC3)

> It's the right thing to offer the most vulnerable in society, whether they're witnesses who are the victims of serious crime or they're defendants who have their own issues … the support to give them the best chance of giving their evidence the best way. (CAC4)

A number of interviewees noted some resistance at first to the changes and it has taken some time for them to bed down. A contrast was drawn across the jurisdictions between 'old-school' barristers who were still quite resistant to change and younger barristers who were more open to embracing it:

> I've had two examples in the past year where I've had to stop [counsel's] cross-examination, get the jury out and say, 'Look, these days … are long gone. You just cannot do this'. And both of them were barristers who were in their 70s. (ABJ2)

> You used to get a lot of, 'I think you know me and I think you can trust me to ask proper questions' or 'I've been doing this for 30 years, I think I know how to ask a question of a child'. And invariably, that was a preamble to not a clue how to ask a question of a child. (ACJ3)

There was also a view that there were differences of approach between 'old-school' judges and judges who were more recently appointed, although there was more consistency now than there used to be because guidance such as the Crown Court Compendium in England and Wales and the Crown Court Bench Book in Northern Ireland was imposing more uniformity. One counsel referred to an 'old-school' judge who dealt with a sensitive vulnerable witness case completely differently from a newly appointed judge who had been doing this sort of work recently and had done all the recent training (AAC3). Another contrasted the 'new breed … who know how to do this and do it properly' with 'some of the old dinosaurs who are just like, "Well, why haven't you put the inconsistency in? Oh, come on, do it properly"' (ABC1). The worst, he said, were 'the older male recorders [part-time judges], particularly the Silks [senior counsel], who generally don't deal with this kind of thing as much, and they are less receptive to it'.

We shall see that interviewees' views on how much change there has actually been on the ground varied according to jurisdiction. What was striking, however, was the degree to which judges and advocates across the jurisdictions appear to have accepted changes that have made considerable inroads into key aspects of traditional cross-examination. Henderson (2014) has argued that the changes target three particular aspects of conventional cross-examination: the use of developmentally inappropriate language to convey key messages to the fact-finder; the use of suggestive questions; and use of cross-examination to confront the witness. As we have seen, cross-examiners are now required to adapt to a best evidence model whereby the function of cross-examination shifts from advocacy towards forensic examination which focuses on facilitating communication with witnesses, restricting suggestion, and, possibly most controversial of all given the association of traditional cross-examination with confrontation, avoiding direct challenge. Although, as we shall see, these changes present advocates with many challenges, none of the interviewees objected in principle to having to adapt their cross-examination of vulnerable witnesses to this best evidence model.

As explored in Chapter 2, another aspect of traditional cross-examination has been the broad discretion given to advocates to cross-examine witnesses on any relevant issues or on any matter affecting a witness's credibility with limited intervention from judges. The new changes have required judges to police the cross-examination of vulnerable witnesses to a much greater degree than hitherto. As one Scottish advocate put it:

> At one time, judges were far less interventionist than they are now. They would generally just sit, be the referee and not really intervene at all unless an extreme situation arose. Whereas now, it's pretty obvious that they do take these matters very seriously and they want to know what is proposed for the taking of the evidence and how it's to be done. (BAC1)

We have seen that judges were observed to intervene with respect to vulnerable witnesses, some quite regularly, and advocates appeared to accept these interruptions without complaint. Some interviewees suggested that this greater judicial intervention has to be seen against the background of a general shift towards judicial case management. In England and Wales, the Criminal Procedure Rules 2020 require judges to take greater control over how cases in general are progressed, overseeing what is agreed and disputed between the parties, and setting time limits on cross-examination.[1] A good example of this was given by one judge who had been in a drugs case, not involving vulnerable witnesses, where a barrister insisted on cross-examining witnesses at length:

> Whereas everyone else was getting up, getting down within 20 minutes having their case done. And after an hour, he's still there covering old ground. And then eventually you just have the jury out and you say, 'Mr X, you've dealt with this, it's gone on far too long, I'll give you an extra 10 minutes'. He comes back saying, 'You can't do that', and you say, 'Well, actually I can. Look at the criminal procedure rules, you've got to focus your cross-examination now'. (ABJ2)

There was a consensus among interviewees, borne out in our linguistic analysis in Chapter 6, that the most dramatic adaptations have taken place in relation to young children. Interviewees across the jurisdictions referred

1 See Crim PR 3.2(2)(c), 3.13(d); *R v Simon* [2018] EWCA Crim 3086; *R v Lally (Mark Stephen)* [2021] EWCA Crim 1372.

to the strict manner in which judges police the cross-examination of young children, refusing to allow them, according to one counsel, to be any longer than maybe an hour, an hour and a half and broken into maybe 20–25-minute sections: 'so maybe like three short sessions and that's it' (CAC3). Judges have been greatly assisted in this policing role by two innovations – the use of intermediaries and ground rules hearings (GRHs) – which strike at the heart of traditional cross-examination in other ways.

As discussed in Chapter 4, the use of intermediaries to interrupt and query counsel's cross-examination constitutes a revolutionary break from tradition as this is the first time anyone other than the judge or opposing counsel has been permitted to do this in a criminal trial. Yet previous research in England and Wales has found that although there was naturally at first a certain level of tension produced by the advent of a new player in court (Henderson, 2015a), intermediaries have gradually garnered the support of judges and lawyers (for example, Cooper and Mattison, 2017). Interviewees in England and Wales said that it took a while for the relationship between intermediaries and counsel to bed down. One judge said that when she first started, intermediaries 'were trying to justify their existence and a number of them were interrupting and interventionist' but now 'we've all rather calmed down … we were all rather nervous at one another' (ACJ2). Another judge explained that before questions were submitted in advance and there was discussion of what the questions were, there was a 'perception that the registered intermediary sat in the room saying "No, he can't answer that. Stop. You have to rephrase that"' which 'did break down the flow of things' (AAJ2). But she noted that had now changed.

Judicial interviewees in England and Wales tended to be more enthusiastic about the use of intermediaries than advocates, one judge commenting that advocates 'may not say overtly but they certainly give the impression that the intermediary on occasion is cramping their style', but they had had to accept that they were here to stay (ABJ4). For their part, however, most advocate interviewees admitted they had come to accept that intermediaries could be useful:

> At first advocates did not like being told how to do their job. Whereas now I think they realise that actually they really can help them do their job and then therefore there's more acceptance. And then as we've got more used to that, the intermediary has had to be less involved because we as advocates now know how to question someone. (ABC1).

As noted in Chapter 4, intermediaries have been used in Northern Ireland for almost ten years. There was an acceptance on the part of most judicial and counsel interviewees that their reports could be useful in advising how to question the most vulnerable witnesses but there was a feeling that they could be too interventionist at trial. One judge (CAJ2), who was broadly in favour of them, said that some were not sufficiently broadly experienced to know when to step in and when not to step in during the trial process, but another judge (CAJ4) said this was something that came with training and experience. According to one counsel:

> Sometimes you know, say someone is asked a question in cross-examination and they're just mulling it over and they're sort of thinking before they answer and sometimes you get an intermediary who would intervene, 'Could you repeat that question in a different way or something?' And there's no need for it because you can sort of see that the person is just thinking about what they're going to say here and I know they're trying to be helpful, but then it's like, it can throw the whole flow of cross-examination. (CAC3)

We have seen that the use of intermediaries is still evolving in Ireland. At the time of the interviews there was no formal scheme in place and much reliance was placed on experienced intermediaries who had been trained in Northern Ireland. Interviewees were overwhelmingly positive about the added value they brought to cases. In one of the observed cases (D008) discussed in Chapter 5, defence counsel opposed the appointment of an intermediary for a young adult with a level of understanding equivalent to a five-year-old on the ground that the witness was able to cope without an intermediary in her police interview. But the objection was overridden by the trial judge, who granted the appointment as a special measure. A judicial interviewee recalled one case where defence counsel resisted the appointment of an intermediary for a vulnerable adult but the appointment was upheld by the Court of Appeal. In her view, 'once counsel experience it, they realise that it isn't something really to be feared because … counsel really aren't trained to deal with vulnerable witnesses either … ultimately everybody sees it as an advantage, but obviously people have to get used to it' (CAJ2).

In Chapter 4, we saw that judges and advocates expressed some strong opinions about the overuse of intermediaries which was underpinned by a narrow understanding of intermediaries' skill sets. But there was universal acceptance of their use in certain cases, particularly for children under nine or witnesses with specific communication difficulties. It was also salient that there was little objection to them being allowed to interrupt the free flow of question and answer to facilitate communication. Several counsel and intermediaries noted that intermediaries were intervening less at trial because counsel now disclose their questions and have them agreed upon in advance.

This potentially erodes another element of the principle of party control; advocates have never been required to reveal in advance their line of questioning, let alone have their questions pre-approved by a judge. At one level GRHs are simply an extension of judicial case management that has emerged in recent decades throughout the UK jurisdictions requiring judges to set a timetable for the progress of the case to increase efficiency. One judge described it as an 'elaborate directions hearing' where 'you should be discussing the issues in the case, the length of time witnesses are going to have to give evidence, the nature of the way in which they will give evidence, whether special measures are required and so on' (AAJ3). According to several interviewees, however, the requirement that counsel submit written questions in advance for pre-approval prompted considerable resistance at first in England and Wales. Once again, however, it was striking how this innovation has come to be accepted. Although there was still a 'natural reluctance', as one counsel intimated, to have 'your homework marked by somebody else' (ACC1), interviewees in England and Wales considered that there was now a general acceptance of the need to write questions down for the most vulnerable witnesses. As one put it, 'That cri de cœur, "Why should I do this? it's outrageous that I should put my questions down", I haven't heard that for a long time' (AAC2).

The practice of providing written questions in advance appears to be still evolving in Scotland and Northern Ireland, although it would seem that practitioners are generally open to it for the most vulnerable witnesses. A defence advocate in Scotland mentioned that while he had no objections to writing down themes and topics in advance, he had reservations about writing questions 'word for word'. He explained,

> the whole point of advocacy is you have to react to the answer you're given and therefore, setting out the questions in such a precise and rigid way might make no sense whatsoever because when you create these questions, you're assuming certain answers or types of answers which you may not get and you may have to probe a bit more. (BAC1)

A judge in Northern Ireland noted that this had also been a common complaint made by advocates there, but in his view 'there is no reason why you cannot put down the areas and the primary questions that you want to ask' (CAJ3). In Ireland the practice still seems to be uncommon. One counsel said he did not object to it in certain cases involving very vulnerable witnesses. For instance, in one case, he had been required to write down questions for a witness who was both deaf and mute. However, he was sceptical about an approach which required a list of questions routinely for vulnerable witnesses, which he saw as 'the thin edge of the wedge' because 'you have to be guided by the answers that you get and this will inform any further probing' (DAC4).

With the exception perhaps of Ireland, however, advocates now appear to accept that written questions may be necessary in cases of very vulnerable witnesses provided judges are willing to permit further questions in response to how the written questions are answered. But advocates had two lingering concerns about written questions. One was that they were giving away questions that would get back to the witness. Criminal Practice Directions in England and Wales require that where questions are to be committed to writing and subject to judicial editing, with or without input from an intermediary, then, as a general rule, the proposed questions must be shared with the other parties to the trial.[2] A Scottish advocate depute said that 'the idea of keeping everything, and not forewarning anybody about your lines of question' had 'kind of dissipated over the years and people were a bit more accepting of all of this', partly because Scotland's 'rape shield' legislation now required complainers to be told what lines of questioning are going to be asked (BAC2). But according to a judge in England and Wales:

> If you're dealing with a 16-year-old streetwise girl who says she's been raped outside a nightclub, you will have a lot of resistance from certain advocates who do not want to give you advance notice of the questions that they want to ask her … Say, for example, there is something they want to challenge her about, about some CCTV where she's seen in the bar area doing something which she denied doing and it would affect her credibility. (ABJ2)

The other concern on the part of counsel was that judges could be too prescriptive about cutting down questions at GRHs. A particular example was when 'you're asking a question because there is information that you have that the judge is not privy to because it's in your defendant's proof of evidence and you need to ask that witness because you know the defendant is going to say something else later down the line' (ACC1). The judge will say, 'Well, you don't need to ask this' but 'actually, I do but I don't really want to tell you too much about it'. A Scottish advocate depute also said the judge could interfere too much in how they wish to conduct their questioning of the witness. He gave the example of asking a witness about where a town clock was as this could be a useful reference point when he wished the witness to describe where various incidents took place, but the judge had said there was no need to ask about the town clock as it was something that could be agreed in evidence.

[2] Criminal Practice Directions 2023 6.1.5.

Challenges for advocates

To say that advocates have come to accept many of the changes to traditional cross-examination is not to say that they have not experienced considerable challenges. As we have seen in the previous chapter, many of these challenges have been at the level of modifying the way they would traditionally put questions to witnesses. A number of interviewees said they were under no illusion that it was easy to change the habits of a lifetime. One barrister in England and Wales who had much experience of delivering advocacy courses said that '[t]here can be comfort in routine and repetition which means if you are making mistakes, you continue to make the same mistakes' (ABC3). There was a view that it can be particularly difficult for the more experienced to shed old habits:

> We've had this adversarial system. We're all used to it, and we're all trained in it, and it's very difficult for, I would speak for I think both my colleagues on the defence side and my fellow prosecutors, to suddenly have this soft soap approach because we're not used to it. Probably certainly my vintage, I'll never, we'll never get used to it. Obviously the new ones, the new intake will probably have a different approach. (CAC3)

Even when counsel had undergone vulnerable witness training, as a number of interviewees had in England and Wales, there was a feeling that there was a lot left to learn. One counsel considered that it was easy for the training to become a mere 'tick-box' mechanism: 'The worst problem that lawyers have is thinking they know something. Whereas it's the unknown unknowns. And it's very easy to characterise yourself as having done the training but then having a disconnect between having done it and putting it into action' (ABC3).

Another counsel considered that the training had given barristers 'a toolkit, a basic toolkit, to be able to say no … that question is too complicated or that question is irrelevant or we can deal with that material in a different way' but what it had not done was produce a 'a more sophisticated understanding of the way in which we should be communicating with people' (ACC1). In his words, 'the language skills of a child of six or seven who's vulnerable by virtue of being six or seven but is perfectly intellectually able would be completely different from a woman of 25 who's got intellectual difficulties but who's got a lot more life experience'. Yet they tend to be dealt with in exactly the same way and, equally, if somebody has got no intellectual difficulty but they have got massive trauma problems then again 'we tend to say, "Well, no tag questions and they'll need breaks every 20 minutes", as though that solves the problem'.

As we saw in Chapter 6, one particular conundrum that advocates face is how far to go in putting the defendant's version of the facts to the witness during cross-examination, known as 'putting the case'. We have seen that one of the rules of traditional, conventional cross-examination is that where counsel intends to challenge or contradict any aspect of a witness's evidence, they are under a duty to pursue a line of questioning against that witness until they are deemed to have 'put their case' (*Browne v Dunn* (1894) 6 R 67). In *R v Lubemba* ([2014] EWCA Crim 2064 [45]) the English Court of Appeal appeared to question whether it was necessary to put the case to vulnerable witnesses, stating that advocates 'cannot insist upon any supposed right "to put one's case" or previous inconsistent statements' to them. There was a consensus on the part of both judicial and advocate interviewees that the practice of not putting the case at all had gone too far. According to one judge:

> Certainly, when the toolkits were first introduced it went, I think, far too much one way, and judges were effectively being encouraged to say, 'You don't put your case at all, that there is to be no challenge, you're not to suggest to any of the witnesses that they're making this up'. And I think that the pendulum swung too far that way. I think now at the moment we've centred it again and if it's an appropriate challenge and if it can be dealt with sensitively and appropriately, and in a very limited way, judges allow it, and I think the process is far better for it. (AAJ2)

The Court of Appeal has since clarified that it remains a 'general duty to ensure the defence case is put fully and fairly and witnesses challenged where that is possible' (*R v RK* [2018] EWCA Crim 603). However, although one judge told us that judges now expect the case to be put, some interviewees reported that practice is still uncertain. Many counsel had a sense that there was a degree of unpredictability, with some judges saying they want the case put and others saying, 'you can't put your case at all'. One counsel gave an example of a 15-year-old whom he thought could cope with it being suggested to her that she had talked to her sister, and this had affected her testimony, but some judges would say, 'No, you can't say that' (AAC5). Yet the counsel who had met the witness before the trial considered the girl was bright enough to know that the defendant was denying what she was saying (AAC5).

When the case is required to be put, there were also challenges in terms of how exactly that task could be effectively accomplished with vulnerable witnesses. As we saw in Chapter 6, The Advocate's Gateway advises against cross-examiners suggesting that witnesses are lying or confused. However, this can be difficult for counsel when the case hinges on the witness being untruthful. Judges and counsel acknowledged that intermediaries can be immensely helpful in advising on how to present the case to specific witnesses. They described a careful balancing act: putting the case strongly enough to allow the witness to respond effectively, while also protecting the witness from the trauma of a direct challenge. As one judge put it,

> not putting the case from a defence perspective that's fantastic. You don't get a contradiction and you get, 'This is a defendant in a difficult situation. The child's vulnerable. These are the questions we would like to have asked but we haven't been …' The defendant becomes at a disadvantage in the eyes of everybody. (AAJ3)

From the prosecution point of view, however, not putting the case in a direct enough way to a vulnerable complainant can disadvantage the prosecution case as 'you can lose some of that … indignation or … shock or confusion … because if you ask a child, "Well did X really happen?" and the child says "Yeah", then that's it … So, it doesn't always have the same impact, I don't think' (AAJ1). A judge explained:

> The unfairness is that [the complainant] doesn't have the opportunity to address the central plank of the defence which is either she's lying or she's mistaken or it wasn't Bob it was Jimmy who did it … or whatever the central plank of the defence is … Later the defence are going to sort of say to the jury, well you know, she was a bit uncertain about the colour of the bed clothes and the wallpaper and all that sort of stuff. And her mum said that she didn't always trust her to tell the truth, or whatever other bits of stuff they've got in the case to disparage her. And yet she … hasn't had the opportunity to deal with a central plank of the defence case. (ACJ3)

Some advocates took the view that not putting the case directly enough could go so far as to affect the outcome of the case, especially in cases involving very young witnesses where there was a real tension between exposing witnesses and victims to challenge in order to make them more believable or watering down cross-examination to protect complainants and witnesses at the risk of offenders avoiding justice. Defendants may be acquitted in these cases on the basis of 'a handful of really namby-pamby questions', as the complainant's evidence 'lacks the bite' to convict the defendant (ACC3). One counsel described a case where there was extremely limited cross-examination of a very young child of seven or eight, involving three or four questions and when the defendant was acquitted, he remembered thinking, 'I'm not really sure that that was right … He really had the benefit of not having had his case put to a witness' (AAC2).

We saw in Chapter 3 that some advocate interviewees went so far as to question whether cross-examination should continue at all for very vulnerable witnesses and have embraced more radical solutions such as questions being put instead by an intermediary as a 'sort of follow-up ABE' rather than cross-examination in a courtroom. Certain Scottish advocates considered this was the best way of achieving best evidence in these kind of cases (for example, BAC2, BAC4), and, as we shall see in the next chapter, there have been moves to develop the *Barnahus* approach in Scotland, although there are no imminent plans to make changes to the current arrangements for evidence on commission.

The extent to which interviewees appeared willing to consider radical solutions to enable best evidence was particularly salient, given that many of these would involve a fundamental departure from the core tenets of traditional cross-examination such as 'putting the case', and in the case of a 'pure' *Barnahus* approach even preventing advocates cross-examining the witness at all. Notably, however, these radical solutions were only tolerated in relation to the most vulnerable witnesses. The idea of adopting radical solutions for the less vulnerable witnesses met with more resistance when these disrupted advocates' more traditional working practices. As noted in Chapter 3, one of the changes that advocates in England and Wales found most disruptive was the use of pre-recorded cross-examination. There were complaints, as we have seen, about the listing problems it had caused and the extra workload it entailed. As one judge put it: 'When a surgeon goes in to perform an operation … he isn't going to leave another operation halfway down the corridor … and pop in and do this one because it's a child and then go back to the other one' (ABJ1).

However, we also observed that for some counsel, pre-recorded cross-examination went beyond mere inconvenience and posed a threat to the traditional conduct of trials. What unnerved them was not just the erosion of the traditional orality principle, where witnesses give live evidence in open court. Other special measures, such as the use of pre-recorded examination-in-chief, are now an accepted feature of giving evidence across the UK and Ireland. The concern was that pre-recorded cross-examination requires advocates to present their case to witnesses before the trial, effectively isolating the main witness from the rest of the trial. There was an acceptance that this was less of a challenge when the witness was a child, as there may not be much to put to such witnesses. However, in sexual offence cases involving older witnesses, pre-recorded cross-examination often takes place before sufficient material has come to light, as complainants often disclose information in stages.

Notably there were fewer complaints from advocates in Scotland about capturing the evidence of vulnerable witnesses in advance of trials through evidence on commission. The practice of capturing the evidence of sexual offence complainers in this manner has only recently been introduced in Scotland. Practitioners face similar challenges here to those faced by practitioners in England and Wales during section 28 hearings. However, there appeared to be less resistance in Scotland to taking evidence on commission compared to the use of pre-recorded cross-examination in England and Wales. This raises intriguing questions about how cultural change has been driven across different jurisdictions and what lessons this may offer for promoting the acceptance of best practices.

Drivers of cultural change

Although there was a consensus that much had changed and practitioners generally welcomed these changes, there was a difference of emphasis across the jurisdictions on how much change there had been on the ground. Interviewees in England and Wales were more inclined to refer to a 'wholesale change' of approach (AAJ1, AAJ2). According to one judge in England and Wales, it had been 'very slapdash' at first but in her view generally advocates now are really good at sticking to the 'simple issues and all the fluff of cross-examination has just gone' (ABJ2). Another judge said that people had railed against the changes at the beginning and said that they would be impossible to implement, but then they realised that the changes do not fundamentally prevent you from putting your case or from asking the things you want to ask and 'actually, you are probably getting better evidence as a result of it' (AAJ1). One counsel said that when he started out, 'the phrase vulnerable witnesses didn't exist', but now the position had changed beyond recognition. He said that when he has conferences with vulnerable witnesses, it is important to explain to them that the kind of hectoring or bullying or effectively trying to trip up and trick witnesses which they may have seen in a television drama 'is not what you would experience in court and will just not be tolerated any longer' (AAC2).

Interviewees in other jurisdictions were more muted about the pace of change. One judge in Scotland noted that while there had been a change in advocates' approaches, it had not been voluntary and had been brought about by the senior judiciary taking a bold and firm line over the last 6–7 years, stamping out as unacceptable 'the bullying, belittling of witnesses, endless cross-examinations, you know, going for days' (BAJ1). There were other more critical views in the Irish jurisdictions. One judge in Northern Ireland said that there had been a marked difference since 1999 but it had been a 'slow improvement … with still pockets of bad practice' (CAJ2). Another commented, 'As far as the treatment of vulnerable witnesses is concerned, it's an uphill battle, right? It's how I would see it. I think the representatives … intellectually they know how these things should be done. But, on the ground, there's relatively little change' (CAJ4).

A judge in Ireland said that the pace of change had been incredibly slow. Although there had been an acceptance on the part of the legal profession of the need to modify very entrenched habits in order to elicit reliable evidence from vulnerable witnesses, 'on a day-to-day basis the emphasis on the part of defence counsel … is more inclined towards confusing the witness, and endeavouring to get the answer that suits the case they're making rather than getting a more reliable and factually accurate answer' (DAJ1). She considered that the pace of change was slow even in children's cases, where there had most definitely been a shift in terms of court style, but there was still quite a confrontational approach involving 'a lot of the pitfalls of … overly complicated questions … leading questions, tagged questions … closed questions'. Moreover, it was not just the 'old school' who were guilty of such practices. She gave an example of a case where a very junior counsel was 'committing all of the cross-examination offences' that older counsel are accused of.

Apart from children's cases, there was an acknowledgement across the jurisdictions that much had also changed in relation to the questioning of witnesses to sexual offences. But again there were different perceptions regarding the pace of change. One judge in England and Wales commented that in the sexual offences cases she had done in the last few years the lawyers had stuck very much to the new approach 'because we're used to it' (ABJ2). Another judge, however, contrasted the experience of vulnerable witnesses with what she called 'ordinary' complainants in sexual offences cases who still felt bruised and feel 'as though they've been through the ringer a bit and the mangle a bit' (ACJ3).

According to a solicitor advocate in Scotland:

> There's no such thing as just a vulnerable witness, there's all categories and people can lie in a big broad spectrum and if somebody's at the more capable end as a deemed vulnerable witness, for example a complainer in a rape case, then … still relatively robust cross-examination takes place, but that's policed pretty well by the judiciary here. (BAC3)

Interviewees in Northern Ireland reported that cross-examination could still be very unnerving and there was room for improvement in the questioning of adult sexual offences complainants:

> I will do a very high percentage of cases with vulnerable complainants in sex cases. And I see them on both sides. I see my other defence colleagues and I see what they do … and some do it very well and some also have a long way to go, yeah. A long way to go. (CAC1)

> [Adult] complainants still do say to me afterwards, you know, 'Oh, that was terrible' or 'I didn't know he could do this' … Has there been a

> softening generally with adults with no vulnerabilities? I don't really think so … taking maybe extra breaks and things like that … but that's as much for the benefit of the jury as it is for the witness. (CAC3)

Across the jurisdictions, there was a consensus that societal attitudes towards vulnerable witnesses have influenced the approach of judges and advocates. While legal systems can sometimes be insulated from societal changes, the jury system can act as a counterbalance, graphically described as injecting 'lay acid' into the system (Bankowski, 1988: 20). One counsel noted that jurors, representing a broad cross-section of the public, 'don't accept bombastic directions to accept or reject evidence' and 'if at any point you appear to be bullying a witness or just using your position as a member of the court to attack someone on their evidence without any foundation to that attack then you just look appalling' (ACC3). Another counsel observed that the culture has shifted away from the 'stereotypical badgering counsel' because jurors are unlikely to be swayed by aggressive tactics, especially towards children or vulnerable witnesses. Such behaviour could cause jurors to dislike both the advocate and their client (DAC1). There was also a perception that juries are now less accepting of rape myths compared to 15 or 20 years ago. A barrister in England and Wales recalled an early case in his career where counsel held up the complainant's underwear to suggest she was dressed to have sex, implying consent. At that time, the counsel said, there would have been a significant number of jurors who might have nodded along with that, but if you said that to a jury now, 'one: the judge even in your speech would interrupt you, and two: you could expect an audible response really, some of the jurors telling you where to get off' (ACC3).

Apart from societal attitudes generally, interviewees across the jurisdictions pointed to a number of factors that have been catalysts of change: the Toolkits in The Advocate's Gateway, the judgments of appellate courts endorsing the Toolkits, greater judicial management, ground rules hearings, intermediaries, and training. A number of interviewees in Scotland, Northern Ireland, and Ireland also referred to the various reviews on sexual offences that have been carried out (Gillen Review, 2019; O'Malley Review, 2020; Dorrian Review, 2021) as important catalysts of change. According to a judge in Northern Ireland, Gillen had given 'a tremendous impetus' to driving a new approach to cross-examining vulnerable witnesses (CAJ2).

Interviewees in England and Wales, and Scotland, agreed that a key driver of cultural change was the senior judiciary's determination to implement reforms through appellate court judgments, practice directions, and judicial training. One judge in England recalled a former Lord Chief Justice and other senior judges trying to change the culture by producing a video which made the point that 'actually a bullying cross-examination isn't a proper cross-examination' (ACJ2). A number of judicial interviewees noted that the leadership of senior judges empowered the judiciary to take the bold steps necessary to enforce the changes. The role of the Court of Appeal in particular was pivotal in making judges much more confident now 'about setting time limits, about scrutinising the proposed questions and about challenging them' (AAJ3). Without appellate guidance, judges would otherwise be in a difficult position when counsel are flagrantly breaking the rules of the Toolkits because 'the greatest fear for any judge is that there is a conviction and that is overturned because you have intervened too much, or you're accused of this, that or the other, because then the complainant has to go through the whole thing again' (CAJ4). One counsel also referred to the practice direction requiring judges to give juries directions about myths and stereotypes as having made 'a massive difference' in influencing the cross-examination of sexual complainants (ACC3). The directions were typically given at the end of the trial and practitioners seemed well aware of their potential to influence the jury:

> If you went in heavy in cross-examining a witness, especially a vulnerable witness about why they hadn't walked into their local police station and said 'I've been attacked by my husband' the morning after something had happened, you knew that what was going to happen was that you were going to be taken out at the knees by the judge's legal direction at the end of the case, do you see what I mean? (ACC3)

A judge in Scotland said that there had been a 'huge cultural push' since 2015 from the senior judiciary to change the approach to cross-examination, which had been very significant (BAJ1). It meant that 'judges like me, first instance judges, know that if I apply these rules I will be supported on appeal. Whereas I wouldn't have been confident of that 15 years ago'. She stated that the prosecution, defence, and judiciary had been very slow to catch up with changes and it was only when there was leadership from the top which included 'some quite savage criticism of judges who have failed to apply the rules that things changed and judges who wanted to apply the rules were give a lot of confidence'. One judge in Northern Ireland, by contrast, lamented the absence of any 'robust judgments from the Court of Appeal' in that jurisdiction, which 'would make things better' (CAJ4).

Interviewees highlighted the significant role that resident judges in specific court centres in England and Wales, as well as recorders in Northern Ireland, have played in reinforcing changes and setting an example. An advocate in England mentioned a judge in one of the areas piloting pre-recorded cross-examination, who took a leading role in vulnerable witness training. Similarly, a judge in Northern Ireland expressed her and another judge's eagerness to train the Bar to 'mould attitudes and change culture' (CAJ3).

She noted that she and a group of judges were 'leading from the front', and counsel appearing before her no longer needed reminders to consult The Advocate's Gateway because 'the good ones are all getting the message' (CAJ3).

While there was a consensus that the push from senior judges, resident judges, and recorders was instrumental in driving cultural change, some interviewees in England pointed to the transformative effect of vulnerable witness training, which had been rolled out by the Bar Council in 2017. As one counsel explained:

> In the space of a few months, awareness of the modern way that you're supposed to cross-examine a vulnerable witness just increased kind of infinite fold across the legal profession it seemed to me, and all of a sudden, judges across the piece were talking about, knowledgably about, the dos and the don'ts of cross-examination and expecting advocates to know. So that, for me, that was where the sea change occurred. (AAC3)

Although, as we have seen, there is a danger that training can become merely a tick-box exercise, a number of interviewees noted that it was beneficial not only in educating judges and advocates on how best to question vulnerable witnesses, but also in driving home the potentially traumatic effect on victims if questioning is not handled sensitively. One Irish judge referred to a video that was circulated as part of judicial training into how to conduct a very poor cross-examination, by contrast with the way it should be done according to best practice, and how there were a lot of techniques discussed in that particular video which would obviate the need for the vulnerable witness to be pressed in relation to matters in dispute (DAJ1). Another judge in England and Wales referred to a training course where she had seen a video in which a doctor had interviewed some adult women after they had given evidence and how traumatised they were by it; how they felt like they were being accused, that they were the ones on trial:

> Some of them you could understand why they might feel like that because there wasn't a conviction. Others, even after a conviction, still felt like that. Felt like they'd been violated all over again in some respects, which is interesting I thought. Because I don't think, when you've been in law for 20 years and you've been on this side of the fence, that you necessarily understand what it feels like to be a victim and what it feels like to be in the witness box. (AAJ2)

Several judges supported the requirement that judges must be 'ticketed' before being assigned to RASSO cases, meaning they must attend a course on serious sexual offences. Similarly, in England and Wales, advocates must undergo training before prosecuting such offences. A judge in Northern Ireland (CAJ2) suggested that mandatory training for all counsel involved in vulnerable witness cases would ensure they understand their responsibilities and that failing to adhere to questioning principles could constitute a breach of professional conduct.

However, there was also a belief that fostering a collaborative approach, as opposed to a disciplinary one, could be effective in changing legal culture. Such an approach involves everyone working together towards the common goal to do justice to the case. As one counsel in Ireland put it, 'everybody, in truth, is looking for solutions as opposed to problems' (DAC4). Despite differing perspectives and desired case outcomes, his experience was that 'nobody is being obstructionist, nobody is seeking to create trouble, everybody recognises that the system must work, and the best way to achieve it is through collaboration, working together, as opposed to simply being difficult'.

One way of instilling such an approach would be to organise joint training events which bring judges, advocates, and intermediaries together so that they can share experiences and learn about the experiences of other professional groups.[3] Another would be to establish court users' groups comprising judges, advocates, intermediaries, police, prosecuting agencies, witness services, and representatives from support groups to develop consistent practices towards issues such as familiarisation visits, the use of intermediaries, GRHs, and pre-recorded cross-examination. An exemplar in this respect is the court user group in Scotland that was chaired by a judge with representatives including prosecution and defence lawyers to identify problems, solve them, and develop shared understandings and good practice for making and deciding evidence on commission applications (Lord Beckett, 2023). In England, by contrast, there was a common perception among judges and advocates that the top-down nature of the roll-out of pre-recorded cross-examination to adult sexual complainants meant insufficient thought had been afforded to practical ramifications, such as the impact on the fairness of proceedings, and whether section 28 hearings were always necessary for more mature teenagers or for victims of historic sexual abuse.

Another factor that may account for the greater acceptance of taking evidence on commission in Scotland was that Scotland would seem to have invested in making it work more smoothly. As we saw in Chapter 3, the use of bespoke suites for taking evidence on commission meant there was no

[3] See Fairclough et al (2023), who recommend that intermediaries and the legal profession are brought together in a training environment to iron out misperceptions and promote a strong, respectful relationship.

need to pre-book time slots in courtrooms, which prevented other court business being undertaken. The recording and editing of the evidence on commission was also done by an in-house team rather than by an external service provider, which seemed to result in greater efficiency, with fewer technical problems and postponements.

Vulnerable defendants as outliers?

Although various steps have been taken across the jurisdictions to drive the pace of cultural change in the cross-examination of vulnerable witnesses, in Chapter 6 we noted instances where there was a disparity of treatment between vulnerable witnesses and vulnerable defendants (see also Cooper et al, 2024). There was a consensus among a number of interviewees that there has not been enough effort to change the culture of cross-examination of vulnerable defendants and that a marked contrast exists between the treatment of vulnerable witnesses and defendants. One judge commented: 'I don't think at the moment it seems to be applying across the board. I still find that defendants are being cross-examined in a more robust fashion' (ABJ4). According to another judge, cross-examination is adapted for vulnerable defendants 'to an extent, but much less so than it is with vulnerable prosecution witnesses' (ABJ3). Advocates gave examples of how vulnerable defendants were given no concessions in cross-examination, with one prosecution counsel admitting that the way he cross-examined vulnerable defendants was 'just worlds apart' from the way in which a defence barrister is allowed to cross-examine a vulnerable witness. One counsel told us that in his experience, prosecution counsel are not case managed in the same way as defence counsel (ABC1) and an intermediary observed that defendants 'are asked a lot more questions … It's almost like questioning for questioning's sake, at times' (ABR1).

The asymmetrical treatment of vulnerable witnesses and vulnerable defendants regarding special measures, at least in England and Northern Ireland (see Chapters 1 and 2), would therefore seem to have carried through into the manner in which vulnerable witnesses and defendants are cross-examined (Cooper at al, 2024). Various explanations can be given for this. One advocate said that although 'a huge percentage of defendants have mental health problems' (ACC4), there is an absence of information on just what defendants' vulnerabilities are and so accommodations are not made. One Scottish prosecutor posited that the criminal justice profession is so accustomed to defendant vulnerability that it has become the norm: 'actually, you see it so often that you stop seeing it' (BAC4). Counsel in England and Wales highlighted the structural obstacles to identification of the precise nature of a defendant's vulnerabilities. The prosecutor and judge are reliant on defence counsel to alert them to any issues, but the defence team are not well equipped to pick up on them. This differential treatment, however, is not simply explicable as a product of structural failure to identify need. Some interviewees described a criminal justice system lacking in commitment to equal treatment in terms of facilitating best evidence and a culture where, as Hoyano (2010) observed in relation to special measures support,[4] defendants are seen as less deserving of assistance to give their best evidence:

> I think for me, as a practitioner, the culture there is really very different and very far behind the way that we treat witnesses. (AAC4)

> If you're a witness, the chances are you are a victim, and you are therefore always treated more favourably than somebody who is accused of stabbing someone, hurting someone, sexually abusing them. (ABC1)

This was a point also made by practitioners in Scotland, with one solicitor advocate highlighting a similar level of inequality in reporting that 'the accused person or the defendant is very much an afterthought in most of the thinking and most of the planning', acknowledging that 'we're not really where we should be for the accused' (BAC4).

The view that there is a hierarchy between 'more deserving' vulnerable witnesses and 'less deserving' vulnerable defendants is illustrated particularly vividly in England and Wales. We saw in Chapter 4 that there was a reluctance to recognise that vulnerable defendants are as deserving of intermediary support as vulnerable witnesses. Consequently, GRHs are rarely held for vulnerable defendants. Even where an intermediary is appointed and a GRH is held, intermediaries reported that judicial directions to share and review prosecution questions for the defendant are infrequent. Although the English Court of Appeal has recognised the principle that defendants must be able to participate effectively in their trial in order to receive a fair trial (see Chapter 2), what would seem to be required is a greater push towards *equality* of participation for vulnerable defendants and vulnerable witnesses throughout the criminal process.

One step in this direction would be to change legislation to adopt the principle that vulnerable defendants are given the same access to special measures as vulnerable witnesses (see Fairclough, 2018a). This would include the same access to intermediaries by amalgamating the separate intermediary schemes for witnesses and defendants in England and Wales (see also Fairclough et al, 2023), with greater focus on whether defence

[4] See also Fairclough (2018b: 472).

intermediaries should be appointed before trial and for the duration of the trial itself.[5]

Above all, though, what seems to be needed is a greater cultural push from the judiciary and the legal profession for equality of treatment between vulnerable defendants and witnesses. Notably, there has been a different attitude from the beginning towards the appointment of defence intermediaries in Northern Ireland and Ireland. One intermediary in Northern Ireland explained that that there is 'a very strong sense here of human rights which I think is founded in the years and years of struggle that the legal profession has had in dealing with what some call a terrorist situation, and others call our little conflict' (CAR2). In his view, 'a very dynamic legal service had evolved in Northern Ireland with legally bright solicitors' practices setting up all over the place and providing an excellent service to their clients'. So when the idea of intermediaries being appointed began to be discussed, there was a strong view from solicitors that even though intermediaries were officers of the court, if the prosecution were going to have one, the defence should have one too. As a result, the registered scheme in Northern Ireland applies to both vulnerable witnesses and defendants and 'it wouldn't have moved off the ground, nor should it have, in my view, if it hadn't been a service for all'. It is also salient that in Ireland graduates from the recently established postgraduate Professional Diploma in Intermediary Studies are eligible to be placed on a panel to work as registered intermediaries (RIs) for both vulnerable witnesses and defendants (Delahunt, 2024). Judicial and counsel interviewees were also noticeably open to the idea that the defence may need an intermediary throughout the trial for vulnerable defendants to understand the issues and give instructions.

This ethos of equality in relation to access to intermediaries has carried through in Northern Ireland by the issue of protocols for vulnerable witnesses and defendants, which, as we saw in Chapter 3, applies the principle of best evidence to all witnesses, including the accused.[6] The protocols adopt identical criteria for when vulnerable witnesses and defendants should be assessed by a RI and for when a GRH should ordinarily be held. Notably, they also require that in the case of vulnerable witnesses *and* defendants, GRHs must be held *before* the trial to give legal representatives 'sufficient time to adapt their questions to the witnesses' needs'.[7] The protocols also set

[5] The Advocate's Gateway (2024) calls for holding a GRH for vulnerable defendants before the trial and, if the defendant later elects to give evidence, a second GRH should be arranged specifically to discuss how questioning should be conducted. See www.theadvocatesgateway.org/_files/ugd/1074f0_395da62674464adbabfccc9e2fa43827.pdf.

[6] Practice Direction No 2/2019 Annex A, A2.1, B2.1.

[7] Ibid, cf A5.2 and B5.2.

out identical requirements for both vulnerable witnesses and defendants in relation to the issues to be considered at the GRH and for the production of a trial practice note setting out any directions given or agreements made at the GRH, including 'where appropriate, formulated questions to be provided to the court in advance'.[8]

Broader cultural change and cross-examination

A further question is whether there has been a change of culture more broadly when it comes to the cross-examination of non-vulnerable witnesses. We have seen that judicial case management has led to stricter time limits on cross-examination than hitherto. Other changes to criminal procedure and evidence would seem to have altered advocates' approaches to cross-examination. Some interviewees pointed to how changes in rules of evidence such as restrictions on the admissibility of sexual history evidence and bad character evidence had had an effect in making cross-examination generally more forensic and less focused on the character of the complainant or the defendant.

A number of interviewees referred to the effect that rape shield legislation has had, not only in restricting the questions that can be asked, but also in making advocates think about questions which previously they would have asked, so that 'questions such as, "You were wearing a short skirt?" were asked at one time and are not asked now' (BAJ4). There was also a broad consensus that there was a greater awareness of the sort of rape myths that permeate sexual offences cases. As one counsel put it: 'We've moved a long, well we should have moved a long way, [from] the attitude that the female's clothes weren't ripped and she wasn't injured and she wasn't crying or distressed immediately after what had happened' (CAC1). Restrictions on bad character evidence more generally have also led to a pushback against putting witnesses' and defendants' character on trial during cross-examination. As one counsel put it:

> Someone's previous convictions, you are most likely to do that in a written document, which goes before the jury as part of agreed facts and you would make your comments about them in a speech, as opposed to saying to someone, 'Well, you're a burglar and a thief, aren't you?' Or, 'You're no better than you should be, are you? That's basically what you are'. I mean to someone in the new world, all of that would tend to be by agreed facts.[9] (ABC3)

---

[8] Ibid, cf A5.4–5 and B.5.4–5.

[9] For more on the tendency to admit character evidence by agreement, see Thomason (2021).

Alongside restrictions on the admissibility of character evidence, there has been a significant expansion of disclosure rules over the years. According to one experienced counsel in Northern Ireland (CAC2), this shift has made disclosure the focal point of trials, rather than cross-examination. With the availability of extensive information from primary, secondary, and third-party sources, there is now much greater potential to challenge the prosecution's case. In the past, counsel's primary strategy was to break down the witness's account. Cross-examination as to credit had much broader scope, allowing almost any question (CAC2). He recalled his first criminal trial, where senior counsel's opening question to the complainant was, 'Isn't it the case that your aunt has spent some time in a mental hospital?', with the complainant confirming 'Oh yes'. However, such a question would be 'totally unthinkable now … But that was perfectly permissible at the time … As time has gone on more information has been available to the cross-examiner, it's a much more clinical or forensic process' (CAC2).

This interplay between disclosure and cross-examination illustrates how cross-examination has been undergoing change in respect of non-vulnerable as well as vulnerable witnesses. Some advocates referred to the fact that there had been a change in the training towards encouraging a more focused approach in all cross-examination away from out-and-out advocacy with no holds barred. An advocate who had considerable experience of training on advocacy courses said that there had been a shift in the direction of what he called the 'Hampel method' of cross-examination, which he described as 'a more focused, forensic' approach to cross-examination which meant asking only what you needed to ask (ABC3). A Scottish solicitor advocate drew a contrast between the approach of practitioners steeped in older ways, who think they have to challenge every witness on absolutely everything, and his approach:

> So, you're trying to do, I suppose, kind of like the doctor, first do no harm. You certainly don't want to make the case any worse for your client. And that can happen if you blunder into it without having prepared properly. You want to lay the groundwork for the defence case that is to come, and then to highlight the areas where there are problems with the credibility or the reliability of the witness. (BAC4)

While the approach to cross-examining vulnerable witnesses has to be seen in the context of changes to cross-examination more broadly, there was also a view that the cross-examination of vulnerable witnesses has had a spillover effect on the cross-examination of non-vulnerable witnesses. One counsel considered that there was no conscious crossover, but because of the approach that was now taken with vulnerable witnesses there was a realisation that there were better ways of cross-examining witnesses in general and judges were more impatient of the old-style 'battering ram' kind of cross-examination than they used to be (ACC1). A judge considered there were transferable skills – breaking things down into topics and putting thought into a logical sequence of cross-examination, giving rather more thought to precise language, and concentration on getting as much information as possible in as few questions as possible – so that, 'if you do several cases with vulnerable witnesses, where you submit specific questions in advance, and then you go and do a case where you cross-examine an adult, I think some of that bleeds over' (AAJ2).

A number of judges and advocates considered that there was much to be said for transferring these skills to non-vulnerable witnesses as cross-examination can be more effective ultimately. As one judge put it:

> Good questioning is good questioning. You know, you identify the issues, you plan your cross-examination, you tailor it to the issues, you tailor it to the witness, and you go through it. Nothing is ever gained by repetition. Often things are lost in repetition. Nothing's ever gained by sloppy, ill-thought-out questions. So, I cannot see a downside to this. (AAJ3)

Another judge said she was a 'massive fan' of the new style of cross-examination, which was really no more than the way cross-examination used to be conducted:

> For 30, 40 years, we've had a very lazy style of cross-examination in the UK in general, where counsel is like a performing seal for want of a better word. No question of a witness is ever capable of an answer because in fact what it is, is a closing speech to the jury with the words 'isn't that right?' tied on at the end. (CAJ2)

She gave an example where there was a contradiction between two witnesses about whether a car was black or grey. With the witness who says it was black, there is no need to say to them that another witness will say it is grey:

> I need to have the professional discipline to establish with you that you're absolutely, completely and utterly convinced that it's black because it reminded you of your friend Joe who has a very black car just like that. And then I need to establish with [the other witness] that it was shiny, metallic grey, and then I close to the jury, 'These two witnesses cannot both be right. One is mistaken or both are mistaken. Either way, ladies and gentlemen, you cannot be sure.' That's advocacy. (CAJ2)

Another judge was optimistic that the new style of cross-examination of vulnerable witnesses would come to prevail because it was 'more effective and structured and therefore easier for the jury to understand' (CAJ3). There was a difference between the cross-examination of a child and an adult but 'it doesn't have to be fundamentally different' (CAJ3).

There is still a notable difference between the cross-examination of vulnerable and non-vulnerable witnesses, as supported by our linguistic analysis in the previous chapter. Interviewees contrasted the 'good old-fashioned advocacy' techniques that were still used with 'normal' adult witnesses – using 'the tone of their voice and the choice of their language to display their incredulity of the evidence that's being given, jumping around sometimes to discombobulate … wanting them to forget or accusing them of lying' (ABC1) – with the 'completely different skill set' required for child witnesses where a much less emotive approach is taken and 'you have to do things far more chronologically' (for example, ABJ2, ABC1). An advocate in Ireland mentioned that the discipline of asking focused questions to vulnerable witnesses had improved his cross-examination of other witnesses (DAC3). However, there was a difference in approach: with non-vulnerable witnesses, advocates might use them to weave a broader narrative, 'spreading the seeds' for their closing argument, whereas 'in a child sex case, you're not going to be doing that with a child'.

This raises intriguing questions about the extent to which the culture of cross-examination can be completely changed away from the advocacy model of cross-examination in an adversarial system where advocates will want to use witnesses to put their case to the jury. One intermediary who had a lot of experience of the family courts as well as the criminal courts considered that cross-examination was very different in the family courts. In her view, in the family courts 'the quality of the process is better because it's not so much about it being adversarial. It's about finding out the truth' (CAR2). She considered that the judges in these courts 'really seem to want to have a level playing field and they want to make sure that everyone is supported in understanding the cross-examination and giving their best evidence'. The absence of the jury meant that there was also less 'playing to the gallery' in family cases:

> So when a barrister is cross-examining or is taking their defendant through the evidence in chief, obviously, they're communicating with the defendant, but there's a lot of performing for the jury in terms of their body, their language, how they look, you know, how they look at a jury after a defendant's given their answer. And you don't have that performing in the family courts because it's a private court. There is no public gallery. There is no jury. And it's the judge.

In the final chapter we consider whether there needs to be more fundamental change in the criminal process if vulnerable witnesses and defendants are going to be truly enabled to give their best evidence.

8

Cross-Examination in Transition

This book has mapped the changes that have taken place to the way in which cross-examination is being conducted for the most vulnerable witnesses in adversarial criminal trials. But it is important to be aware that there are respects in which cross-examination more generally has been undergoing transition in recent decades. It has for a long time been a deep-seated part of lawyers' folklore that cross-examination is the centrepiece of the adversarial trial on which cases are won or lost. However, cross-examination of lay witnesses has diminished in significance as alternative forms of evidence have reduced the traditional reliance on oral evidence. It is true that the rise in child abuse cases, coupled with changes in the competency rules, has meant that children's evidence is now more common than hitherto. In 2011, Plotnikoff and Woolfson estimated that there had been a 60 per cent increase in the numbers of young witnesses being called to court. However, over 25 years ago the interdepartmental review of the treatment of vulnerable and intimidated witnesses, *Speaking Up for Justice*, which recommended changes in the competency rules, drew attention to the many different types of evidence that may make it less necessary to rely on the oral evidence of witnesses, such as forensic evidence and CCTV in public places (Home Office, 1998). To this may be added the heavy reliance that is now placed in criminal investigations on digital evidence given the rise of social media and the use of mobile phone footage. As mentioned in Chapter 5, in two of the 25 rape and serious sexual offences (RASSO) trials we observed that three child complainants were not called as witnesses and the case was proved by other evidence. Of course, other evidence will be presented by police officers and forensic scientists who will undergo cross-examination, but this itself marks a shift in the focus of cross-examination away from lay witnesses towards professional and expert witnesses.

In the previous chapter we noted that the conduct of cross-examination generally has also been undergoing change. As new case management systems drive greater efficiency and create pressure for counsel to agree facts, and time limits are imposed on cross-examination, the days are gone when counsel had freedom to contest every point against their case. We also saw there is a view that disclosure has replaced cross-examination as the centrepiece of the trial, providing defence counsel with much more information with which to challenge prosecution evidence, with the result that there is less reliance on denigrating the credibility of witnesses in cross-examination. The rules of evidence have also limited the degree to which character evidence and sexual behaviour evidence can be used to impugn witnesses' credibility.

We did not measure the extent to which cross-examination continues to be the centrepiece of adversarial criminal trials generally, but it would seem to be the case that its significance has been reduced in cases involving the most vulnerable witnesses. Our observations, backed up by interviewees, suggest that steps are routinely taken to curtail the length of cross-examination, and the use of intermediaries and GRHs means that the substance and nature of cross-examination are much more effectively policed. This chapter considers whether the changes that we have discussed throughout this book are succeeding in their aims of making cross-examination less stressful for witnesses and more conducive to them giving their best evidence. It also explores what further steps might be taken to drive change in this direction.

Improving the witness experience

It has been argued that when special measures were introduced three decades ago, the primary motivation arose out of 'an intrinsic concern for the humane treatment of the vulnerable in court' (Fairclough, 2021: 1067). The Pigot Committee (Home Office, 1989: para 2.14) considered that radical changes were needed if the courts were to treat children in a 'humane and acceptable way'. Pigot stopped short of criticising cross-examination practice, but there has since been an abundance of evidence which has shown that the kinds of questions vulnerable witnesses face in court can make cross-examination itself a painful experience. The question then arises whether the changes that we have discussed in this book have made cross-examination any less painful.

It is important to bear in mind that however much the tone and content of cross-examination may have changed, witnesses' and defendants' experience of it will be coloured by their general experience of the court process. Back in 1989, Pigot's concern for the welfare of children who have to give evidence in court stemmed from court delays which induce a 'sense of insecurity and uncertainty' and the intimidating atmosphere of having to give evidence in public (Home Office, 1989: para 2.10). Despite the introduction of special measures such as giving evidence by live link outside the courtroom, Plotnikoff and Woolfson (2012) considered that 20 years on there had been little progress on these two principal concerns and our research suggests this continues to be the case.

In 2018, a Young Witness Initiative protocol between the police, Crown Prosecution Service (CPS), and Her Majesty's Courts and Tribunals Service (HMCTS) was launched to fast-track cases involving witnesses under the age of ten so as to expedite the trial proceedings.[1] There has also been a successful pilot in Belfast Crown Court to fast-track serious sexual offences involving child witnesses under 13.[2] But delays caused by a backlog of cases and exacerbated by the COVID-19 pandemic have done little to improve the general experience of vulnerable witnesses in the criminal courts despite the roll-out of section 28 in England and Wales and the extension of taking evidence on commission in Scotland to include sexual complainants.

In 2016, an ambitious programme was launched in England and Wales to modernise the courts and tribunals system and improve access to justice for users of its services, including vulnerable groups (see Lord Chancellor et al, 2016). But the dominant narrative in much of the literature continues to highlight the immense difficulties that vulnerable witnesses experience in the court process and that giving evidence remains a traumatic experience for many such witnesses. A recent report by Victim Support found that although some recent innovations such as the introduction of independent sexual violence advisers (ISVAs) have been positive, overall the experience of victim-survivors of sexual violence before, during, and after the trial was profoundly negative (see Moroz and Dinisman, 2024). Many of the challenges align with our observations of trials involving various vulnerable witnesses, which were often disrupted by numerous adjournments, with the effectiveness of special measures also being undermined by inadequate technology. In England and Wales in particular we observed trials being delayed because of the poor quality of Achieving Best Evidence (ABE) recordings and pre-recorded cross-examinations having to be postponed when the recording failed.

Clearly, there is much work still to do to improve the quality of recordings and the environment where witnesses provide their evidence, and to reduce the disruption and delays in trials caused by incompatible IT systems and poor-quality footage.[3] Turning to the cross-examination experience itself, however, a central finding of our research is that courtroom practice of

---

1 www.cps.gov.uk/sites/default/files/documents/publications/police-cps-hmcts-ywi-protocol-2018.pdf.

2 See Protocol to Expedite Serious Sexual Offence Cases in Belfast and Antrim between PSNI, PPS, NICTS, DOJ, LSANI, Law Society of NI, Bar of NI, NSPCC Young Witness Service and Victim Support NI's Child Independent Sexual Violence Advocates (ChISVA). Issued on 2 September 2019 and extended to Antrim Crown Court on 1 September 2022.

3 Our final report to the Nuffield Foundation made a number of recommendations along these lines (Jackson et al, 2024: Part 5).

cross-examination differs considerably from the bleak mainstream narrative that witnesses continue to be bullied and berated by advocates. Legal professionals and intermediaries believe that changes to cross-examination, including GRHs and intermediaries, have improved the cross-examination experience of vulnerable witnesses and this was borne out in our trial observations and linguistic analysis. But it may be that the delays that witnesses have to endure before giving their evidence and the ordeal of coming to court to give evidence overshadow any benefits that have been achieved in the actual manner in which they are cross-examined. While we saw many instances of good practice, many inconsistencies were also apparent in terms of the use of intermediaries, the conduct of GRHs, and adherence to the principles set out in The Advocate's Gateway and in the Inns of Court Advocacy guidance. Overall, the landscape is patchy and incongruous, suggesting that witnesses' experiences of cross-examination are likely to be unpredictable and subject to significant variation.

The impact of the changes would seem to have been most marked in the cases of young children who provided the impetus for the original rulings of the English Court of Appeal on the need for cross-examination to change. For example, the average length of cross-examination for child witnesses was 12 minutes. By contrast, we found that the length of cross-examinations for complainants in sexual offence trials was longer than for vulnerable witnesses in other trials, although the average length of 46 minutes was less than much mainstream narrative has suggested. In the recent Victim Support survey, victim-survivors complained that the length of their cross-examinations, which varied from five hours to two days, made the whole experience more arduous (Moroz and Dinisman, 2024: 39). In our research, very few child witnesses were directly challenged as liars, although, as we have seen, one child defendant was challenged in this manner. There were differences in perception among interviewees on the extent of the improvement there has been in the cross-examination experience of sexual offence complainants, and we did, albeit infrequently, observe instances where adult sexual offence complainants were explicitly accused of lying by defence counsel.

Of course, it is important to be aware when surveying witnesses' experience of cross-examination that few witnesses will positively enjoy testifying under any conceivable procedural arrangement (Cooper and Roberts, 2005). It is also important to acknowledge that for victim witnesses as well as defendants there is more at stake than just the experience of giving evidence. For all witnesses, the shorter the time they undergo cross-examination and the 'softer' it is, the less pain they will endure. But for victims and defendants, who both have a stake in the outcome of the proceedings, it may be more in their interests to endure the short-term pain of being challenged under cross-examination in order to have their voice fully heard. The need to ensure that vulnerable witnesses are treated humanely does not just entail protecting them from an intimidating environment and unnerving questioning. As Cooper and Roberts (2005: 19) note, the principle entails affording 'due consideration and respect to victims and other witnesses' genuine interests and concerns'.

This resonates with the emerging international right of witnesses, victims, and defendants to be able to participate effectively in any legal proceedings. The significance of effective participation was highlighted by one counsel in our research who said that 'very often now you deal with witnesses and their experience of the process is that it's so anodyne that they [think], "Well, when am I actually going to be asked a difficult question?"'. His view was that 'sometimes we are better to support a witness well through a difficult process than to make the process so easy that they don't get a chance to tell their story properly' (ACC1). A judge pondered the potential tension between the negative experience of giving evidence and the eventual prospect of justice being secured:

> If the question is what's worse for the witness, being slightly upset or confused in the trial, or getting … an acknowledgement that this has happened to them, so that they can get closure … They want to know that someone was brought to justice for it and was punished. If the reality is they're less upset at the trial, but the result is that there is no conviction, which is actually better? … It's [a question] I've asked myself quite a lot. (AAJ1)

Notably, in the recent Victim Support survey, although all the victim survivors described cross-examination as a negative experience, some considered it to be an empowering experience once it was over. They felt they had their day in court and were able to stand up and tell the story of what had happened to them.

Achieving best evidence

The other motivation for special measures which has carried through to the motivation for the changes to cross-examination has been the need to achieve best evidence. 'Achieving best evidence' has become a mantra among policy makers and judges across the jurisdictions we surveyed and is referenced in the recent reports that examined the conduct of sexual offence cases in Northern Ireland, Ireland, and Scotland (see respectively Gillen Review, 2019; O'Malley Review, 2020; Dorrian Review, 2021). However, the term has been curiously under-theorised in the literature. It first gained prominence among government policy makers in England and Wales, who used it to highlight concern about the system's inability to convict those offending against children and other vulnerable people due to the lack of admissible evidence of good quality. Although *Speaking Up for Justice* (Home Office, 1998) referred to the need to have regard to the emotional trauma of witnesses, the goal of achieving best evidence was written specifically into its term of reference by the requirement 'to encourage vulnerable witnesses including those likely to be subject to intimidation to give evidence of crime and enabling them to give best evidence in court'. Nowhere, however, was the term defined. In its early usage, it seems to have been equated with the need to achieve the best evidence in the case for the prosecution in order to secure a conviction. Although the Youth Justice and Criminal Evidence Act 1999 makes no reference to the term, in the years since its passage it became more synonymous with improving the quality of a witness's evidence whether it ultimately supports the prosecution case or not. Under the Act, judges had to determine whether the use of special measures would be likely to improve the quality of evidence the witness gives, with quality defined in terms of 'completeness, coherence and accuracy' (s 16(5)).

At one level, it can be argued that there is a fundamental conflict between the aims of cross-examination and criminal justice objectives, with government policy focusing on facilitating 'best evidence' and cross-examination aiming at 'persuading witnesses to adopt an alternative version of events or discrediting their evidence' (Plotnikoff and Woolfson, 2012: 22). But as we observed in Chapter 5, it is problematic to equate 'best evidence' with evidence supporting a particular party's case or with accurate or truthful evidence. The courts have seen it instead as eliciting from the witness 'the best evidence of which he or she is capable'.[4] Criminal Practice Directions now require the courts to take 'every reasonable step' to enable 'a witness or the accused to give their best evidence'.[5] Whether it is assessed as credible or not is a matter for the trier of fact. As the Court of Appeal stated in *R v Barker* ([2010] EWCA Crim 4 [40]), 'the purpose of the trial process is to identify evidence that is reliable and that which is not whether it comes from the adult or the child'. This did not mean that there was no place for cross-examination. But it did mean that in the case of young children a fundamental shift in approach was necessary, away from the advocacy model where it is used as a tool of persuasion or denigration towards a more forensic approach where, as we have seen, the Court said that 'short, simple questions' can be used to test whether the child is lying or mistaken. This required the advocate to 'forgo much of the kind of contemporary cross-examination which consists of no more than comment which will be put before the jury in any event from different sources' (at [42]).

[4] See eg *R v Barker* [2010] EWCA Crim 4 [42], cited with approval in *R v Lubemba* [2014] EWCA Crim 2064 [38].

[5] Criminal Practice Directions 2023, 6.1.1.

Achieving best evidence, then, would seem to be best described as a process which enables witnesses of all kinds, whatever their vulnerabilities, to voice their recollection of events in the best way they can. This also has resonance with the right to effective participation. Cross-examination can and should play a role in this process so far as it assists in assessing whether they are voicing their true recollection. The question then is whether the changes that have taken place to cross-examination are contributing to this form of 'best evidence'. Although, as we have seen, achieving best evidence has not been prioritised for vulnerable defendants, it is important to include defendants in debates on how best evidence might be enhanced as it is hard to see why, as a matter of equality of arms, they should be deprived of adaptations that are made for vulnerable witnesses.

However well questions are tailored to the vulnerabilities of the witness, the responses of the witness will be coloured by the timing and context in which they are asked. As Pigot recognised many years ago, many of the factors that impact detrimentally on children's welfare when giving evidence in court, such as delays and an intimidating environment, will also have a mutually detrimental effect on the 'integrity of the evidence' (Home Office, 1989: para 2.9). Interviewees drew our attention to measures that had been taken to support witnesses, such as familiarisation visits to the court and initiatives such as the CPS protocol 'Speaking to Witnesses at Court', where prosecuting counsel explain to witnesses what issues may come up in cross-examination.[6] But it remains unclear what impact these have had on the quality of the evidence that witnesses give during cross-examination.

Another question that was raised by a number of interviewees was whether the move away from giving direct evidence in the courtroom has enhanced the quality of the evidence that vulnerable witnesses give. While interviewees acknowledged that remote testimony had the benefit of not exposing vulnerable witnesses to the ordeal of giving evidence in the courtroom, a number took the view that it did not help them achieve their best evidence because such procedures lack the immediacy of cross-examination, 'where you can put someone on the spot and correspondingly, when a witness comes back at you with an answer, that just completely bowls you over' (ACC3). Recent research discussed in Chapter 3, suggesting that juries experience pre-recorded cross-examination differently than they do other forms of live cross-examination (Thomas, 2024), would seem to caution against the Law Commission's (2023) recommendation that all complainants in sexual offences prosecutions be automatically entitled to pre-record their evidence, including evidence-in-chief, cross-examination, and re-examination. At the same time, we need to be careful about drawing any definitive conclusion

[6] See www.cps.gov.uk/legal-guidance/speaking-witnesses-court.

from such data that there is something inherently defective about pre-recorded cross-examination. As Thomas (2024) acknowledges, one possible explanation for the lower conviction rates found in cases using section 28 evidence is that such cases are 'inherently weaker' than those cases where section 28 is not used. It has also been pointed out, by Thomas (2024) and others (Kyneswood, 2022, 2024), that the differences in conviction rates may be attributable to the poor quality and presentation of pre-recorded evidence under the present arrangements, which would suggest that the emphasis should be on improving the quality, consistency, and presentation of pre-recorded evidence at trial rather than on pausing its roll-out.

Regarding the tone and content of cross-examination, much effort has been expended in training on acquainting legal professionals with the principles set out in The Advocate's Gateway and in the Inns of Court Advocacy guidance. But we saw in Chapter 6 that there is not only some way to go to ensure that there is consistent adherence to these principles; there is also a continuing need to update the guidance to ensure that it is informed by the best linguistic expertise. Not all tagged questions are necessarily confusing for vulnerable witnesses and, conversely, the dangers of questions such as 'do you agree?' need to be reflected in the guidance. So much depends on the vulnerabilities of each witness to be cross-examined, and, as Chapter 4 illustrated, the input of intermediaries was widely acknowledged as valuable as they are uniquely qualified to carry out a case-by-case assessment of the communication challenges each individual witness faces. An alternative (or additional) approach could entail enacting specific legislation to impose a judicial duty (over and above that at common law) to curtail improper or overly aggressive questioning. Such an approach has been followed by several Australian jurisdictions,[7] but has been criticised for its lack of enforcement, with research suggesting that it is 'exercised sparingly and varies from judge to judge' (Cossins, 2020: 236–7).

One point of contention is whether the pendulum has swung too far in the direction of protecting certain vulnerable witnesses, such as children, at the expense of them giving their best evidence. This was neatly summarised

[7] The Uniform Evidence Acts in New South Wales, Victoria, Tasmania, the Australian Capital Territory, and the Northern Territory provide courts with a broad discretion to make any such order that they consider just in relation to the way in which witnesses are to be questioned (s 26), and it may even order that the witness give evidence completely or partly in narrative form (s 29). In addition, section 41 of the Uniform Acts stipulates that the court must disallow any improper questions put to a witness if that question: (a) is misleading or confusing; (b) is unduly annoying, harassing, intimidating, offensive, oppressive, humiliating, or repetitive; (c) is put to the witness in a manner or tone that is belittling, insulting, or otherwise inappropriate; (d) has no basis other than a stereotype (see further Doak et al, 2021).

by one counsel: 'It depends what the purpose of best practice is. If it's to give the witnesses as comfortable an experience as possible, and to help them cope with questions, then yes. Does it actually produce the most powerful and truthful evidence? Not necessarily' (AAC5). This resonates with findings from a study by Carline et al (2020: 64), in which barristers involved in RASSO cases made a distinction between the ABE or investigative interview which is concerned with producing best evidence and barristers' concern with what amounts to 'persuasive or affective evidence' which improves the prospects of their case. Indeed, we saw in the last chapter that several advocates felt that judges had overstepped in managing questions down to the point where witnesses are asked nothing more than the most anodyne of questions with the result that cross-examination did not appear to serve any purpose at all. Although it was accepted that young children can only cope with the simplest of questions, older children and vulnerable adult complainants could often cope with more challenging questions. Again, it would seem that intermediaries have a pivotal role to play in assessing just how probing questions should be.

We were unable to draw definitive conclusions on the extent to which judges are deploying excessive case management at ground rules hearings and there is scope for further research on the way GRHs are managed. We have seen that judges and intermediaries have played a significant role in framing the questions that vulnerable witnesses will be asked. Cross-examination has undoubtedly been undergoing a transition away from the traditional approach, where it was largely an unmediated process of question and answer between advocates and witnesses. A much more forensic approach has been adopted, moving away from a model where questions were interlaced with comment. However, it is too early to conclude that a 'best evidence' model of cross-examination has become the norm in the contemporary trial. No matter how robustly cases are managed by judges, it is important to acknowledge that the criminal trial continues to be based on an adversarial system of party control where it is the parties, not the judge or intermediaries, who initiate the content of the questions asked (Thomason, 2021).

This raises the more fundamental question as to whether the adversarial structure is itself preventing witnesses from giving their best evidence. This concern is not new (Birch, 2000; Ellison, 2001; Doak, 2008); Henderson (2016: 196) has neatly encapsulated the conceptual tension between cross-examination as an 'investigative interview', probing the truthfulness and completeness of the witnesses' evidence, and cross-examination as 'an opportunity for advocacy'. We have seen that efforts have been made to eliminate comment in the cross-examination of vulnerable witnesses. However, as long as the criminal trial remains adversarial, it is doubtful that advocates will allow witnesses the freedom to fully recount their experiences. The ongoing trauma witnesses face while giving evidence also raises concerns about whether the adversarial trial is a suitable forum for witness testimony. In the next section we focus on more radical solutions that seek to maximise the effective participation of vulnerable witnesses, victims, and defendants.

Towards more radical solutions

From victim advocacy to independent legal representation

Over the last 20 years there has been a rise in the role of victim advocacy across many jurisdictions, with professional staff trained to support and advocate for victims, particularly in sexual assault and domestic abuse cases. However, the funding for such schemes has been patchy and different names have been given to the professionals involved – variously described as 'advocates', 'advisers', or 'support workers' – which has not helped to clarify the nature of their role. Statutory provision is made in Scotland for a 'supporter' to sit alongside vulnerable witnesses and in Ireland for complainants in sexual offences to be accompanied by a 'support worker' described as a volunteer or someone employed in an organisation which provides support to victims of crime.[8] But in England and Wales and in Northern Ireland there is only statutory provision for supporters to accompany vulnerable witnesses who give evidence by live link.[9] Beyond this, the court may, through its inherent jurisdiction, permit supporters to accompany witnesses in the courtroom and sit next to them when they give evidence.[10]

A recent report by the Victims Commissioner in England and Wales highlighted the benefits of advocacy for victims navigating a system that is unfamiliar to them (see Welland et al, 2024). But there was inconsistency in the funding arrangements and gaps in advocacy services for those victims, particularly of domestic abuse, who were assessed as medium and low risk. Advocates experienced challenges in terms of perception of their professional status and court officials often appeared unfamiliar with the victim advocate role or purpose. As a result, considerable variability was noted around whether court officials would allow ISVAs to accompany victims into courtrooms. In our observed trials, there was inconsistency in the use of supporters to assist witnesses and on occasion intermediaries appeared to step into a supporting role, which we have seen raises questions about the

8 Criminal Procedure (Scotland) Act 1995, ss 271H and 271L; Criminal Law (Rape) Act 1981, s 6(3)(5); Criminal Justice (Victims of Crime) Act 2017, s 20.

9 Youth Justice and Criminal Evidence Act 1999, s 24(1A); Criminal Evidence (Northern Ireland) Order 1999, art 14 (1A).

10 For commentary, see Law Commission (2023: 7.199). In certain other jurisdictions the 'supporter' need not be human. It has been claimed that the use of therapy dogs/'canine companions' can reduce anxiety for some witnesses and assist with the communication of their evidence (see further Cooper, 2020: 151–4).

boundaries of their role. At present there is no one charged with working to create the conditions in which the vulnerable witness can give the best evidence they are capable of. Intermediaries appear currently to come the closest to fulfilling this role, but intermediary support is not appropriate for all vulnerable witnesses and furthermore it may have implications for the neutral role that we have seen intermediaries pride themselves as playing.

A more radical option might involve the appointment of a state-funded independent legal representative (ILR). Although the use of ILRs is generally debated in the context of rape and sexual offences cases, there is no reason why the mechanism could not also be rolled out to other vulnerable witnesses.[11] While schemes differ in terms of the standing and powers of the representative and the points at which they can intervene in the criminal process, most provide an opportunity for representations to be made on issues pertaining to privacy and dignity, including applications to introduce sexual history evidence, sensitive digital evidence, and other third-party materials (Braun, 2014, 2019; Kirchengast, 2016; Iliadis et al, 2021a). It is thus widely acknowledged that they hold the potential to empower complainants through increasing their sense of voice, control, and validation as well as providing better information (Iliadis, 2020: 100).

Of the four jurisdictions we studied, Ireland is currently the only system which provides for ILRs. First introduced in 2001,[12] the ILR's role is limited to making representations at pre-trial hearings where the defence apply for leave to cross-examine the complainant in relation to her sexual history with anyone other than the accused[13] or where the defence seek to disclose counselling records.[14] Although widely lauded when first introduced, the scheme has been criticised on the grounds of its narrow remit, the inherent constraints of the adversary system, and its potential to perpetuate myths around sexuality and rape (Iliadis, 2020). The O'Malley Review (2020: 69) has proposed to expand the remit of ILRs to empower them to object to a particular line of questioning in cross-examination, though it remains to be seen whether this recommendation will be implemented.

In England and Wales, an attempt was made to amend the Police, Crime, Sentencing and Courts Bill 2021 in order to introduce ILR for complainants in applications to admit evidence of previous sexual behaviour, but this was rejected before the Bill was subsequently enacted (Law Commission, 2023: 367). Recently, however, the Law Commission (2023: 396) has

[11] See eg Iliadis et al (2021b), advocating its use in the context of domestic abuse.

[12] Criminal Law (Rape) Act 1981, s 4A, inserted by the Sex Offenders Act 2001, s 34.

[13] These are known as 'section 3' hearings: Criminal Law (Rape) Act 1981, s 3. Responsibility for enforcement lies with the trial judge.

[14] Criminal Evidence Act 1992, s 19A(9), as amended by the Criminal Law (Sexual Offences) Act 2017.

provisionally recommended (pending consultation) that ILR should be introduced for complainants in sexual offence cases 'for advice, assistance and to make representations on requests and applications for personal records and the admission of under section 41 of the Youth Justice and Criminal Evidence [regarding sexual history evidence]'.

In Scotland, a previous attempt to introduce ILR was thwarted in 2015, although the Dorrian Review (2021: 85–6) triggered a fresh debate in proposing a similar scheme to that of Ireland, whereby the ILR's role would be circumscribed to making representations on applications to admit sensitive records or sexual history evidence. Despite the Review noting that implementing legislation would be required, there seems to be a lack of capacity to do so given the degree of 'stress the criminal justice system is currently under, and the scarcity of legal representation' (Cowan et al, 2024: 12).

Similarly, the Gillen Review (2019: 173) also proposed the introduction of ILRs at GRHs in Northern Ireland, stating that legal representatives should 'resist applications for disclosure' where the relevance of applications to adduce third-party evidence can be brought into question, in addition to opposing applications to admit sexual history evidence and providing general legal support up to (but not including) the point of trial. Like Ireland and Scotland, Gillen's proposals fell short of representation within the trial itself, although the door was left ajar with the possibility that 'consideration be given to and a cost analysis made of extending legal representation during examination-in-chief and cross-examination at the trial itself after the recommendations above … have been piloted and analysed'.[15] More radical forms of ILR where representations can be made during the trial are now in place in other jurisdictions including the International Criminal Court, India, Namibia, and the US military, while many 'quasi-adversarial' jurisdictions such as Sweden, Denmark, and Norway have similar arrangements (Braun 2019; Daly and Smith, 2020).

Juryless trials

As we saw in Chapter 3, there was a general view among interviewees that when the jury is absent during cross-examination, as during pre-recorded cross-examination, there was 'less showboating from the advocates because you're not playing to an audience' (ABC1) and the questioning is 'much shorter, more focused and less confrontational' (ABJ4). According to a Scottish judge, there is something very powerful about the presence of a jury, which is like an audience that inflames 'the theatrical gene' within advocates, and when you take the jury away, they behave very differently (BAJ1). This raises the question whether the jury itself may be an obstacle to achieving best evidence.

[15] Gillen Review (2019: 187). See further Iliadis et al (2021a).

As we have seen, counsel interviewees were acutely aware of the need to gear their questioning to how they think it will be received by the jury. This would seem to have a positive effect in deterring the worst kinds of cross-examination. As one counsel put it:

> Simply being a posh barrister who tells … the witness that they're lying or made it up or they're unreliable. That just doesn't really work anymore. If at any point you appear to be bullying a witness or just using your position as a formal member of the courts to just attack someone in their evidence without any foundation to that attack then you just look appalling. I think the jury take against barristers or other advocates who behave in that way very quickly, and that impression is disastrous and very difficult to reverse. (ACC3)

But as we observed in one trial in Chapter 5, jurors may also turn against defendants when vulnerable complainants, particularly those in RASSO trials, are subject to perfectly proper searching cross-examination.

Apart from the effect the jury has in influencing the tone and content of cross-examination, it is important to note that when the jury is withdrawn, the structure of the trial necessarily shifts away from adversarial presentation of evidence by the parties as professional triers of fact come to exercise a much more pervasive influence over the proceedings than lay triers of fact could ever achieve (Jackson and Doran, 1995: 294). In particular, the focus shifts away from the oral evidence of the witnesses towards other evidence to which professional judges become privy. Spencer (2012: 196) has noted that in cases where children's evidence is tested in the civil courts, judges are able to take a much more 'holistic approach' because both rules of evidence and the method of trial are radically different from those in operation in criminal proceedings. In criminal trials, the focus of attention inevitably centres on the oral evidence of the witness in the form of ABE interviews and cross-examination. In civil trials, judges can consider a mass of documentary evidence, much of it hearsay, which is put together in a file that together with the oral evidence forms the focus of argument. Spencer concluded in the case of young children that 'it is difficult to avoid the conclusion that the methods used in the civil courts to evaluate the truth or otherwise of the evidence … are much more rational than the methods – or to be accurate, the one and only method, namely cross-examination – relied on by the criminal courts' (Spencer, 2012: 198). However, he considered that the 'totemic' regard in which jury trial is held in serious criminal cases made any rational discussion of the merits of jury trial near impossible.

There has been a greater willingness to consider juryless trials in recent years, notably in sexual offence cases (see Gillen Review, 2019; Dorrian Review, 2021; Law Commission, 2023). Other jurisdictions operate jury waiver schemes which enable juryless trials (see Doran and Jackson, 1997), and the time has perhaps come for a more rational debate about the merits of such a procedure. It has to be acknowledged, however, that the 'totemic' regard for jury trials is still strong in a number, although by no means all, common law systems. Another approach would be to reinforce the importance of taking witness testimony (including cross-examination) as early as possible before trial in order to secure early best evidence from witnesses and spare them the ordeal of coming to court by permitting a pre-trial judge to offer a sentence on the basis of the papers and the pre-trial testimony elicited in the case if the defendant were to plead guilty. Defendants would still be able to opt for a full jury trial if they refused to plead guilty, without perhaps the guarantee that the sentence will not be more severe if they are convicted at trial than the one proposed before trial (see Jackson and Weigend, 2022). Several variations on such a model would be possible with the aim of reducing full trials as much as possible in order that witnesses can give their best evidence before trial.

The impact of therapeutic jurisprudence

It is clear that cross-examination can still be traumatic for many vulnerable witnesses, notwithstanding the range of new procedures that have been introduced to mitigate its impact. Proponents of the therapeutic jurisprudence movement, which emerged in the 1990s, have argued that the legal system, its rules, and its actors often undermine the well-being of its users. The movement is underpinned by a central belief that lawyers and policy makers can seek to reduce anti-therapeutic aspects of the legal process while simultaneously enhancing its therapeutic effects by studying the emotions and psychological experiences of victims and offenders (Wexler and Winick, 1998). While lawyers cannot be expected to act as therapists, and trials cannot provide a substitute for psychological interventions, Wexler (2005: 748) contends that justice processes, and their key players, hold the potential to operate as 'change agents', whereby victims and witnesses are offered respect and space to tell their story and air their emotions.

Although the paradigm has not been without its critics (see, for example, Slobogin, 1995; Arrigo, 2004), it has had a significant impact on the course of law reform in subsequent decades, spurring creative and holistic approaches in many spheres (King et al, 2014). Therapeutic jurisprudence has been highly influential in catalysing new streams of research on issues such as vulnerability (for example, Fineman, 2013; Cooper and Norton, 2017; Cooper, 2018; Dehaghani, 2019; Farrugia, 2024) and the potential benefits of trauma-informed approaches (for example, Cossins, 2020; James, 2020). The discourse has underlined the impacts of vulnerability and resilience on an individual and collective level, as evidenced by the ascendancy of health–justice partnerships (Forell and McCarron, 2024); problem-solving courts (Winick, 2002; King et al, 2014); diversionary and rehabilitation initiatives, including restorative justice (Wexler, 2005; Doak, 2011; King et al, 2014); and creating new avenues for victim participation (Erez et al, 2011). Consequently, we now have a much clearer understanding of the specific practices that can distress witnesses and undermine the quality of their evidence, as well as the benefits of new mechanisms which can reduce secondary victimisation and help them to give best evidence.

Given the anti-therapeutic nature of cross-examination, there have been calls to dispense with the process altogether. While the adoption of an inquisitorial model seems implausible in the medium term at least, it has been suggested that evidence in its entirety could be taken in an investigative interview by an independent, trauma-informed examiner (Bowden et al, 2014; JUSTICE, 2019; Cossins, 2020). The Nordic *Barnahus* (Children's House) system was cited by some of our interviewees as an exemplar of best practice in this regard (see Chapter 7; see further Bowden et al, 2014; Council of Europe, 2018). The model is underpinned by an interdisciplinary and multi-agency approach to respond to child welfare concerns and criminal investigations in cases of violence or sexual abuse against children. It is used for both investigative and therapeutic purposes, with the child's best interests placed at the heart of the process (Myklebust, 2017; Council of Europe, 2018). In its purist form in many Nordic jurisdictions, it operates to elicit all the evidence of child witnesses and, increasingly, that of complainants in cases of sexual violence. The interview is conducted at an early stage in the investigation, at a remote location, with an intermediary receiving questions from advocates via an earpiece. It is then played back at trial, without the need for any further involvement of the witness. As Cossins (2020: 252) explains, lawyers and judges who are untrained in child development may lack the specialist knowledge to recognise the signs of stress or confusion and 'are imbued with adversarial modes of interacting with witnesses, something that does not apply to speech therapists, social workers and other professionals employed as intermediaries'.

The model is in the process of being rolled out in Scotland and Ireland, has been piloted in England, and has been recommended (though not yet developed) in Northern Ireland (see further Devaney et al, 2024). However, at the current time there are no imminent plans in any of these jurisdictions to substitute existing provisions on cross-examination with a self-standing investigative interview,[16] despite calls by the Scottish Courts and Tribunals

[16] This has been explicitly ruled out by the Scottish Government (2021: 14): 'Questioning of the witness will still be carried out by defence and prosecution lawyers, with a video recording being played during the trial.'

Service (2016) and the Gillen Review (2019: 146).[17] As noted in the previous chapter, some Scottish interviewees also expressed a preference for the *Barnahus* approach.

Like many of the other initiatives discussed, this would likely be seen in some quarters as an anathema to the adversarial tradition, but evidence on commission in Scotland has shown that evidence in its entirety can be pre-recorded and played to the court without the need for subsequent cross- or re-examination. While Cossins (2020) argues that the adversarial system in its entirety needs to be usurped by a comprehensive trauma-informed system, there is no reason in principle that such an arrangement could not operate within an adversarial context. It would, however, likely require legislation, a code of practice, and an appropriate regime of training and accreditation. Such specialist examiners could be appointed as officers of the court, as intermediaries currently are, with an overriding duty to elicit best evidence. While many intermediaries would be well equipped to fulfil such a role where the witness has difficulties in communication, it could equally be performed by a trauma-informed practitioner or other healthcare professional as appropriate.

Looking towards the future

The underlying adversarial nature of the criminal trial lies at the root of both practitioner and academic concerns around the feasibility of implementing some of the more radical measures discussed. Although the adversarial/inquisitorial dichotomy has some value as a model, the terms should not be used as definitive typologies. In addition to the influence of therapeutic jurisprudence, other trends such as international convergence and 'borrowing' (Schwikkard, 2008; Colson and Field, 2016) and managerialism (McEwan, 2011) have prompted the notion that 'pure systems no longer exist' (Spencer, 2016: 601). These developments bring into question the adversarial/inquisitorial dichotomies that have long characterised national criminal procedures and encouraged greater experimentation with mixed converging models (Jackson, 2021). As outlined in Chapter 2, the current steer on international best practice would appear to align with a notion of 'participatory proof' (see further Jackson, 2005; Jackson and Summers, 2012), and the quest for best practice is no longer restricted to the boundaries of

[17] While acknowledging logistical and resourcing issues in establishing such a scheme, Gillen recommended that all child victims under 16 should be taken by an expert forensic interviewer and pre-recorded with no questioning by lawyers at all in the majority of cases. Such a measure occasionally for child complainants under 18 and for vulnerable adult complainants very occasionally (Gillen Review, 2019: 4.61).

individual nation states (Misileglas et al, 2015). While adversarialism remains ingrained in the legal structures of most common law jurisdictions, in those that we have studied (to a greater or lesser degree), the nature of cross-examination in the criminal courts has undergone a fundamental change in its normative stance towards the quest for best evidence. These changes have acted as a catalyst in re-examining the operation of the courts, the role of lawyers, and the ways in which lawyers of the future are educated, with an increasing focus on alternatives to the conventional adversarial narrative (King et al, 2014: 263). Irrespective of which labels are applied, the adversarial ethos underpinning the criminal justice system shapes how lawyers behave within it (King et al, 2014). Freiberg (2011) has outlined a vision of post-adversarial and post-inquisitorial justice as one in which courts no longer simply resolve disputes or punish offenders, but become places where trauma is healed, offenders are rehabilitated, and societal problems are solved.

The COVID-19 pandemic provided new insights into the reflexiveness and responsiveness of the criminal justice system. The pandemic catalysed the use of video technology in courts and as a result a 'new normal' may be emerging whereby eliciting evidence in this way becomes more mainstream and accepted by parties (Doak and Jackson, 2021; Rossner, 2021). There is a need for more research generally on a broad level as to how such changes may impact upon the value of live cross-examination in general, but also how special measures of all kinds are being implemented; and in particular a need to monitor whether the new procedures governing cross-examination are effecting change on the ground. There remains much more work to do before a comprehensive assessment can be made of the manner in which different kinds of vulnerable witnesses are cross-examined and the impact of recent changes as a whole.

References

International instruments

Council of Europe (1950). Convention for the Protection of Human Rights and Fundamental Freedoms. ECHR. Rome: 4 November 1950

Council of Europe (2011). Convention on Preventing and Combating Violence Against Women and Domestic Violence. Istanbul Convention. Istanbul: 11 May 2011

Council of Europe (2010). Guidelines of the Committee of Ministers of the Council of Europe on Child-Friendly Justice. Strasbourg: 17 November 2010

European Commission (2013). Recommendation of 27 November 2013 on Procedural Safeguards for Vulnerable Persons Suspected or Accused in Criminal Proceedings 2013/C 378

European Union (2010). Directive 2012/29/EU (the Victims' Rights Directive)

International Criminal Court (2019). Rules of Procedure and Evidence *RPE*. The Hague: 4 March 2019

Organization of American States (1969). American Convention on Human Rights. ACHR. San José: 22 November 1969

United Nations (1966). International Covenant on Civil and Political Rights. ICCPR. New York: 6 December 1966

United Nations (1989). Convention on the Rights of the Child. UNCRC. New York: 20 November 1989

United Nations (1998). Rome Statute of the International Criminal Court. New York: 17 July 1988

United Nations (2005). Guidelines on Justice in Matters Involving Child Victims and Witnesses of Crime (GA/RES/2005/20). New York: 22 July 2005

United Nations (2006). Convention on the Rights of Persons with Disabilities. CRPD. New York: 13 December 2006

United Nations (2019). General Comment No 24 (2019) on Children's Rights in Juvenile Justice; CRC/C/GC/24

Legislation

England and Wales

Criminal Justice Act 1992
Criminal Law (Rape) Act 1981
Criminal Law (Sexual Offenders) Act 2017
Criminal Practice Directions 2015
Criminal Practice Directions 2023
Criminal Procedure Rules 2020
Coroners and Justice Act 2009
England and Wales Coronavirus Act 2020
Mental Health Act 1983
Police, Crime, Sentencing and Courts Act 2022
Sex Offenders Act 2001
Youth Justice and Criminal Evidence Act 1999

Ireland

Children Act 2001
Criminal Law (Rape) Act 1981
Criminal Evidence Act 1992
Criminal Law (Sexual Offences) Act 2017
Criminal Justice (Victims of Crime) Act 2017
Criminal Procedure Act 2021
Sex Offenders Act 2001

Northern Ireland

Criminal Evidence (Northern Ireland) Order 1999
Criminal Justice (Northern Ireland) Order 2008
Criminal Justice Act (Northern Ireland) 2013
Justice Act (Northern Ireland) 2011
Police and Criminal Evidence (Northern Ireland) Order 1989
Practice Direction No 2/2019

Scotland

Criminal Procedure (Scotland) Act 1995
Victims and Witnesses (Scotland) Act 2014
Victims, Witnesses and Justice Reform (Scotland) Bill 2023
Vulnerable Witnesses (Scotland) Act 2004
Vulnerable Witnesses (Criminal Evidence) (Scotland) Act 2019

Other international

Criminal Code RSC 1985, C-46 (Canada)

Cases

European Court of Human Rights

Al-Khawaja and Tahery v UK (2012) 54 EHRR 23

Baegen v Netherlands [1995] ECHR, 16696/90

Barbera, Messegue and Jabardo v Spain (1988) 11 EHRR 360

Bocos-Cuesta v The Netherlands [2005] ECHR, 54789/00

Colozza v Italy (1985) 7 EHRR 516

Doorson v The Netherlands (1996) 22 EHRR 330

Finkensieper v Netherlands [1995] ECHR, 19525/92

Kostovski v Netherlands (1989) 12 EHRR 434

Kovač v Croatia [2007]ECHR, 503/05

Mraovič v Croatia [2020] ECHR, 30373/13

SC v United Kingdom (2005) 40 EHRR 10

SN v Sweden [2002] ECHR, 34209/96

Stanford v UK [1994] ECHR, 16757/90

T and V v United Kingdom (1999) 30 EHRR 121

Van Mechelen v Netherlands (1998) 25 EHRR 657

Y v Slovenia [2015] ECHR, 41107/10

Other international

Dowdell v United States, 221 US 325, 330 (1911) (United States)

Osolin v R (1993) 86 CCC (3d) 481 (Canada)

VK v Bulgaria (C/49/D/20/2008) (CEDAW)

England and Wales

Al-Rawi v The Security Service [2011] UKSC 34 [14]

Browne v Dunn (1894) 6 R 67

Hobbs v Tinling [1929] 2 KB 1

Jones v National Coal Board [1957] 2 QB 55

Le Brocq v Liverpool Crown Court [2019] 4 WLR 108 EWCA Crim 1398

Mechanical and General Inventions Ltd and Lehwess v Austin and Austin Motor Co Ltd [1935] AC 346

R v Barker [2010] EWCA Crim 4

R v Biddle [2019] EWCA Crim 86

R v Camberwell Green Youth Court (ex p D a Minor) [2005] 1 WLR 393

R v DL [2019] EWCA Crim 1249

R v *Dean Thomas* [2020] EWCA Crim 117

R v Doolin [1882] 1 Jebb CC 123

R v E [2011] EWCA Crim 3028

R v Farooqi [2013] EWCA Crim 1649

R v Grant-Murray and Others [2017] EWCA Crim 1228

R v Jonas [2015] EWCA Crim 562

R v Kalia (1974) 60 Cr App R 200

R v Lally (Mark Stephen) [2021] EWCA Crim 1372
R v Lawless (1993) 98 Cr App R 342
R v Lubemba; R v JP [2015] 1 WLR 1579
R v *McGill and Hewitt* [2017] EWCA Crim 1228
R v Milton Brown [1998] 2 Crim App R 364
R v Pipe [2014] EWCA Crim 270
R v PMH [2018] EWCA Crim 2452
R v Puddick (1865) 4 F&F 497
R v RK [2018] EWCA Crim 603
R v Sandor Jonas [2015] EWCA Crim 562
R v Sharp [1993] 3 All ER 225
R v Simon [2018] EWCA Crim 3086
R v Smellie (1919) 14 Cr App R 128
R v Wills [2012] 1 Cr App R 2
R v Wood Green Court, ex p Taylor [1995] Crim LR 879
R v X, Y and Z (1989) 91 Cr App R 36
R v W and M [2010] EWCA Crim 1926
R v Yahya Rashid [2017] EWCA Crim 2
TI v Bromley Youth Court [2020] EWHC 1204 (Admin) [2020] Crim LR. 951

Ireland
DPP v O'Driscoll [2022] IECA 4
DPP v MT [2023] IECA 65
DPP v VE [2021] IECA 122

Scotland
Donegan v HM Advocate 2019 JC 81
Inch v Inch (1856) 18 D 997
Begg v HM Advocate [2015] HCJAC 69

Works cited

Adler, Z. (1987). *Rape on Trial.* Routledge and Kegan Paul

Agnew, S.E. and Powell, M.B. (2004). The Effect of Intellectual Disability on Children's Recall of an Event across Different Question Types. *Law and Human Behavior*, 28, 273–294

Aldridge, M. and Luchjenbroers, J. (2007). Linguistic Manipulations in Legal Discourse: Framing Questions and 'Smuggling' Information. *International Journal of Speech, Language and the Law*, 14, 85–107

Andrews, S.J. and Lamb, M.E. (2017). The Structural Linguistic Complexity of Lawyers' Questions and Children's Responses in Scottish Criminal Courts. *Child Abuse & Neglect*, 65, 182–193

Andrews, S.J. and Lamb, M.E. (2018). Cross-Examining Young Alleged Complainers in Scottish Criminal Courts. *Criminal Law Review*, 1, 34–57

Arrigo, B. (2004). The Ethics of Therapeutic Jurisprudence: A Critical and Theoretical Enquiry of Law, Psychology and Crime. *Psychiatry, Psychology and Law*, 11, 23–43

Auld Review (2002). *Review of the Criminal Courts of England and Wales* (Cmnd 9376). HMSO

Bachmaier, L. (2019). Rights and Methods to Challenge Evidence and Witnesses in Civil Law Jurisdictions. In D.K. Brown, J.I. Turner and B. Weisser (eds), *The Oxford Handbook of Criminal Process*. Oxford University Press

Bankowski, Z. (1988). The Jury and Reality. In M. Findlay and P. Duff (eds), *The Jury under Attack*. Butterworths

Bar Standards Board (2024). *Bar Standards Handbook*. www.barstandardsboard.org.uk/the-bsb-handbook.html?part=&audience=&q=c29

Beriqi, R. (2017). Reflections on Certain Witnesses: Protective Measures under the Rome Statute of the International Criminal Court. *European Scientific Journal*, 17, 342–362

Berk-Seligson, S. (1999). The Impact of Court Interpreting on the Coerciveness of Leading Questions. *International Journal of Speech, Language and the Law*, 6, 30–56

Birch, D. (2000). A Better Deal for Vulnerable Witnesses? *Criminal Law Review*, 4, 223–249

Booth, T., Kaye, M. and Wangmann, J. (2019). Family Violence, Cross-Examination and Self-Represented Parties in the Courtroom: The Differences, Gaps and Deficiencies. *University of New South Wales Law Journal*, 42, 1106–1142

Bowden, P., Henning, T. and Plater, D. (2014). Balancing Fairness to Victims, Society and Defendants in the Cross-Examination of Vulnerable Witnesses: An Impossible Triangulation? *Melbourne University Law Review*, 37, 539–584

Bowles, P.V. and Sharman, S.J. (2014). A Review of the Impact of Different Types of Leading Interview Questions on Child and Adult Witnesses with Intellectual Disabilities. *Psychiatry, Psychology and Law*, 21, 205–217

Braun, K. (2014). Legal Representation for Sexual Assault Victims – Possibilities for Law Reform? *Current Issues in Criminal Justice*, 25, 819–837

Braun, K. (2019). *Victim Participation Rights*. Palgrave Macmillan

Brennan, M. and Brennan, R. (1988). *Strange Language: Child Victims under Cross-Examination*. Riverina Murray Institute of Higher Education

Brereton, D. (1997). How Different Are Rape Trials? A Comparison of the Cross-Examination of Complainants in Rape and Assault Trials. *British Journal of Criminology*, 37, 242–261

Brian, D. and Cruickshank, D.A. (2019). Police Officers Giving Evidence: Understanding the Enablers and Challenges of Performance. *Police Journal*, 92, 360–383

Brodsky, S.L., Dvoskin, J.A. and Neal, T. (2017). Temptations for the Expert Witness. *Journal of the American Academy of Psychiatry and Law*, 45, 460–463

Burton, M. (2023). *Domestic Abuse, Victims and the Law*. Routledge

Burton, M., Evans, R. and Sanders, A. (2006). *Are Special Measures for Vulnerable Witnesses Working? Evidence from the Criminal Justice Agencies*. Home Office

Cairns, D. (1998). *Advocacy and the Making of the Adversarial Trial 1800–1865*. Clarendon

Campbell, L., Ashworth, A. and Redmayne, M. (2019). *The Criminal Process* (5th edn). Oxford University Press

Carline, A., Gunby, C. and Murray, J. (2000). *Rape and the Criminal Trial: Reconceptualising the Courtroom as an Affective Assemblage*. Palgrave

Chambers, G. and Millar, A. (1986). *Prosecuting Sexual Assault*. HMSO

Charmaz, K. (2006). *Constructing Grounded Theory: A Practical Guide through Qualitative Analysis*. Sage

Colman, G. (1970). *Cross-Examination: A Practical Handbook*. Juta and Co

Colson, R. and Field, S. (2011). *The Transformation of Criminal Justice: Comparing France with England and Wales; Les Transformations de la Justice Pénale: Une Comparaison Franco-anglaise*. L'Harmattan

Colson, R. and Field, S. (2016). *EU Criminal Justice and the Challenges of Diversity: Legal Cultures in the Area of Freedom, Security and Justice*. Cambridge University Press

Cooper, D. (2005). Pigot Unfulfilled: Video-Recorded Cross-Examination under s 28 of the Youth Justice and Criminal Evidence Act 1999. *Criminal Law Review*, 6, 456–466

Cooper, D. and Roberts, P. (2005). *Special Measures for Vulnerable and Intimidated Witnesses: An Analysis of Crown Prosecution Service Monitoring Data*. Crown Prosecution Service

Cooper, D., Doak, J., Jackson, J., Saunders, C. and Wright, D. (2024). Cross-Examination Compared: The Asymmetric Treatment of Vulnerable Defendant and Non-Defendant Witnesses. *Criminal Law Review*, 9, 609–626

Cooper, P. (2018). 'Moving at a Pace': Towards a New Approach to Vulnerability in Courts and Tribunals? In P. Cooper and L. Hunting (eds), *Access to Justice for Vulnerable People*. Simmonds & Hill

Cooper, P. (2020). Looking Ahead: Towards a Principled Approach to Supporting Participation. In J. Jacobson and P. Cooper (eds), Participation in Courts and Tribunals. Bristol University Press

Cooper, P. and Mattison, M. (2017). Intermediaries, Vulnerable People and the Quality of Evidence: An International Comparison of Three Versions of the English Intermediary Model. *International Journal of Evidence & Proof*, 21, 351–370

Cooper, P. and Norton, H. (2017). *Vulnerable People and the Criminal Justice System*. Oxford University Press

Cooper, P., Backen, P. and Marchant, R. (2015). Getting to Grips with Ground Rules Hearings: A Checklist for Judges, Advocates and Intermediaries to Promote the Fair Treatment of Vulnerable People in Court. *Criminal Law Review*, 6, 420–435

Cooper, P., Dando, C., Ormerod, T., Mattison, M., Marchant, R., Milne, R. and Bull, R. (2018). One Step Forward and Two Steps Back? The '20 Principles' for Questioning Vulnerable Witnesses and the Lack of an Evidence-Based Approach. *International Journal of Evidence & Proof*, 22, 392–410

Cossins, A. (2020). *Closing the Justice Gap for Adult and Child Sexual Assault: Rethinking the Adversarial Trial.* Palgrave Macmillan

Council of Europe (2018). *Protection of Children against Sexual Exploitation and Abuse: Child-Friendly, Multidisciplinary and Interagency Response Inspired by the Barnahus Model.* Council of Europe

Courts Service of Ireland (2024). Registered Intermediaries in the Irish Criminal Justice System: Guidance Document. Courts Service of Ireland. www.courts.ie/acc/alfresco/8a68a59b-d8ab-4dcf-aead-9b8670e4315e/Registered%20Intermediaries%20Register%20Guidance%20Document%20April%202024.pdf/pdf/1

Cowan, S., Keane, E.P. and Munro, V.E. (2024). *The Use of Sexual History Evidence and 'Sensitive Private Data' in Scottish Rape and Attempted Rape Trials.* University of Edinburgh

Cowe, M. and Cavender, S. (2020). *Practical Advocacy in the Crown Court.* Bloomsbury Publishing

Crown Prosecution Service (2021). *Legal Guidance – Special Measures.* CPS

Cusack, A. (2020). Addressing Vulnerability in Ireland's Criminal Justice System: A Survey of Recent Statutory Developments. *International Journal of Evidence & Proof*, 24, 280–306

Cusack, A. (2022). From Special Measures to Separate Legal Representation: Charting Shifts in the Treatment of Victims of Crime with Intellectual Disabilities in Ireland. *Irish Judicial Studies Journal*, 4, 98–115

Daly, E. and Smith, O. (2020). *Scoping Review: Legal and Non-legal Advocacy for Rape Complainants in Adversarial Jurisdictions*. Loughborough University

Damaška, M. (1973). Evidentiary Barriers to Conviction and Two Models of Criminal Procedure: A Comparative Study. *University of Pennsylvania Law Review*, 121, 506–589

Danet, B. and Bogoch, B. (1980). Fixed Fight or Free-for-All? An Empirical Study of Combativeness in the Adversary System of Justice. *British Journal of Law and Society*, 7, 36–60

Davies, E. and Seymour, F. (1998). Questioning of Complainants of Sexual Abuse: Analysis of Criminal Court Transcripts in New Zealand. *Psychiatry, Psychology and Law*, 5, 47–61

Davies, E., Henderson, E. and Seymour, F.W. (1997). In reply to: The Interests of Justice? The Cross-Examination of Child Complainants of Sexual Abuse in Criminal Proceedings. *Psychiatry, Psychology and Law*, 4, 217–229

Davies, E., Henderson, E. and Hanna, K. (2010). Facilitating Children to Give Best Evidence: Are There Better Ways to Challenge Children's Testimony? *Criminal Law Journal*, 34, 347–362

Davies, G. and Noon, E. (1991). *Evaluation of the Live Link for Child Witnesses*. HMSO

De Wilde, B. (2013). A Fundamental Review of the ECtHR Right to Examine Witnesses in Criminal Cases. *International Journal of Evidence & Proof*, 17, 157–182

Dehaghani, R. (2019). *Vulnerability in Police Custody: Police Decision Making and the Appropriate Adult Safeguard*. Routledge

Dehaghani, R., Fairclough, S. and Mergaerts, L. (eds) (2023). *Vulnerability, the Accused, and the Criminal Justice System: Multi-jurisdictional Perspectives*. Routledge

Delahunt, M. (2024). *Vulnerable Witnesses and Defendants in Criminal Proceedings*. Clarus Press

Dennis, I. (2010). The Right to Confront Witnesses: Meaning, Myths and Human Rights. *Criminal Law Review*, 4, 255–274

Devaney, J., Mitchell, M., Alaggia, R. and Gray, C. (2024). Papering Over the Cracks or Rebuilding the System: Opportunities and Challenges for the Barnahus Model. In S. Johansson, K. Stefansen, E. Bakketeig and A. Kaldal (eds), *Justice and Recovery for Victimised Children: Institutional Tensions in Nordic and European Barnahus Models*. Palgrave Macmillan

Doak, J. (2008). *Victims' Rights, Human Rights and Criminal Justice*. Hart

Doak, J. (2011). Honing the Stone: Refining Restorative Justice as a Vehicle for Emotional Redress. *Contemporary Justice Review*, 14, 439–456

Doak, J., and Doak, L. (2017). Non-verbal Victims in the Adversarial Criminal Process: Communication, Competency, and Credibility. *Northern Ireland Legal Quarterly*, 68, 451–468

Doak, J. and Jackson, J.D. (2021). Cross-Examination: In Search of a New Normal. *The Barrister Magazine*. https://barristermagazine.com/cross-examination-in-search-of-a-new-normal/

Doak, J., Jackson, J.D., Saunders, C., Wright, D., Gómez Fariñas, B. and Durdiyeva, S. (2021). *Cross-Examination in Criminal Trials: Towards a Revolution in Trial Practice?* Nottingham Trent University

Doran, S. and Jackson, J. (1997). The Case for Jury Waiver, *Criminal Law Review*, 3 155–172

Dorrian Review (2021). *Improving the Management of Sexual Offence Cases: Final Report from the Lord Justice Clerk's Review Group*. Scottish Courts and Tribunals Service

Drake, K. (2010). The Psychology of Interrogative Suggestibility: A Vulnerability during Interview. *Personality and Individual Difference*, 49, 683–688

Du Cann, R. (1993). *The Art of the Advocate* (2nd edn). Penguin

Ellison, L. (2001). *The Adversarial Process and the Vulnerable Witness.* Oxford University Press

Ellison, L. (2007). Witness Preparation and the Prosecution of Rape. *Legal Studies*, 27, 171–187

Ellison, L. and Munro, V.E. (2014). A 'Special' Delivery? Exploring the Impact of Screens, Live-Links and Video-Recorded Evidence on Mock Juror Deliberation in Rape Trials. *Social & Legal Studies*, 23, 3–29

Ellison, L. and Munro, V.E. (2017). Taking Trauma Seriously: Critical Reflections on the Criminal Justice Process. *International Journal of Evidence & Proof*, 21, 183–208

Equality and Human Rights Commission (2020). *Inclusive Justice: A System Designed for All.* EHRC

Erez, E., Kilchling, M. and Wemmers, J.A. (eds) (2011). *Therapeutic Jurisprudence and Victim Participation in Justice: International Perspectives.* Carolina Academic Press

Ericson, K.I. and Perlman N.B. (2001). Knowledge of Legal Terminology and Court Proceedings in Adults with Developmental Disabilities. *Law and Human Behavior*, 25, 529–545

Fairclough, S. (2018a). Speaking Up for Injustice: Reconsidering the Provision of Special Measures through the Lens of Equality. *Criminal Law Review*, 1, 4–19

Fairclough, S. (2018b). Using Hawkins' Surround, Field and Frame Concepts to Understand the Complexities of Decision Making in Crown Courts. *Journal of Law and Society*, 45, 457–485

Fairclough, S. (2021). The Lost Leg of the Youth Justice and Criminal Evidence Act (1999): Special Measures and Humane Treatment. *Oxford Journal of Legal Studies*, 41(4), 1066–1095

Fairclough, S. (2023). Section 28 Pre-trial Cross-Examination: Barristers' Experiences and Perceptions of Its Wider Use in Practice. *Archbold Review*, 5, 5–10

Fairclough, S., Taggart, J. and Backen, P. (2023). Lost in Translation? Perceptions of Defendant Intermediaries in the Legal Profession. *Criminal Law Review*, 7, 437–458

Farrugia, L. (2024). *Exploring Vulnerability in the Criminal Justice System in England and Wales.* Taylor & Francis

Fielding, N. (2006). *Courting Violence.* Oxford: Oxford University Press

Fielding, N. (2013). Lay People in Court: The Experience of Defendants, Eyewitnesses and Victims. *British Journal of Sociology*, 64, 287–307

Fineman, M.A. (2008). The Vulnerable Subject: Anchoring Equality in the Human Condition. *Yale Journal of Law and Feminism*, 20, 177–191

Fineman, M.A. (2013). *Vulnerability: Reflections on a New Ethical Foundation for Law and Politics*. Routledge

Flynn, E. (2015). Disabled Justice? Access to Justice and the UN Convention on the Rights of Persons with Disabilities. Routledge

Forell, S. and McCarron, E. (2024). Health Justice Partnership: Access to Justice Meets Health Equity. *Alternative Law Journal*, 49, 168–173

Frank, J. (1949). *Courts on Trial: Myth and Reality in American Justice*. Princeton University Press

Freiberg, A. (2011). Post-adversarial and Post-inquisitorial Justice: Transcending Traditional Penological Paradigms. *European Journal of Criminology*, 8, 82–101

Friedman, R. (1998). Hearsay and Confrontation: Thoughts from across the Water. *Criminal Law Review*, 10, 697–709

Giannini, M.M. (2016). The Procreative Power of Dignity: Dignity's Evolution in the Victims' Rights Movement. *Drexel Law Review*, 9, 43–100

Gillen Review (2019). *Report into the Law and Procedures in Serious Sexual Offences in Northern Ireland*. Department of Justice

Godfrey, B., Richardson, J.C. and Walklate, S. (2022). The Crisis in the Courts: Before and Beyond Covid. *The British Journal of Criminology*, 62, 1036–1053

Gooding, P. and O'Mahony, C. (2016). Laws on Unfitness to Stand Trial and the UN Convention on the Rights of Persons with Disabilities: Comparing Reform in England, Wales, Northern Ireland and Australia. *International Journal of Law, Crime and Justice*, 44, 122–145

Goodman, G., Taub, E.P., Jones, D., England, P., Port, L., Rudy, L. and Rado, L. (1992). *Testifying in Criminal Court: Emotional Effects on Child Sexual Assault Victims*. University of Chicago Press

Grande, E. (2019). Transplants, Translations, and Adversarial-Model Reforms in European Criminal Process. In D.K. Brown, J.I. Turner and B. Weisser (eds), *The Oxford Handbook of Criminal Process*. Oxford University Press

Green, S. (2007). Crime, Victimisation and Vulnerability. In S. Walklate (ed), *Handbook of Victims and Victimology*. Routledge

Greer, D.S. (1971). Anything but the Truth? The Reliability of Testimony in Criminal Trials. *British Journal of Criminology*, 11, 147–154

Grohovsky, J.A. (2000). Giving Voice to Victims – Why the Criminal Justice System in England and Wales Should Allow Victims to Speak Up for Themselves. *Journal of Criminal Law*, 64, 416–430

Gudjonsson, G.H. and Henry, L. (2003). Child and Adult Witnesses with Intellectual Disability: The Importance of Suggestibility. *Legal and Criminological Psychology*, 8, 241–252

Hamlyn, B., Phelps, A., Turtle, J. and Sattar, G. (2004). *Are Special Measures Working? Evidence from Surveys of Vulnerable and Intimidated Witnesses* (Home Office Research Study 283). Home Office

Hanna, K. and Henderson, E. (2018). '[Expletive], That Was Confusing, Wasn't It?' Defence Lawyers' and Intermediaries' Assessment of the Language Used to Question a Child Witness. *International Journal of Evidence & Proof*, 22, 411–427

Hanna, K., Davies. E., Crothers, C. and Henderson, E. (2012). Questioning Child Witnesses in New Zealand's Criminal Justice System: Is Cross-Examination Fair? *Psychiatry, Psychology and Law*, 19, 530–546

Hayes, D. and Bunting, L. (2013). 'Just Be Brave': The Experiences of Young Witnesses in Criminal Proceedings in Northern Ireland. *Child Abuse Review*, 22, 419–431

Heffer, C. (2005). *The Language of Jury Trial: A Corpus-Aided Analysis of Legal–Lay Discourse*. Palgrave Macmillan

Henderson, E. (2014). All the Proper Protections – The Court of Appeal Rewrites the Rules for the Cross-Examination of Vulnerable Witnesses. *Criminal Law Review*, 2, 93–108

Henderson, E. (2015a). Communicative Competence? Judges, Advocates and Intermediaries Discuss Communication Issues in the Cross-Examination of Vulnerable Witnesses. *Criminal Law Review*, 9, 659–678

Henderson, E. (2015b). Theoretically Speaking: English Judges and Advocates Discuss the Changing Theory of Cross-Examination. *Criminal Law Review*, 12, 929–948

Henderson, E. (2015c). A Very Valuable Tool: Judges, Advocates and Intermediaries Discuss the Intermediary System in England and Wales. *International Journal of Evidence & Proof*, 19, 154–171

Henderson, E. (2016). Taking Control of Cross-Examination: Judges, Advocates and Intermediaries Discuss Judicial Management of the Cross-Examination of Vulnerable People. *Criminal Law Review*, 3, 181–205

Henderson, H., Lamb, M. and Rafferty, A. (2019). The Discussion of Ground Rules Issues in Pre-trial Preparation for Vulnerable Witnesses in English Crown Courts. *Criminal Law Review*, 7, 599–610

Henry, L.A., Crane, L., Millmore, A., Nash, G. and Wilcock, R. (2021). Intermediaries and Cross-Examination Resilience in Children: The Development of a Novel Experimental Methodology. *Applied Cognitive Psychology*, 35(6), 1387–1404

High Court of Justiciary (2017). *Practice Note No 1: Taking of Evidence of a Vulnerable Witness by a Commissioner*. Scottish Courts and Tribunal Service

High Court of Justiciary (2019). *Practice Note No 1: Vulnerable and Child Witnesses: Written Questions*. Edinburgh: Scottish Courts and Tribunal Service

Hirst, M. and Sahyouni, S. (2020). Effective Legal Representation for Participating Victims: Principles, Challenges and Some Solutions. In R. Jasini and G. Townsend (eds), *Advancing the Impact of Victim Participation at the International Criminal Court: Bridging the Gap between Research and Practice*. ESRC/University of Oxford

Home Office (1989). *Report of the Advisory Group on Video Evidence*. HMSO

Home Office (1998). *Speaking Up for Justice: Report of the Interdepartmental Working Group on the Treatment of Vulnerable or Intimidated Witnesses in the Criminal Justice System*. Home Office

Hostettler, J. (2006). *Fighting for Justice: The History and Origins of Adversary Trial*. Waterside Press

Hoyano, L. (2000). Variations on a Theme by Pigot: Special Measures Directions for Child Witnesses. *Criminal Law Review*, 4, 250–272

Hoyano, L. (2010). Special Measures Directions Take Two: Entrenching Unequal Access to Justice. *Criminal Law Review*, 5, 345–367

Hoyano, L. (2021). Postage Stamp Justice? Virtual Trials in the Crown Court under the Police, Crime, Sentencing and Courts Bill. *Criminal Law Review*, 12, 1029–1050

Hoyano, L. and Rafferty, A. (2017). Rationing Defence Intermediaries under the April 2016 Criminal Practice Direction. *Criminal Law Review*, 2, 93–105

Hunter, G., Jacobson, J. and Kirby, A. (2018). *Judicial Perceptions of the Quality of Criminal Advocacy* (Project Report). Solicitors Regulation Authority

Iliadis, M. (2020). *Adversarial Justice and Victims' Rights: Reconceptualising the Role of Sexual Assault Victims*. Routledge

Iliadis, M., Smith, O. and Doak, J. (2021a). Independent Separate Legal Representation for Rape Complainants in Adversarial Systems: Lessons from Northern Ireland. *Journal of Law and Society*, 48, 250–272

Iliadis, M., Fitz-Gibbon, K. and Walklate, S. (2021b). Improving Justice Responses for Victims of Intimate Partner Violence: Examining the Merits of the Provision of Independent Legal Representation. *International Journal of Comparative and Applied Criminal Justice*, 45, 105–114

Inns of Court College of Advocacy (2022). *Advocacy for Vulnerable People and Children (Criminal Course), National Training Programme. The* 20 Principles of Questioning. Inns of Court College of Advocacy

Jack, F. and Zajac, R. (2014). The Effect of Age and Reminders on Witnesses' Responses to Cross-Examination-Style Questioning. *Journal of Applied Research in Memory and Cognition*, 3, 1–6

Jackson, J.D. (2005). The Effect of Human Rights on Criminal Evidentiary Processes: towards Convergence, Divergence or Realignment? *Modern Law Review*, 68, 737–764

Jackson, J.D. (2021). The Case for a Hybrid Jury in Europe. In S.K. Ivković, S. Diamond, V.P. Hans and N.S. Marder (eds), *Juries, Lay Judges and Mixed Courts*. Cambridge University Press

Jackson, J.D. (2023). Rethinking the Orality/Confrontation Paradigm in a World of Remote Evidence. *Criminal Law Review*, 4, 265–285

Jackson, J.D. and Doran, S. (1995). *Judge without Jury: Diplock Trials and the Adversary System*. Clarendon

Jackson, J.D. and Summers, S.J. (2012). *The Internationalisation of Criminal Evidence: Beyond the Common Law and Civil Law Traditions*. Cambridge University Press

Jackson, J.D. and Weigend, T. (2022). Witness Evidence in Pre-trial and Trial Procedure. In K. Ambos, A. Duff, A. Heinze, J. Roberts and T. Weigend (eds), *Core Concepts in Criminal Law and Criminal Justice* (Vol 2). Cambridge University Press

Jackson, J.D., Doak, J., Saunders, C., Wright, D. and Cooper, D. (2024). *Mapping the Changing Face of Cross-Examination in Criminal Trials*. Nuffield Foundation

Jacobson, J. and Cooper, P. (eds) (2020). *Participation in Courts and Tribunals*. Bristol University Press

Jacobson, J. and Talbot, J. (2009). *Vulnerable Defendants in the Criminal Courts: A Review of Provision for Adults and Children*. Prison Reform Trust

Jacobson, J., Hunter, G. and Kirby, A. (2015). *Inside Crown Court: Personal Experiences and Questions of Legitimacy*. Bristol University Press

James, C. (2020). Towards Trauma-Informed Legal Practice: A Review. *Psychiatry, Psychology and Law*, 27, 275–299

Judicial College (2024). *Equal Treatment Bench Book*. HMCTS

JUSTICE (2019). *Prosecuting Sexual Offences*. JUSTICE

Keane, E. and Davidson, F. (2018). *Raitt on Evidence: Principles, Policy and Practice* (3rd edn). W. Green

Kebbell, M.R. and Johnson, S.D. (2000). Lawyers' Questioning: The Effect of Confusing Questions on Witness Confidence and Accuracy. *Law and Human Behavior*, 24(6), 629–641

Kebbell, M., Hatton, C.L. and Johnson, S.D. (2004). Witnesses with Intellectual Disabilities in Court: What Questions Are Asked and What Influence Do They Have? *Legal and Criminological Psychology*, 9, 23–35

Kebbell, M., Evans, L. and Johnson, S.D. (2010). The Influence of Lawyers' Questions on Witness Accuracy, Confidence, and Reaction Times and on Mock Jurors' Interpretation of Witness Accuracy. *Journal of Investigative Psychology and Offender Profiling*, 7, 262–272

King, M., Freiberg, A., Batagol, B. and Hyams, R. (2014). *Non-adversarial Justice*. Federation Press

Kirchengast, T. (2016). *Victims and the Criminal Trial*. Palgrave Macmillan

Krähenbühl, S. (2011). Effective and Appropriate Communication with Children in Legal Proceedings According to Lawyers and Intermediaries. *Child Abuse Review*, 20, 407–420

Kyneswood, N.S. (2022). *The Application of Section 28 and Related Measures in Sex Offence Cases: Is Pre-recorded Cross-Examination Achieving Best Evidence for Intimidated Complainants?* University of Warwick (Doctoral dissertation)

Kyneswood, N.S. (2024). Supplementary Written Evidence Submitted to the HC Justice Select Committee Inquiry: *The Use of Pre-recorded Cross-Examination under Section 28 of the Youth Justice and Criminal Evidence Act 1999* (PRE0037, 5 March 2024)

Lara, C.E. (2011). Child Soldier Testimony Used in Prosecuting War Crimes in the International Criminal Court: Preventing Further Victimization. *Southwestern Journal of International Law*, 17, 309–330

Langbein, J.H. (1978). Torture and Plea-Bargaining. *University of Chicago Law Review*, 46, 3–22

Langbein, J.H. (2003). *The Origins of Adversary Criminal Trial*. Oxford University Press

Law Commission (2023). *Evidence in Sexual Offence Prosecutions*. Consultation Paper 259. Law Commission

Lazer, S. (2021). *The Principle of Orality: An Analysis of the Principles Governing the Prevalence of Direct Oral Testimony in the English Adversarial Trial System and the Impact of Reforms to Reduce Its Status*. University of Huddersfield (Doctoral dissertation)

Lees, S. (1996). *Ruling Passions: Sexual Violence, Reputation and the Law*. Open University Press

Loftus, E.F. (1975). Leading Questions and the Eyewitness Report. *Cognitive Psychology*, 7, 560–572

Lord Beckett (2023). Untitled Address to the Conference on *Adversarialism, Participation and Voice in the Criminal Process*, 22–23 June 2023. University of Limerick

Lord Chancellor, Lord Chief Justice and Senior President of Tribunals (2016). *Transforming Our Justice System*. Ministry of Justice

Lord Chief Justice's Office (2019). *Practice Direction No 2/2019: Case Management in the Crown Court including Protocols for Vulnerable Witnesses and Defendants*. Lord Chief Justice's Office

Lord Judge, LCJ (2013). *Half a Century of Change: The Evidence of Child Victims*. Toulmin Lecture in Law and Psychiatry. King's College London

Maley, Y. (1994). The Language of the Law. In J. Gibbons (ed), *Language and the Law*. Longman

McBarnet, D. (1983). Victim in the Witness Box – Confronting Victimology's Stereotype. *Contemporary Crises*, 7, 293–303

McEwan, J. (2011). From Adversarialism to Managerialism: Criminal Justice in Transition. *Legal Studies*, 31, 519–546

McGlynn, C. (2017). Rape Trials and Sexual History Evidence: Reforming the Law on Third Party Evidence. *Journal of Criminal Law*, 81, 367–392

McGonigle Leyh, B. (2011). *Procedural Justice? Victim Participation in International Criminal Proceedings*. Intersentia

Mehrabian, A. (1972). *Nonverbal Communication*. Aldine-Atherton

Ministry of Justice (2023). *Registered Intermediary Procedural Guidance*. Ministry of Justice

Ministry of Justice and National Police Chiefs' Council (2022). *Achieving Best Evidence in Criminal Proceedings: Guidance on Interviewing Victims and Witnesses, and Guidance on Using Special Measures*. Ministry of Justice

Misileglas, V., Alldridge, P. and Cheliotis, L. (2015). *Globalisation, Criminal Law and Criminal Justice*. Hart Publishing

Molina, J. and Poppleton, S. (2020). *Rape Survivors and the Criminal Justice System*. Victims Commissioner

Moroz, A. and Dinisman, T. (2024). *Suffering for Justice: Sexual Violence Victim-Survivors' Experiences of Going to Court and Cross-Examination*. Victim Support

Morrison, J., Forrester-Jones, R., Bradshaw, J. and Murphy, G. (2019). Communication and Cross-Examination in Court for Children and Adults with Intellectual Disabilities: A Systematic Review. *International Journal of Evidence & Proof*, 23, 366–398

Morrison, J., Bradshaw, J. and Murphy, G. (2021). Reported Communication Challenges for Adult Witnesses with Intellectual Disabilities Giving Evidence in Court. *International Journal of Evidence & Proof*, 25, 243–263

Munro, V. (2018). *The Impact of the Use of Pre-recorded Evidence on Juror Decision Making: An Evidence Review*. Scottish Government

Munro, V., Weare, S., O'Doherty, L., Carter, G., Hudspith, L., Sleath, E., Brown, S., Cutland, M. and Perot, C. (2024). 'It's the Judicial Equivalent of Robbing Peter to Pay Paul' – The Implementation Gap in Section 28 Youth Justice and Criminal Evidence Act 1999. *International Journal of Evidence & Proof*, 29(1), https://doi.org/10.1177/13657127241259800

Myklebust, T. (2017). The Nordic Model of Handling Children's Testimonies: Exploring the Nordic Barnahus Model. In S. Johansson, K. Stefansen, E.K. Bakketeig, and A. Kaldal (eds), *Collaborating against Child Abuse: Exploring the Nordic Barnahus Model*. Palgrave Macmillan

O'Kelly, C.M.E., Kebbell, M.R., Hatton, C. and Johnson, S.D. (2003). Judicial Intervention in Court Cases Involving Witnesses with and without Learning Disabilities. *Legal and Criminological Psychology*, 8, 229–240

O'Malley Review (2020). *Review of Protections for Vulnerable Witnesses in the Investigation and Prosecution of Sexual Offences*. Department of Justice

Oireachtas Joint Committee on Justice (2021). *Report on Victims' Testimony in Cases of Rape and Sexual Assault*. Oireachtas Éireann

Owusu-Bempah, A. (2018). The Interpretation and Application of the Right to Effective Participation. *International Journal of Evidence & Proof*, 22, 321–341

Osuwu-Bempah A. (2020). Understanding the Barriers to Defendant Participation in Criminal Proceedings in England and Wales. *Legal Studies*, 40, 609–629

Plotnikoff, J. and Woolfson, R. (2004). *In Their Own Words: The Experiences of 50 Young Witnesses in Criminal Proceedings*. NSPCC

Plotnikoff, J. and Woolfson, R. (2009). *Measuring Up? Evaluating Implementation of Government Commitments to Young Witnesses in Criminal Proceedings*. Nuffield Foundation

Plotnikoff, J. and Woolfson R. (2011). *Young Witnesses in Criminal Proceedings*. Nuffield Foundation and NSPCC

Plotnikoff, J. and Woolfson R. (2012). 'Kicking and Screaming': The Slow Road to Best Evidence. In J.R. Spencer and M. Lamb (eds), *Children and Cross-Examination: Time to Change the Rules?* Bloomsbury Publishing

Plotnikoff, J. and Woolfson, R. (2015). *Intermediaries in the Criminal Justice System*. Bristol University Press

Plotnikoff, J. and Woolfson, R. (2019). *Falling Short? A Snapshot of Young Witness Policy and Practice*. NSPCC

Podsakoff, P.M., Mackenzie, S.B. and Podsakoff, N.P. (2012). Sources of Method Bias in Social Science Research and Recommendations on How to Control It. *Annual Review of Psychology*, 63, 539–569

Rape Crisis Ireland (2018). *Hearing Every Voice – Towards a New Strategy on Vulnerable Witnesses in Legal Proceedings*. Rape Crisis Ireland

Roberts, A. (2019). The Frailties of Human Memory and the Accused's Right to Accurate Procedures. *Criminal Law Review*, 11, 912–933

Roberts, P. (2022). *Roberts and Zuckerman's Criminal Evidence* (3rd edn). Oxford University Press

Rock, P. (1993). *The Social World of an English Crown Court: Witnesses and Professionals in the Crown Court Centre at Wood Green*. Clarendon Press

Rossner, M. (2021). Remote Rituals in Virtual Courts. *Journal of Law and Society*, 48, 334–361

Rush, E., Quas, J.A. and McAuliff, B.D. (2012). Child Witnesses' Experiences of Distress in Criminal Courts: Sources, Consequences and Solutions. In M.K. Miller and B.H. Bornstein (eds), *Stress, Trauma, and Well-Being in the Legal System*. Oxford University Press

Saks, M.J. and Spellman, B.A. (2016). *The Psychological Foundations of Evidence Law*. New York University Press

Sanders, A. and Jones, I. (2007). The Victim in Court. In S. Walkate (ed), *Handbook of Victims and Victimology*. Routledge

Saunders, C. (2018). Rape as 'One Person's Word against Another's': Challenging the Conventional Wisdom. *International Journal of Evidence & Proof*, 22, 161–181

Schwikkard, P.J. (2008). *Possibilities of Convergence: An Outside Perspective on the Convergence of Criminal Procedures in Europe*. Kluwer

Scottish Courts and Tribunals Service (2016). *Evidence and Procedure Review: Next Steps*. SCTS

Scottish Government (2021). *The Foundations for Bairns' Hoose (Scottish Barnahus)*. Scottish Government

Scottish Government (2023). *Vulnerable Witnesses Act: Section 9 Report*. Scottish Government

Scottish Law Commission (1990). *Report on the Evidence of Children and Other Potentially Vulnerable Witnesses* (Report 125). Scottish Law Commission

Segovia, D.A., Strange, D. and Takarangi, M.K. (2017). Trauma Memories on Trial: Is Cross-Examination a Safeguard against Distorted Analogue Traumatic Memories? *Memory*, 25, 95–106

Shapland, J. and Hall, M. (2007). What Do We Know about the Effects of Crime on Victims? *International Review of Victimology*, 14, 175–217

Sixsmith, A. (2024). Safeguarding the Procedural Rights of Young Defendants in England and Wales: The Role of Neuroscience. In H. Wishart and C.M. Berryessa (eds), *Neurolaw in the Courtroom: Comparative Perspectives on Vulnerable Defendants*. Taylor & Francis

Slobogin, C. (1995). Therapeutic Jurisprudence: Five Dilemmas to Ponder. *Psychology, Public Policy and Law*, 1, 193–219

Smith, O. (2018). *Rape Trials in England and Wales: Observing Justice and Rethinking Rape Myths*. Palgrave MacMillan

Smith, O. and Skinner, T. (2012). Observing Court Responses to Victims of Rape and Sexual Assault. *Feminist Criminology*, 7, 298–326

Spencer, J.R. (2012). Conclusions. In J.R. Spencer and M. Lamb (eds), *Children and Cross-Examination: Time to Change the Rules?* Bloomsbury Publishing

Spencer, J.R. (2016). Adversarial vs Inquisitorial Systems: Is There Still Such a Difference? *International Journal of Human Rights*, 20, 601–616

Spencer J.R. and Flin, R. (1993). *The Evidence of Children* (2nd edn). Blackstone

Stone, M. (1984). *Proof of Fact in Criminal Trials*. Sweet & Maxwell

Taggart, J. (2021). 'I Am Not Beholden to Anyone ... I Consider Myself to Be an Officer of the Court': A Comparison of the Intermediary Role in England and Wales and Northern Ireland. *International Journal of Evidence & Proof*, 25, 141–162

Taggart, J. (2022). Vulnerable Defendants and the HMCTS Court Appointed Intermediary. *Criminal Law Review*, 6, 432–447

Temkin, J. (2000). Prosecuting and Defending Rape: Perspectives from the Bar. *Journal of Law and Society*, 27, 219–248

Teubner, G. (1992). The Two Faces of Janus: Rethinking Legal Pluralism. *Cardozo Law Review*, 13, 1443–1462

The Advocate's Gateway (2015a). *Planning to Question a Child or Young Person*: Toolkit 6. The Advocate's Gateway

The Advocate's Gateway (2015b). *Witnesses and Defendants with Autism: Memory and Sensory Issues*: Toolkit 15. The Advocate's Gateway

The Advocate's Gateway (2019). *Intermediaries: Step by Step*: Toolkit 16. The Advocate's Gateway

The Advocate's Gateway (2024). *Ground Rules Hearings and the Fair Treatment of Vulnerable People in Court*: Toolkit 1. The Advocate's Gateway

Thomas, C. (2023). Juries, Rape and Sexual Offences in the Crown Court 2007–21. *Criminal Law Review*, 3, 197–222

Thomas, C. (2024). Written Evidence to the HC Justice Select Committee Inquiry: *The Use of Pre-recorded Cross-Examination under Section 28 of the Youth Justice and Criminal Evidence Act 1999* (PRE0029, 9 January 2024)

Thomason, M. (2021). Admitting Evidence by Agreement: Recalibrating Managerialism and Adversarialism in Crown Court Trials. *Criminal Law Review*, 9, 727–752

Tkačuková, T. (2015). A Corpus-Assisted Study of the Discourse Marker 'Well' as an Indicator of Judges' Institutional Roles in Court Cases with Litigants in Person. *Corpora*, 10, 145–170

Valentine, T. and Maras, K. (2011). The Effect of Cross-Examination on the Accuracy of Adult Eyewitness Testimony. *Applied Cognitive Psychology*, 25, 554–561

Victim Support (1996). *Women, Rape and the Criminal Justice System*. Victim Support

Welland, S., Murray, S., Storry, M. and Poppleton, S. (2024). *Going Above and Beyond: Mapping the Provision and Impact of Victim Advocacy in the Criminal Justice System*. Victims Commissioner

Wemmers, J.A. (2012). Victims' Rights Are Human Rights: The Importance of Recognizing Victims as Persons. *Temida*, 15(2), 71–83

Wexler, D.B. (2005). Therapeutic Jurisprudence and the Rehabilitative Role of the Criminal Defense Lawyer. *Thomas Law Review*, 17, 743–774

Wexler, D.B. and Winick, B.J. (1996). *Law in a Therapeutic Key: Developments in Therapeutic Jurisprudence*. North Carolina Academic Press

Wheatcroft, J.M. and Ellison, L.E. (2012). Evidence in Court: Witness Preparation and Cross-Examination Style Effects on Adult Witness Accuracy. *Behavioral Sciences & Law*, 30, 821–840

White, R., Bornman, J. and Johnson, E. (2015). Testifying in Court as a Victim of Crime for Persons with Little or No Functional Speech: Vocabulary Implications. *Child Abuse Research in South Africa*, 16, 1–14

Wigmore, J.H. (1940). *Evidence in Trials at Common Law*. Little, Brown & Company

Winick, B.J. (2002). Therapeutic Jurisprudence and Problem-Solving Courts. *Fordham Urban Law Journal*, 30, 1055–1103

Wood, M., Lepanjuuri, K., Paskell, C., Thomson, J., Adams, L. and Coburn, S. (2015). *Victim and Witness Satisfaction Survey*. Crown Prosecution Service

Woodbury, H. (1984). The Strategic Use of Questions in Court. *Semiotica*, 48, 197–228

Wright. D., Jackson, J., Doak, J., Saunders, C. and Cooper, D. (2025). Signposting Topics in the Cross-Examination of Vulnerable Witnesses. In T. Grieshofer and K. Haworth (eds), *Language and Justice: Communication in Legal Practice*. Cambridge University Press

Zajac, R., O'Neil, S. and Hayne H. (2012). Disorder in the Courtroom? Child Witnesses under Cross-Examination. *Developmental Review,* 32, 181–204

Zajac, R., Westera, N. and Kaladelfos, A. (2018). The 'Good Old Days' of Courtroom Questioning: Changes in the Format of Child Cross-Examination Questions over 60 Years. *Child Maltreatment*, 23, 186–195

Zydervelt, S., Zajac, R., Kaladelfos, A. and Westera, N. (2017). Lawyers' Strategies for Cross-Examining Rape Complainants: Have We Moved beyond the 1950s? *British Journal of Criminology*, 57, 551–569

Index

References to figures appear in *italic* type; those in **bold** type refer to tables.
References to footnotes show both the page number and the note number (159n5).

D